Eric Jackson PERRIN

THE BIRTH DIAMOND©
Hindu and Sufi
Evolutionary Sacred Karmic Numerology

BOOK AND WORKBOOK

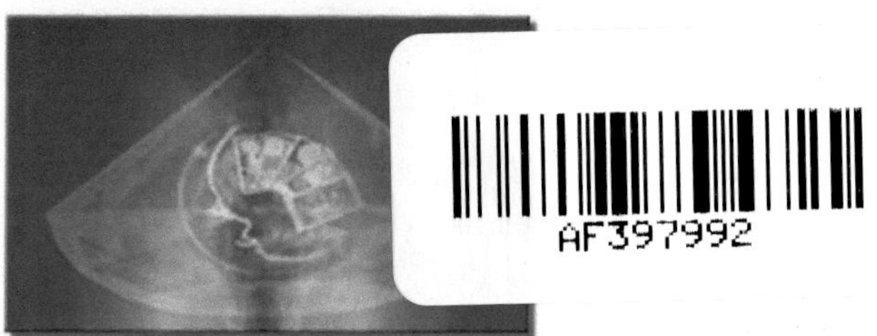

To discover who you are, your Soul Structure, your evolutionary path so as to become the best version of yourself!

Gratitude

A very warm thank you to my GranMa Marguerite Bennasar Ballester and Mother Marie-Christine Jackson

To Denise, Georges, Denis, Corinne, Elodie, Nathalie, Hélène, Carole, Marie-Hélène and Stephan

To Nadine Kaiser and Gilles Guyon

A special thank you to the « Art of Living Foundation », who works so that humanity on Earth can find well being, joy, health and spiritual growth,
All with a beautiful smile

Without them this tool would not exist

Also a very warm thank you to all the friends who helped me check
The efficiency of this self-knowledge tool
Version 4 – JUNE 2022

Legal information

© 2012 –2022 Eric Jackson Perrin
www.coaching-evolution.net

Published by Eric Jackson Perrin
69300 Caluire et Cuire – France

Printed in Germany by BoD – Books on Demand

ISBN: 979-10-94871-911

Legal deposit: September 2016

****

Summary

Introduction

The Birth Diamond is a self-knowledge tool and a tool that can be used for coaching. It's a tool for inner growth. Anayone who wants to know more about themselves can use it. The first 22 numbers fill up 24 inner spaces within you called houses. Each number represents a series of key words. The Birth Diamond chart is like a map of your soul that reveals the structure of who you are and your evolution plan. It describes your soul's plan and architecture by showing the 24 main facets of yourself.

It enables you to have a symbolic and synthetic vision of your potential, of your identity, of your behavioral schemes and of your evolutionary path. It is like a bundle of keys that can open the doors to your interior spaces. It is like a personal a specific inner village with 24 houses that can be fully occupied and settled. The goal of the birth Diamond is to help you become the best version of yourself, which is the supreme goal of every human soul.

Experiencing the Bith Diamond allows you to know more about your inner life. It reveals landmarks that guide you though life and help you make the best of your life. It enhances self-awareness, common sense and self-love. It helps you accept who you are and accept others as they are. As a spiritual being created by life or rather by "The Source of all life", you are a wonderful person, a raw diamond that seeks to shine through every one of its facets. When each facet is experienced in complete awareness and expressed in its best form so that it really belongs to you, your "inner Diamond" or "spiritual body" shines like a sun. You then gradually become the best version of yourself and you succeed.

It can for exemple reveal your needs, your resources and your challenges, your contradictions and your solutions but also where you come from, who you really are and where you are going and how to get there here and now. It can help you to see the connection between your inner life and what you create in the outside world, the goals and needs of your soul and thus to become more aware. This leads to making relevant choices and meaningfull decisions, to implementing actions that convert your goals into achievements and to creating a new and more meaningful life.

The Birth Diamond comes from various Christian and Islamic traditions, which themselves come from India and China. It also comes from different English, American, Canadian and French cultural trends. It built up with a Mayan and Scandinavian cosmological structure, with the western astrological house system, with "the spirit" of Mr and Mrs. Hurley's "Diamond pointed Tarot spread" created in 1974 in California and with specific numerological data.

It combines the 12 astrological houses and 12 numerological components, enabling you to represent an astrological chart in a numerological manner and to bring the numbers to life using imagery from the traditional "Tarot de Marseille" deck. Just like an astral chart, it show one way of considering the soul's structure, but in a more specific and concise manner.

The name « Birth Diamond » and the structure of the tool were invented in 2011/2012 in France by Eric Jackson Perrin (Expert in numerology, astrology and I-Jing). The Tarot Deck used here is the Universal Tarot Deck created by Bruno de Nys in the south of France. It is available on his website. It can be displayed in two ways. Some peopme prefer the classical way and others the astrological display.

Graphical displays of the Birth Diamond
Classical display

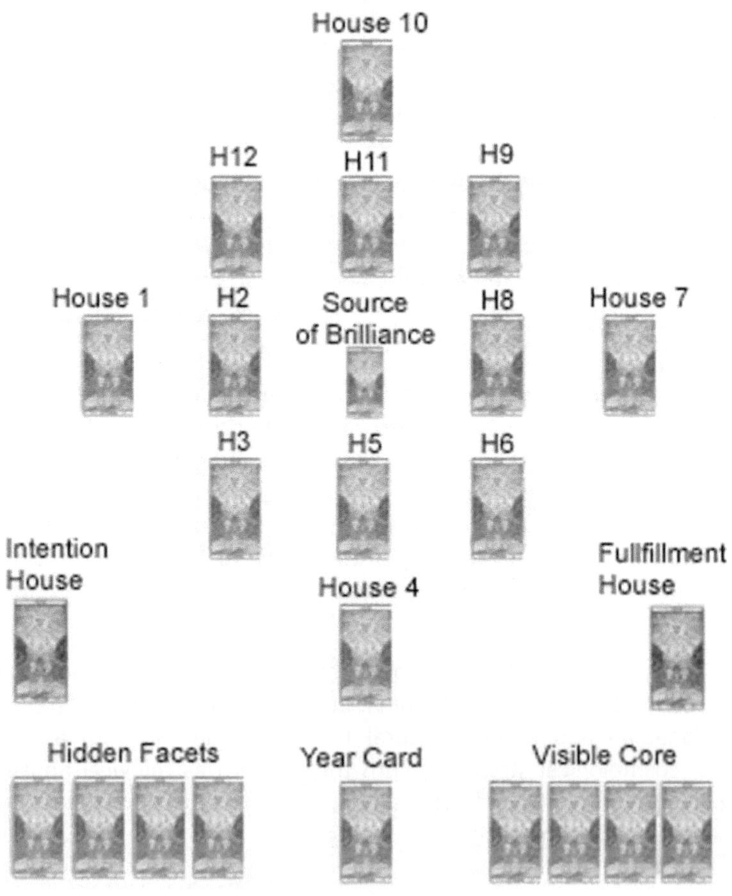

Birth Diamond - Astrological presentation

Astrological Diamond

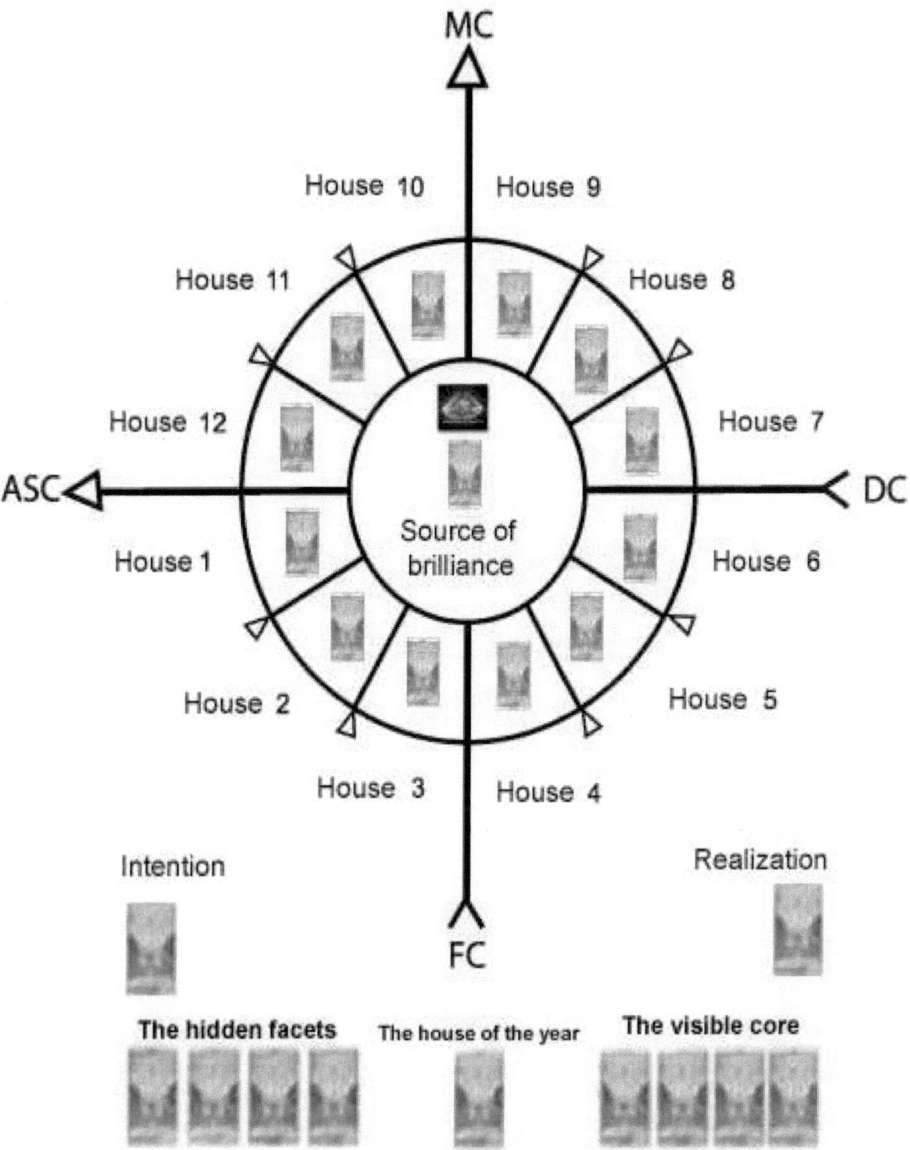

Creation : Eric Jackson PERRIN

The Birth Diamond - Classical Display

Date of Birth :
First Name :
Family Name :

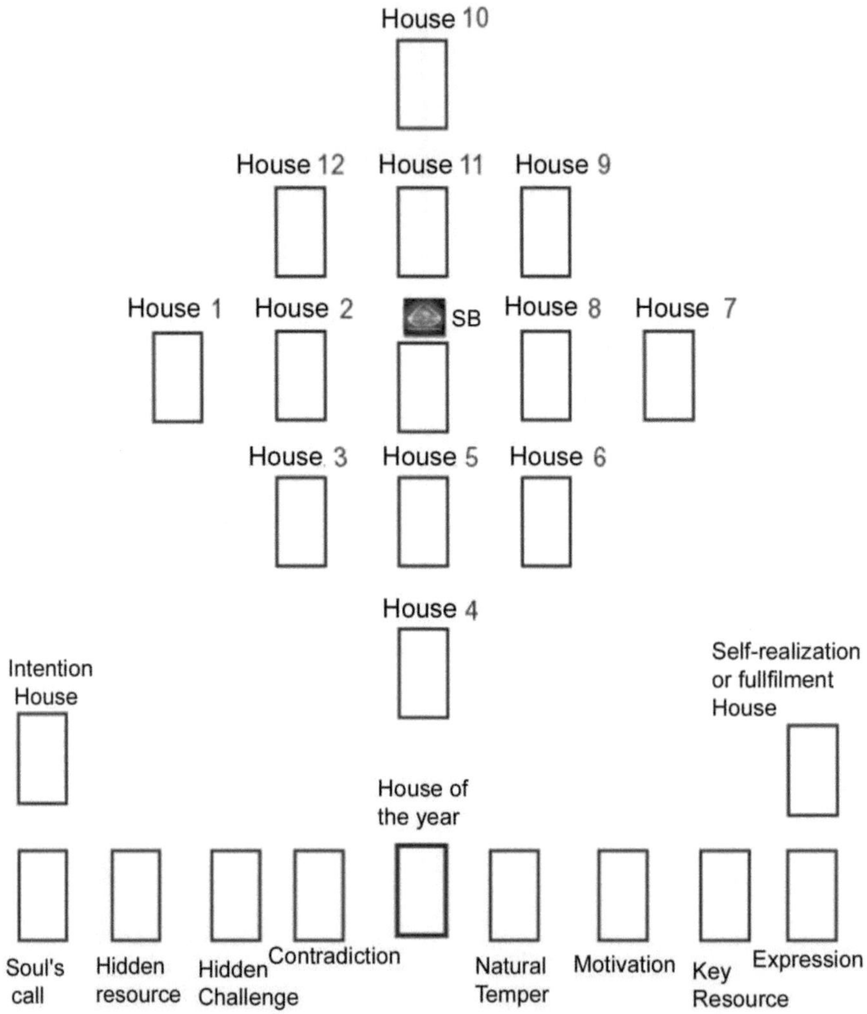

Creation : Eric Jackson PERRIN

10

The Birth Diamond's 24 houses

The Birth Diamond is made up of two parts, its heart above and its foundation below. We will now define each house and see how to calculate the number that dwells in it in the next chapter.

The core or heart of the Diamond: Houses of life sectors

It is made up of the thirteen areas or inner living spaces called "houses » or « life sectors". The words "houses" and "life sectors come from astrology. At the very center of the core lies a special area called the Source of Brilliance that shows how you can express the best of yourself, how you can be brilliant. The definitions and the positions of the first 12 houses are the same as in an astrological chart. Thay are as follows.

House 1 or Ascendant: The major state of mind that you have come to experience, the way in which you assert who you are and start things, your appearance, the image of yourself that you show to others, your weapons, your strength, the masks you put on to exert "an ascendant" on the world.

House 2: How you experience incarnation, your wealth, your main resources, the way you handle matter and money, your relation to pleasure, to money and to your physical body, your artistic abilities or the way you put things into shape.

House 3: Your way of thinking, of learning, of communicating and of adapting to your environment, the way you move and create movement in your life. Your sales intelligence.

House 4 or "Bottom of sky": Your origins, your past, your roots, your family heritage, your childhood and its conditionings, your subconscious mind, what you have deep inside yourself, your dwelling place and your source of well-being.

House 5: Your deep self, personal marks, awareness of yourself, creative power and creations, your need and ability to succeed, your willpower, how you express what's in your heart.

House 6 : Your technical intelligence, how you adapt to the world of matter, your sense of service, your search for well being, health and hygiene, your recurring problems caused by a tendency to try and find solutions with the small mind.

House 7 or "Descendant": How you move away from your center to interact with others and create relationships, your couple, partnerships or rivalries, the opposite but complementary part of you that you tend at first to reject, making it a source of adversity and your main challenge that you must transform into an ally.

House 8: What is hidden inside you, your search for initiation and for your deep truth, the dark side of you that needs to be brought to light, the hidden treasures you have inside you, how you eliminate toxins, your crisis and transformations, how you express sexuality, your unconscious feminine part, your discoveries and revelations.

House 9: How you find your place in society, thrive and blossom, explore space, travel, undertake studies, express your authority and power to do your work, negotiate and do business, your behavior at your workplace, your philosophy or life and your spiritual research.

House 10 or "Midsky": Your ambitions, how you become aware of the laws of life and how you organize your destiny, your relation to structures and organizations, your career, your major achievements, your major life lesson, your path towards your deep inner truth and how you gain wisdom and inner peace.

House 11: Your psychological and technological intelligence, how you express your uniqueness, experience group activities and adapt to modern life and it's technologies, how you experience helping others and being helped, the compulsory solutions you must apply to free yourself, experience inner freedom and do your part to create a better word.

House 12: What makes you suffer, how to go from suffering to delight and bliss thought acceptance, compassion and love, the tests that make you grow, your spiritual evolution, your source of faith, your ancestral and soul memories, your mystical experiences where you can experience unity with God, the end of your story and what you leave behind.

The Diamond's foundation: It is made up of nine houses plus two special houses called intention and realization. If you look at the diagram page 10, you will see that on the left, you have the facets that are initially hidden or non-conscious until they are revealed and used. These facets are named "the soul's intention", "the Soul's Call", "the Hidden Resource", "the Hidden Challenge" and "the Contradiction". On the right, you have the dominant parts of the character, the visible core.

These are psychological schemes and resources that are always available for you to express. You tend to use them consciously to experience what you have come to do on Earth. Your visible core is made up of your "the natural temper", "your deep motivation number", "your key resource number" and "your expression number". The "Self-realization number" or "fulfillment number" summarizes the Birth Diamond. At the center of the Diamond's foundation, you have the "House of the year" or "annual number". It describes the climate or dominant energy existing during a year, from birthday to birthday.

Using the Birth Diamond as a tool for coaching:

Coaching is a process where you firstly define goals in every part of your life, goals that make you grow towards self-realization. You then find the necessary resources and act to achieve your goals and to reach the destination you have chosen. With time and some effort, coaching enables you to express the best of who you are.

To use the Birth Diamond as a tool for coaching, you can first choose a house and then read the text describing it. You can grasp the meaning of a house by becoming aware of its purpose. You can then observe that each house is a part of you, a part of your inner village. You can then read the text describing the number that dwells in that house. It is then necessary to become aware of how you personally experience the specific number/ number existing in each specific house. You can then answer the following questions:

What are your goals in life? Choose one! How are you expressing the part of your Birth Diamond you have chosen to put your attention on? Are you expressing the full potential of the number/number existing in that house? What awareness does your defining of the number/number in the chosen house generate in relation with your goal? What is your main awareness? In relation with your main awareness and with your goal, what actions can you undertake to make things progress? When precisely can you do what you have decided to do? When would you like to do a check-up, with yourself or with a coach, to acknowledge and validate the results obtained and to go on to the next step, or to deal with a problem or an obstacle encountered when putting your plan into action? This coaching process helps you to promote your qualifications and to move forward in your life.

Chapter 1: Putting together a Birth Diamond chart manually.

To calculate the 24 numbers that make up the Birth Diamond, all you need to do is add and subtract numbers. You can photocopy and use the matrix on page 10 or download it from my website. Here is the address. https://www.coaching-evolution.net/FICHIERS/DN-CNDUSA.pdf

You can also purchase on my website, a small software that enables you to calculate and print out the Birth Diamond with the 24 numbers in the 24 houses as in the examples at the end of this book.

The Birth Diamond is based on a cycle of 22. There are 22 numbers in a tarot deck. So when you obtain a number between 1 and 22, you keep that number. **From 23 onwards, you add the two numbers to obtain a new number between 1 and 22.** 23 then becomes 2+3=5. Zero equals 22 so if you subtract two numbers and get zero, you then write 22. The letter H stands for house. It is important to calculate the various numbers in a specific order as shown below and in the technical file a few pages down.

Step 1: House **1** or Ascendant: To calculate the number in House 1: This number is your day of birth reduced to a number equal to or inferior to 22. A person born on the 24th has number 6 in house 1 as 2+4 adds up to 6. You can place it in the rectangle just below the title House 1.

For people born between midnight and sunrise: Many civilizations consider that the day begins at sunrise. My experience of the Birth Diamond revealed that for people born between midnight and sunrise, calculating the Birth Diamond for the day before the official day of birth can be very explicit. It's as if these people are impacted by both the numerological energy of their official birth date and that of the day before. You can try and see. It is however advisable to use the official bithdate first and only later check out the other chart.

Step 2: House **8**: To calculate the number in House 8: This number is the month of birth from 1 (January) to 12 (December). Place the month of birth number in the rectangle just below the title House 8.

Step 3: House **9**: To calculate the number in House 9: This number is the year of birth. You obtain it by adding the 4 numbers that make up the year. Example: 2011 = 2+0+1+1=4. Place the year of birth number in the rectangle just below the title House 9.

Step 4: House **10** or life path: To calculate the number in House 10: The number in house 10 is obtained by adding your whole birth date. Example: 28/12/1963 = 2+8+1+2+1+9+6+3=32=5. Place the date of birth number in the rectangle just below the title House 10.

Step 5: House **2**: To calculate the number in House 2: This number is obtained by adding the day of birth reduced to a number between 1 and 22 and the month of birth. You can also calculate it by adding the number in house 1 to the one in house 8. H2=H1+H8. Place this number in the rectangle just below the title House 2.

Step 6: House **3**: To calculate the number in House 3: This number is obtained with the month of birth and the year of birth. You calculate it by adding the number in house 8 to the number in house 9. H3=H8+H9. Place the number in the rectangle just below the title House 3

Step 7: House **7**: To calculate the number in House 7: This number is obtained with the month of birth and the year of birth, that is, House 8 and House 9. You calculate it by subtracting the smaller of the two numbers from the bigger one. H7=H9-H8 or H9-H8. Place the number belonging to House 7 in the rectangle just below the title House 7.

Step 8: House **5**: To calculate the number in House 5: This number is obtained by adding the number in House 2 to the one in House 7. H5=H2+H7. Place the number belonging to House 5 in the rectangle just below the title House 5.

Step 9: House **6**: To calculate the number in House 6: You obtain this number by subtracting the number in House 5 from the number 22. H6=22-H5. Place this number in the rectangle just below the title House 6.

Step 10: House **4**: To calculate the number in House 4: This number is obtained by adding together the numbers in houses 6, 7 and 9. H4=H6+H7+H9. Place this number just below the title House 4.

Step 11: House **11**: To calculate the number in House 11: This number is obtained by adding together the numbers in houses 1, 8, 9 and 10. H11=H1+H8+H9+H10. Place the number belonging to House 11 in the rectangle just below the title House 11.

Step 12: House **12**: To calculate the number in House 12: This number is obtained by adding together the numbers in houses 2, 8 and 10. H12=H2+H8+H10. Place this number in the rectangle just below the title House 12.

Step 13: Source of brilliance: To calculate the SB number: It is obtained by adding together the numbers in houses 2 and 10. SB=H2+H10. Place the SB number in the rectangle just below the letters SB.

Step 14: Soul intention: To calculate the soul intention number: It is obtained by adding together the numbers in houses 8, 9 and 10. SI=H8+H9+H10. Place the SI number in the rectangle just below the picture of the Diamond and the letters Intention.

Step 15: Soul's call: To calculate the Soul Call number: This number is obtained by adding the value of all the vowels in your first name and family name. The numerical values of all the letters are shown below. You use the family name you have now but it may also be interesting to check out the family name you had at birth if it's different from the one you have now. Place the Soul Call number in the rectangle above the title Soul Call, on the bottom left of the Birth Diamond.

1	2	3	4	5	6	7	8	9
A	B	C	D	E	F	G	H	I
J	K	L	M	N	O	P	Q	R
S	T	U	V	W	X	Y	Z	

Example: John Wayne = 6+1+7+5=19 (Tarot number 19 = The Sun).

Step 16: Hidden Resource: To calculate the hidden resource number: You obtain it by adding the last two numbers of the full birth year. Place the hidden resource number in the rectangle above the title Hidden Resource, on the bottom left of the Birth Diamond. **Example:** 1998 = 9+8=17.

Step 17: Hidden Challenge: To calculate the hidden challenge number: You obtain it by subtracting the number in House 1 from the one in House 9 or vice versa i.e. you calculate it by subtracting the smaller of the two numbers from the bigger one. Hidden Challenge=H1-H9 or H9-H1. Place this number in the rectangle above the title Hidden Challenge.

Step 18: Contradiction: To calculate the contradiction number: This number is obtained by adding the numbers in houses 6 and 7. Contradiction=H6+H7. Place the contradiction number in the rectangle above the title Contradiction.

Step 19: Number of the year : To calculate the annual number: You add the number in House 2 the universal numerological year.

The universal numerological year is the year that begins at your birthday of the current year. If we are in 2021, the universal numerological year is 2+0+2+1=5.

Example: A person born on December the fifth, or 05/12, has, in his or her Birth Diamond, number 17 in House 2 (5+12=17). His or her annual number for the year 2021 (2+0+2+1=10), for example, is number 10 (17+5=22). This number can be visually represented by The Fool (Tarot Number 22). This number/number and what it symbolizes will be brought to life between the 5th of December 2021 and the 5th of December 2022. Place the annual number in the rectangle, at the bottom center of the Birth Diamond, just below the title House of the year.

Step 20: Natural temper: To calculate the natural temper number: You can sometimes obtain it by adding the numbers in houses 2 and 3, but House 2 comes from House 1+House 8 and that House 3 comes from House 8+House 9 so **Natural Temper = H1+H8+H8+H9**. Place the natural temper number in the rectangle above the title Natural Temper.

Step 21: Deep Motivation: To calculate the deep motivation number: This number is obtained by adding together the numbers in houses 1, 5 and 8. Motivation = H1+H5+H8. Place this number in the rectangle, at the bottom right of the Birth Diamond, just above the title Motivation.

Step 22: Key Resource number: To calculate the key resource number: This number is obtained by adding together the numbers in houses 2, 10 and 11. Key Resource = H2+H10+H11. Place the key resource number in the rectangle, at the bottom right of the Birth Diamond, just above the title Key Resource.

Step 23: Expression number: To calculate the expression number: This is obtained by adding all the vowels and all the consonants of the first name and the family name. Expression= vowels + consonants of the complete name. Place the expression number in the rectangle, at the bottom right of the Birth Diamond, just below the title Expression.

Step 24: Self Realization number or Fulfillment number: It is obtained by adding the expression number and the number in House 10. Self-Realization=House 10+ Expression. Place the Self-Realization number in the rectangle, at the bottom right of the Birth Diamond, just below the title Self-Realization. Now that you have learnt the meanings of each house or life sector and how to calculate the 24 numbers that fit in the 24 houses, it is now time to learn the meanings of the 22 numbers.

TECHNICAL FILE – PUTTING TOGETHER THE BIRTH DIAMOND

Birth Diamond's core

HOUSE 1: Day of birth. HOUSE 8 : Month of birth
HOUSE 9: year of birth. (1968 = 1+9+6+8=24 and 2+4=6)
HOUSE 10: Day+Month+Year.
HOUSE 2: H 1 + H 8. HOUSE 3: H 8 + H 9.
HOUSE 7: H 8 – H 9. HOUSE 5 : H 2 + H 7
HOUSE 6: 22 – M 5. HOUSE 4 : H 6 + H 7+ H 9
HOUSE 11: H 1 + H 8 + H 9 + H 10.
HOUSE 12 : H 2 + H 8 + H 10
CENTER OF THE DIAMOND: Source of brilliance number: H 2 + H 10.

Birth Diamond's foundation

Soul Intention number: H8+H9+H10
Soul's call number: Sum of vowels of first name and family name.
Hidden resource number: sum of year of birth's last two numbers
Hidden challenge number: H 1- H 9 or H 9- H 1
Contradiction number: H6+H7

Annual number: H 1 + H 8 + numerological year (2017=2+0+1+7).

Natural temper number: H 1+ H 8 + H 8 + H 9.
Motivation number: H 1 + H 5 + H8.
Key Resource number: H 2 + H 10 + H 11
Expression number: Numerical value of first name and family name.
SELF-REALISATION NUMBER: Expression number + House10

1	2	3	4	5	6	7	8	9
A	B	C	D	E	F	G	H	I
J	K	L	M	N	O	P	Q	R
S	T	U	V	W	X	Y	Z	

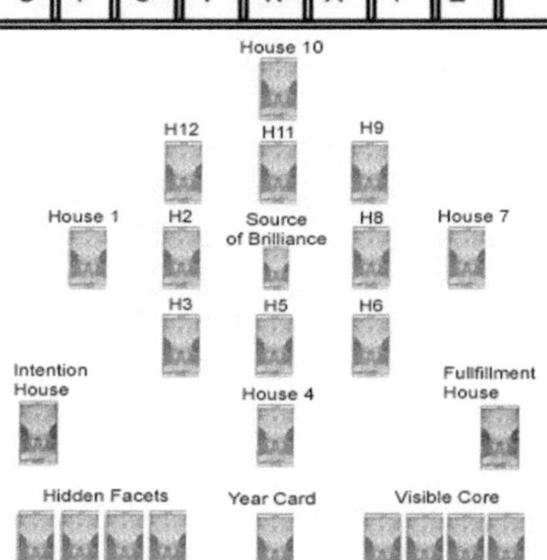

Chapter 2: The meaning of the 22 numbers.

Most people just consider the first 22 numbers to be just numbers having no specific meaning. In China and letter in Europe however, these numbers have been personified and named as living beings, as archetypes, ideas, objects and symbolic people and then gathered within a data system is called Tarot, a word meaning "evolution path". The 22 numbers have been illustrated using images, printed out on cards called "Arcanum", a word meaning "secret teachings". In this chapter, you will find the questions asked, within you, by each number/number and a summary of each number/number's strengths and weaknesses. This will help you grasp the essence of each number and to the keywords related to them. The idea is to consider a number as a life form. The symbolic name given to each number is written beside it. Number 1 is for example called the Acrobat or the Magician.

Explanation concerning the icons: A human being adapts to reality using his 5 senses or perceiving tools which are sight, hearing, touch, smell and taste. Most people (about 70% of the population) use sight to adapt. This means they are mostly receptive to images. They need to imagine and to use images to understand, to feel and to adapt to reality. The visual symbols at the end of each text are there to help feel and channel the vibrations or energy of each number. You are free to create other icons.

Number 1 – The Acrobat or Magician

The Acrobat's or Magician's questions within you: What is my intention? What are my goals and motivations? What tools and skills do i have in my hands and what can i do/create with them? What world and life do I want to create? What would I like to manifest in my reality and what resources do I have to do that? How can I be a magician by using my creative power? Do I have the required energy, abilities and skills to do this? Where can I start?

The weaknesses of this number: I have trouble starting out, motivating myself, acting, being brave, having the required energy, managing the energy I have, knowing what to do, expressing my inner child, being a happy and enthusiastic person, finding the right tools or being able to use them correctly. There is impatience, illusions and lack of experience.

The strengths of this number: I act, undertake and do what needs to be done with energy, confidence, efficiency and joy so as to achieve my goals. I express my creative power and my inner child, in the present moment, to start up new endeavors and to assert who I am. I do so using appropriate tools, smartly and with joy and enthusiasm.

Icons representing number 1:

Number 2 – The High Priestess or the Seer

The High Priestess's questions within you: What do i feel? What are my beliefs, souvenirs and screens? What's in my subconscious and in the depths of my soul? What mould must I imagine and what information must I find to give birth to this new situation? What must I give birth to? What data system and belief system am I using? Does it reflect true reality or does it deform and misinterpret it and if so how?

The weaknesses of this number: I have trouble having faith, expressing my emotions and imagination, giving birth to myself, making my wishes come true, seeing what lies in the invisible realms, not hiding information, finding the right keys and becoming free from secrets. There may be a family secret and a problem with one's mother or Grandmother.

The strengths of this number: I see and can reflect what lies in the invisible realms. I wait patiently and prepare what needs to be prepared. I give birth to what's in the subconscious. I look at what is here and now or within one's memories deeply and thoroughly. I find and give the right keys and relevant information. I give teachings. I unveil and reveal what is hidden or I hide what needs to be kept secret. I call upon the power of faith, imagination and relevant thinking to adapt. I take care of administrative management and of life.

Icons representing number 2:

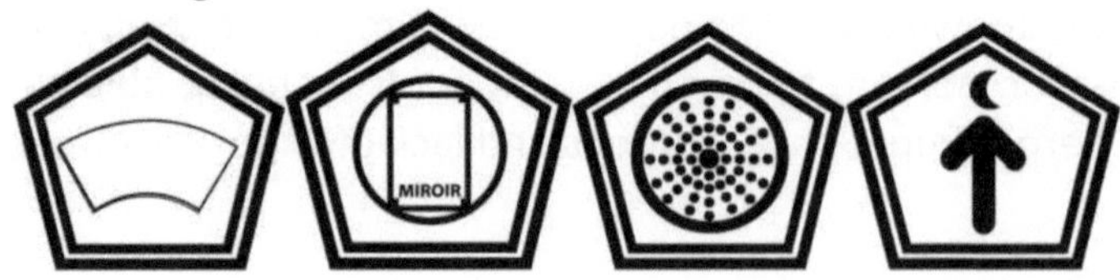

Number 3 – The Empress

The Empress's questions within you: How do I want to adapt? What do I need in order to adapt? Who or what do I want to take care of? What do I want to communicate and express? What must I understand? What must I hear and listen too? What do I need to do to organize and handle the situation efficiently?

The weaknesses of this number: I have trouble learning, understanding, feeling listened too, communicating, saying what needs to be said, doing what I say and saying what I do, undertaking studies, telling the truth, getting organized efficiently, putting things into form, adapting and expressing feminine values. There may be confusion, misinterpretation, excessive frivolity and a problem with one's mother.

The strengths of this number: I synchronize my thoughts, my feelings, my speech and my actions. I express myself with authority, social intelligence, style and elegance. I analyze, communicate, put things into form and adapt smartly and efficiently. I organize and manage the environment I'm in.

Icons representing number 3:

Number 4 – The Emperor

The Emperor's questions within you: What can I do to take my place, do my job as required, be legitimate, build my empire or play my role correctly within someone else's empire ? How can I protect my empire? What are the existing rules in the present situation? How can I organize, manage and master the current situation? What needs to be put into order? To whom or to what am I giving my personal power too?

The weaknesses of this number: I have trouble being self-confident, taking my place, accepting authority or expressing it, feeling or being legitimate, accepting society's rules and building my empire. There may be disorder, havoc, rigidity, confinement, abusive authority, materialistic attitudes, violence, territory issues and a problem with one's father.

The strengths of this number: I express my authority, my ability to organize and my personal power to take my place and do my job, to symbolically build my empire or to play my role in someone else's empire. I structure, circumscribe, allow or forbid and achieve. We have here great work power, discipline, rigor, stability, legitimacy and great confidence.

Icon representing number 4:

Number 5 - The High Priest or Expert

The High Priest's questions within you: What is the meaning of the current situation? What are its teachings? What advice do I need to take or to give? What am I aware of? What do I need to feel safe, protected and blessed? What is guiding me? What is in my heart? What is my philosophy of life?

The weaknesses of this number: I have trouble with finding or giving the right meaning to what is happening, understanding how to organize my life, having faith, accepting the educational system as it is, finding, receiving, incorporating or giving appropriate teachings and education, feeling safe, protected and blessed by life. There may be dogmatism, intolerance, moral rigidity, religious fanatism, wrong advice, proselytism and lack of unity and benevolence.

The strengths of this number: I learn to master a data system and spiritual laws. I find, incorporate and give relevant teachings as well as faith and confidence. I give meaning. I bless and give myself and other permission to succeed. I bring comfort and reassurance. I make a situation official and legal. I unite and counsel, with authority, expertise, benevolence and with spiritual strength.

Icon representing number 5:

Number 6 – The lover or the lovers or the two paths

The Lover's questions within you: How can I make the right choices? What is the right choice? What conscious or non-conscious desire is influencing my choice? What are my true desires? What truly brings me pleasure, joy and happiness? What do I like and don't like and why? How do I relate to people? What sustains and nourishes my desire to be happy? How can I balance opposites? Am I joyful and happy? How can I create a happy life?

The weaknesses of this number: I have trouble being centered within myself as i tend to center myself on others, hearing my own desires, making the right choices, expressing my artistic abilities, being committed to a relationship and living in harmony with others. There may be hesitation, immaturity, emotional dependency, a fashion victim tendency and excessive naivety.

The strengths of this number: I listen to my true desires and to those of others so as to make the right choices. I express my senses, my social intelligence, my charm and my artistic abilities in order to serve, to create beauty and harmony and in order to bring about joy and happiness. I choose. I act with commitment. I love and am in love. I create harmonious relationships and a harmonious love relationship.

Icons representing number 6:

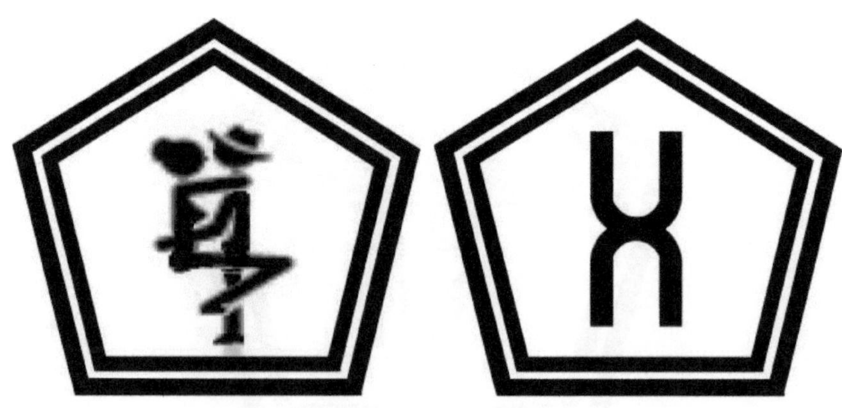

Number 7 – The Chariot

The Chariot's questions within you: What is my goal? Does it solely depend on me? What will I gain by achieving it? When will I know that I have achieved it? What is preventing me from achieving it? What are the advantages and inconvenients in achieving my goal? What resources and means do I need to achieve it? What must I do to achieve it? What is my mission? Where must I go? With what strategy and action plan? What stimulates me, what motivates me and drives me forward? What victory do I need to obtain? How can I best manage my life?

The weaknesses of this number: I have trouble looking within, settling down, defining the right goal, implementing the appropriate strategy and action plan, finding my way, mastering and maintaining my trajectory, expressing my personal power, undertaking, succeeding and being victorious. There may be functional blockages, a lack of confidence, breakdowns, impulsivity, impatience or excess speed.

The strengths of this number: I look within, check things out and define appropriate goals. I undertake the necessary actions using the appropriate means and resources, the right strategy and an efficient organization in order to be successful. I handle the situation, express my entrepreneurial spirit, move where I must and manage projects. I'm fully in charge of my life. I am ready, willing and able.

Icons representing number 7:

Number 8 - Justice

Justice's questions within you: Who or what am I judging and according to what laws? What do I believe to be true? Do I comply with the rules? What can I do to comply with the law and existing rules? Why are things happening this way? What law or underlying order is in action? What must I balance and what are my debts? How can I strike a balance between two opposite elements? What must I decide and determine? What is right for me to be or to do? What role am I playing within society? How can I improve my social life? How does my social life contribute to the harmonious flow of the society I live in?

The weaknesses of this number: I have trouble having a social life and expressing myself within society, living in an orderly and balanced manner, expressing rightness and truth, seeing what is right or accepting order and structures. There may be wounds of injustice, partiality, victimization, imbalance, coldness, harshness, a tendency to be excessively procedural or to live in an illegal manner and sometimes a difficult karma.

The strengths of this number: I become aware of the underlying order in the world and of the principle of balance. I create order, truth, beauty, art, rightness, harmony, partnership, a fulfilling social life, contracts and legitimacy so as to participate in the world around me. I analyze, weigh, measure, assess, decide and make necessary adjustments. I discipline myself, act legally and organize things with rigor and precision so as to live in harmony with who I truly am.

Icons representing number 8:

Number 9 – The Hermit

The Hermit's questions within you: His questions are deep and existential questions. Where do I come from? Who am I? Where should I go and what must I do to go there? Why? When? Where? What does this mean? Is it really true when I observe deeply? What is my deepest truth and who am I without it? What's left when I've withdrawed one thing after another? How can I find inner peace? What can I achieve?

The weaknesses of this number: I have trouble interiorizing, isolating myself from external influences, being silent, building, seeing the truth or seeing things from a distance, looking at life in a deep manner, letting go, being honest, being simple, being on time, taking time, being alone, respecting myself, working hard, evolving, moving forward towards inner peace and expressing wisdom. There may be sadness, shyness, a tendency to remain in confinement, austerity, severity, ascetism, an excessive slowness, stubbornness, rigidity, heaviness and a weighed down aspect.

The strengths of this number: I define long term goals, go deep within, isolate myself from the surroundings, meditate, observe, seek and question. I work hard, build what needs to be built and handle building sites? I move forward along the path towards my deep inner truth and towards inner peace. I become wise and can then guide and enlighten others. There is depth, an important time factor, the ability to handle time, a sense of truth and a joyfully lived solitude.

Icons representing number 9:

Number 10 – The Wheel of destiny or of Fortune

The Wheel's questions within you: What repeated patterns do I express and how can I get out of them? What are the events that changed my life and why? What makes me evolve and what makes me regress? How can I make the wheel of life turn the right way? How does it work? What is the cause of what is happening now? What changes would I like to create in my life? What are the things that change and what remains always the same? How can I adapt by using my technical intelligence? How can I serve life?

The weaknesses of this number: I have trouble getting out of my repeated schemes, understanding how life and the laws of abundance work, moving myself to do what must be done, ceasing to think all the time, adapting, serving, being practical and making the wheel turn the right way. There may be blocks and sometimes a difficult karma.

The strengths of this number: I use my technical, practical and organizational intelligence as well as my ability to understand cycles and to deal with numbers to transform unharmonious repeated patters, to try my luck, to adapt smartly, to innovate, to start again differently, to buy and sell, to be the master of my life and to serve. There is an understanding of life and an ability to make the wheel of destiny turn the right way.

Icons representing number 10:

Number 11 – Strength or the power of love

The Strength's questions within you: What vision do I have of the current situation? What do I honor? What makes me vibrate? What are my strengths and weaknesses? What makes me stronger? What are my strongest desires? What must I confront and overcome? What must I tame and master? How can I express the best of myself and succeed? How can I embody and express the power of love? What is my heart telling me? What is the symbolic meaning of what is happening? What symbolic actions can I undertake?

The weaknesses of this number: I have trouble centering myself, being connected to my heart, being fully in my body, loving myself, managing my strength, my aggressiveness and my inner violence, defining goals, expressing my personal power, being independent and succeeding. There may be a tendency to nurture power based relationships, pride, boastfulness and sometimes cruelty.

The strengths of this number: I focus my attention on my vision, my awareness and my heart. I center myself in body and heart and connect myself to "The Source of all Life". I seek clarity, define goals, express with confidence the power of love and my creative power and use my will power. I discipline myself so as to master myself and my life, be autonomous, succeed, heal what must be healed and become the best version of myself or the queen or king of my inner kingdom.

Icons representing number 11:

Number 12 – The hanged man

The Hanged man's questions within you: What am i clinging to? What force or current is driving me forward? What is limiting my freedom? What am I waiting for? What ancestral memories or past life memories must I transform? What meaning can I give to the current situation? What must I let go off? What belief or perception must I reverse or turn upside down? What must I sacrifice and for what? How can I untie or unknot the situation? What is making me suffer? How can I move from suffering to peace, joy, felicity and bliss? What brings me deep joy and delight? What are my deepest dreams? How can I find God and connect to "The Source of all life"?

The weaknesses of this number: I have trouble freeing myself from ghost like ancestral memories, taking spiritual laws into account, accepting people and situations as they are, meditating, letting go, ceasing to be like a wanderer and getting out of chaos, vagrancy, passiveness, immobility, victimization, suffering, illness or fear of betrayal. There may be blocks and things to unknot, autistic tendencies, confinement, addictions, a tendency to flee and to always complain and depression.

The strengths of this number: I reverse my points of views and beliefs, open up to spiritual reality and to unconditional love, accept people and situations as they are, let go, give the appropriate meaning to the current situation, connect with people and with life, allow things to flow, bring relief to the sufferings and misery of people, free myself from ancestral memories or past life memories by giving back, with love and respect, what belongs to my ancestors so as to live my own life. I forgive, bring delight to places and people and heal trough prayer, though the power of faith, spirituality and Christ like love.

Icons representing number 12:

Number 13 – The unnamed number or the reaper

The unnamed number's questions within you: What am I not? Who am I or what am I? What, within me, is dead, dark, sleeping or forgotten? Where am I hurt? What is my problem? What must I forget, abandon and for what? What's on the other side? How does it end? What is death? How can I die in full awareness and experience eternity? What never changes? What needs to be changed and how can I change it? What must I put an end to? What will I do when I arrive in life hereafter? How can I experience nothingness and what lies beyond it? How can I handle my ability to see subtle energy and what is invisible?

The weaknesses of this number: I have trouble surviving, getting out of ignorance, shadows, of my grave, of misery and of pain, crossing the void, embodying myself in life, seeing behind appearances, being lucid, feeling safe and secure, regenerating, disconnecting from my past, ceasing doing sabotage, playing dead, devaluing or undervaluing myself. I have trouble putting an end to what must be ended and transforming myself so as to experience my eternal nature and my deep inner truth. There may be deep anxieties, a genetic code or identity issue or an issue with dead people, with death or with life hereafter.

The strengths of this number: I learn to dive deep inside, into darkness, into nothingness so as to clearly see what is invisible, subtle energy and the required evolution path to get to the heart of the matter, become aware of my essence and experience eternity. I become aware of my true identity and of life hereafter. I become lucid and authentic. I learn how to abandon the past, how to put an end to what must be ended, how to do astral travel, how to die and become reborn, rebuilt and regenerated. I solve problems and work on structure.

Icons representing number 13:

Number 14 – The angel

The Angel's questions within you: What excesses need to be tempered? Where must I create or restore harmony, hope and find solutions? What must I improve or heal in my life? What do I want or need to ask my "Guardian Angel"? Where can I help or where do I need help? What networks am I in? Who or what am I connected too? Who are my friends?

The weaknesses of this number: I have trouble connecting to the universe, making things flow, being harmonious and embodied in life, using my psychological or technological intelligence, handling technology, working within a team or a network, finding solutions, having hope, making progress, becoming free, autonomous and independent, getting out of virtuality and concepts, making friends, adapting to the modern world, defining goals, finding the required energy, living freely, helping other or accepting help and being an Angel.

The strengths of this number: I connect myself to "The Source of all life" and use my intuition, my logic, my ability to communicate and to avoid excesses, my sincerity, my purity of heart, human values, my psychological or technological intelligence to work within a group or a network so as to bring about hope, help, relief and healing, to find relevant solutions and to create progress, freedom, serenity and success.

Icons representing number 14:

Number 15 – Passion or the devil

Passion's questions within you: Where is there a flaw? How do I sabotage myself and my life and what can I do to fix this? What makes me feel distress, anxiety and misery? Where am I like a slave? To what am I chained or bonded to? What needs to be brought to light, recognized and loved? What makes me feel passion? What means do I have or use to exert pressure on others? What must I change? How can I control the situation? How can I earn money?

The weaknesses of this number: I have trouble getting out of ignorance, shadows, fear, dependency, slavery, illegitimacy, misery, rejection, betrayal, perversity, manipulation, jealousy, obsession, possessiveness, despair or complicated situations. I have trouble seeing behind appearance, being lucid, feeling safe, having faith in life, devaluing or undervaluing myself, sabotaging my life, changing, expressing my personal power, living a satisfying sex-life, doing what makes me feel passionate, earning money and mastering the world of matter.

The strengths of this number: I am lucid, passionate, daring, bold and fearless. I see clearly in the dark. I can see and reveal existing flaws in people or within a situation. I create emotion, passion and suspense. I am connected to my instincts and deep intuition. I seduce, maneuver, spellbind, dominate using my mighty intelligence, express my need to earn money, to have a fulfilling sex-life and to use my personal power so as to serve life with humbleness and master the world of matter. I forge metal and my life.

Icons representing number 15:

Number 16 – The Tower

The Tower's questions within you: To whom or what am I connected too? What gives me structure? What languages do I master? What structures need to be changed? What am I confined in? From what do I need to free myself from? What shocks me? What makes me explode? How can I connect to "The Source of all life, become enlightened and experience God? What do I need to be aware off? What can I do to foster my soul' growth towards completion and inner peace?

The weaknesses of this number: I have trouble asking existential questions, diving inwards to find God, being connected to my divine nature, being aware, finding the right words to express myself, using language, a technological or psychological intelligence, breathing or getting out of my confinements, getting started again after a chock or a fall, adapting to the modern world or to new situations, finding my place within a group, doing teamwork and evolving harmoniously with universal laws. There may be emotional chocks, a disaster, violence, blindness, unpredictable or excessive behavior and sometimes a tendency to see things oversize.

The strengths of this number: I withdraw deep within myself, in my tower and focus on nothingness, light and silence in order to become awareness and fully aware, to become connected with God and with "The Source of all life", deconstruct and reconstruct, free and heal what needs to be freed and healed and then explode with bliss and experience illumination, a new vision and my spiritual nature. I use my understanding of structure as well as my technological or psychological intelligence to clearly express myself, to master languages or networks and to adapt to the modern world.

Icons representing number 16:

Number 17 – The Star or Venus

The Star's questions within you: What do I need to feel well physically? Am I seeing the beauty in myself, in people and in nature? What can I give to others and to life? What can I do to bring delight to others and to create a better world? Who or what do I need to forgive? What do I need to live happily on Earth? What inspires me? What fills me with joy? What gives me hope? What part of me needs to be reconnected with life and joy? What resources do I have and how do I manage them? What is the best version of me and what can I do to become it? What is my best possible future? What can I do to create abundance in every sector of my life?

The weaknesses of this number: I have trouble getting back up after having being put on my knees, being connected with joy, happiness and with "The Source of all life", embodying in life, seeing beyond form, avoiding overeating and what brings physical pleasure, letting go of my illusions, not being naïve, lazy, emotional, incoherent or stupid, defining goals, doing what needs t be done to get results, being brave, adapting to change and to the unknown and turning my life into a work of art.

The strengths of this number: I connect within my heart to the Source of all joy and of all life, to unconditional love, to the fairies, to the truth, to Mother Nature and to the Stars (Astronomy and Astrology). I live my life fully and with joy, express my sensuality and my intuition. I use my social intelligence and my ability to manage money, resources and matter. I express my artistic abilities to create beauty, harmony, hope, peace of heart, abundance, bliss and life. I bring about hope, joy, happiness, inspiration, delight and spiritual love in the hearts of people.

Icon representing number 17:

Number 18 – The Moon

The Moon's questions within you: What am I feeling? How are my subconscious, my memories and my past impacting the current situation? What makes me feel scared? Why am scared so often? What do I need to recharge my batteries and to feel well? Which part of my past must I clean up? What makes me feel truly nourished? What gate must I cross to experience a new life? What makes me dream? What are my dreams and what can I do to make them come true?

The weaknesses of this number: I have trouble expressing my emotions or motherly love, going from a state of emotional stress to a state of wellness and peace, avoiding emotional blackmail, getting out of the dark night of the soul, stopping feeling anxious or managing my fears, not being excessively emotional, incoherent or chaotic, avoiding clinging on to illusions, denials and lies, recharging my batteries, healing the wounds of my soul, nourishing myself at all levels, seeing my true dreams or making them come true, using my intuition and my imagination correctly and taking care of myself, of my family, of my home and of life.

The strengths of this number: I create, perpetuate and take care of life by expressing motherly love towards others, by being spontaneous, natural and sympathetic, by living my dreams, by recharging my batteries when necessary though safe-havens (water, food, a home, habits, sleep, music and family or intimate relationships). I work on my memories and on what is corrupted. I clean up my past. I nourish myself on all sides and at all levels. I express my emotions, my feelings, my imagination, my sensitivity and my intuition. I make things flow. I create warm, happy and intimate relationships. I live happily on Earth in a state of wellness.

Icons representing number 18:

Number 19 – The Sun

The Sun's questions within you: What do I see when I look at things with a child's eyes and with my heart? What are my goals and intentions? What do I value? What brings me great joy? What is important for me? Where must I put light? What must I clarify? What is my heart saying to me? What do I want? What part of me must I love more? How do I express the love in my heart? How can I organize things to be successful and express the best version of myself?

The weaknesses of this number: I have trouble connecting with my heart and with others, loving myself and others, enhancing and praising myself, using my will power, being autonomous, defining appropriate goals and organizing myself to achieve them, seeing myself in a positive manner, presenting a good image of myself, seeing things clearly and positively, being warm hearted and generous, not being self-centered and selfish, not having luxurious tastes, not acting like a megalomaniac, not being dependant on others to have a positive image of myself, expressing my authority without being totalitarian or like a monarch, creating a happy life and shining like a sun.

The strengths of this number: I connect with my heart and live according to it. I connect with the Source of all love and share with others. I see the positive aspects of things, create and perpetuate a happy life and I take care of life and others with warmth, fatherly love, gratitude and generosity. I create special relationships and bring joy, happiness and delight where I go. I am aware that I am pure awareness and I do my best to express my vitality, my inner light and the best version of myself. I enlighten and educate children and those who are ignorant. I define appropriate goals and implement the efficient organization and solutions to achieve them, to master the situation so as to succeed and shine like a sun.

Icons representing number 19:

Number 20 – Judgment or the Archangel

The Judgment's questions within you: What do must I remember? What must I do to access eternal life? What changes must I implement in my life? Which new world or dimension can I go into? What call did i hear or not hear? What would help me resuscitate and revive? If I die tomorrow, what would I regret having done or not done and if I had a second chance, what would I do and how would I do it? When in my life did I have the feeling of starting off a new life?

The weaknesses of this number: I have trouble revealing myself to myself, giving the right advice or messages, not judging others or not misjudging, experiencing a higher vision, becoming aware of life hereafter, listening to the signs of time, not living in a world of lies and fiction, not being confined in a grave, becoming aware of what is sacred, having faith, praying, vibrating with love, handling complex projects, using technology, implementing necessary changes, freeing myself from past memories, adapting to the unknown, giving myself or others a second chance, healing and rising like a phoenix from ashes.

The strengths of this number: I develop a higher, quantic, sacred and multidimensional vision of reality, of life, of the human body and soul and of space and time. I express the power of prayer and faith, handle complex projects, adapt to the unknown, use highly advanced cutting edge technologies or concepts based on vibration, waves, sound, images or atoms so as to pass on messages though books, websites, conferences or teachings, so as to reveal what needs to be revealed and so as to create significant life experiences that bring about deep changes, inner freedom, a second chance, awareness of the afterworld, an awakening of the soul, rebirth, renewal, total healing and resurrection.

Icons representing number 20:

Number 21 – The world

The World's questions within you: What is my vision of the world? What is my place or role in this world and what is my life mission? What must I achieve? How could I experience total achievement and satisfaction? How can I find God and experience a feeling of complete inner unity? What must I finish, complete and end in a blaze of glory? How can I make joy and happiness triumph? How can I turn my life into a piece of art?

The weaknesses of this number: I have trouble not being overwhelmed or suffocated by the world, getting out of my own world, broadening my vision, loving foreign people or lands, adhering to laws and customs, taking universal laws into account, unfolding, thriving and blossoming, embodying in the world of matter, living according to an ideal, defining goals, getting organized efficiently, summarizing, finding and incorporating teachings and education that lead to success, lifting up my soul, expressing my personal power, using my brains and my ability to create social networks, finding solutions and adapting to modern life, expressing my potential, being a wise person and accomplishing my destiny.

The strengths of this number: I find and incorporate the appropriate teachings and education. I organize, manage, achieve, engineer and express my full potential. I embody myself in the world of matter with joy so as to create abundance. I define relevant goals and implement an efficient organization to achieve them. I do what is required to uplift my soul. I use my psychological or technological intelligence to find solutions, to help and to implement progress. I open up to the world, to foreign people and lands. I play my role in the world and take customs, rules and etiquette into account. I become aware of universal spiritual laws, of wisdom and place my awareness inside the center of my heart, in my spiritual body. I experience God, bliss and total fulfillment.

Icons representing number 21:

Number 22- The Fool or The Genius or the Freeman

The Fool's or Genius's questions within you: What makes me free? Where am I free and where am I not? In what circumstances have I been stupid and what were the secondary benefits? Who or what drives me crazy? Where am I unique? What can I do to move forward and express my uniqueness? What risks am I willing to take? What leap of faith must I take?

The weaknesses of this number: I have trouble becoming free from my always thinking mind and from the impact of past life memories or ancestral memories, going beyond form and superficiality, finding relevant landmarks, understanding how the soul, the world, societies and life works, adapting to society and to the educational system, becoming aware of my rights and duties, becoming an adult or a responsible person, getting out of confusion, wandering, chaos, silliness, non rational behavior and madness, not being weird and bizarre, finding my place in the world, not living in the margins, serving life, becoming truly free and living as a free and happy person.

The strengths of this number: I move beyond family, educational and social structures. I get out of the box and open up new paths. I connect myself with the universe, with the stars, with "The Source of all life", with faith and with the genius that lies within me. I express my creative power and my uniqueness to master the world of form and matter, to serve life, to become free from any past influences or memories, to break the bonds of karma, to seek adventure, to explore new lands and travel worldwide, to bring delight to people and places, to return to my true home within the spiritual body and to live in a state of grace, as a free, joyful and happy person on Earth.

Icons representing number 22:

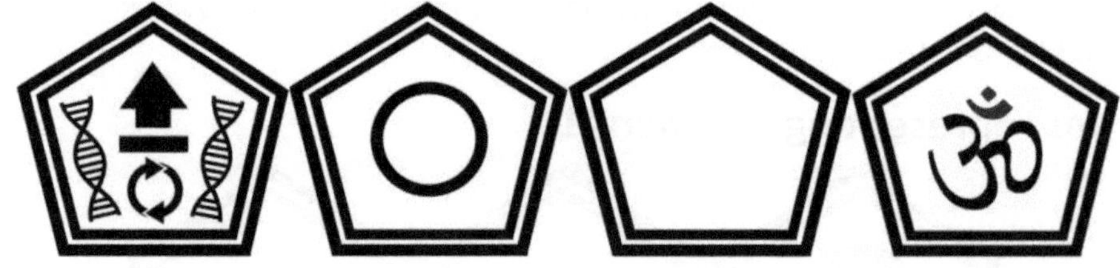

Chapter 3: Keys on how to interpret the Birth Diamond.

To correctly interpret the Birth Diamond, it is very important to know each number and house very well, by grasping its essence, its purpose, its luminous side and its dark side. You can then "see" how each number expresses itself within you and within others and you are free to choose its best possible expression.

Here are the key landmarks to interpret the Birth Diamond.

1: The Birth Diamond's goal is to bring all the different parts of you together in your heart, to become more aware and then to shine the best of who you are using the Source of Brilliance at the centre. This is done by expressing each number in its best possible form in a manner fully adapted to your evolutionary path.

2: The first level of interpretation consists of interpreting the numbers/numbers in the different houses.

3: A number is bonded to its house and tends to be expressed in the field or life sector corresponding to the house. It is very important to observe and clearly identify how one personally expresses each number, thought what beliefs, what experiences and what events.

4: There are no "good" or "bad" numbers! Every number has a purpose in the scheme of life's evolution. What is important is how you choose to express a given number and how you use the number to grow and move closer to your deep inner truth by working on your inner life (your memories, your beliefs, your choices and your actions). However, some numbers can be expressed more or less easily, naturally and in a positive manner depending on the house they occupy.

5: At the beginning of a person's life, the numbers that tend to be expressed in a positive manner, that bring help and solutions, but not always with very much awareness, are the numbers located in houses one, two, five, nine, eleven, in the source of brilliance house, in the hidden resource house, in the contradiction house, in the key resource house and in the self realization house. Problems, issues, blocs, hindrances and what one forbids oneself to be or do are usually shown by the numbers in houses Four, Six, Seven, Eight, Twelve, Hidden Challenge house and Contradiction house.

6: A second level on interpretation firstly takes into account similar numbers existing twice, three, four or five times in the Birth Diamond. A number existing two or four times suggests tension, excesses and a potential inner conflict that needs to be dealt with while a number existing three or five times suggests strong natural abilities to express the number positively, fully, but not always with a high degree of awareness.

7: Even if a number exists three times, the suggested qualities may not be expressed in the person's life because something is blocking them. That something can be a belief, a past experience or a memory. Or it may just be that the number and the house it occupies just don't naturally fit together. Coaching can then be suggested in order to help express it in its best possible form, through an increased awareness. In the same way, a potential inner conflict due to the existence of two or four similar numbers can sometimes be naturally overcomed, especially if the houses involved can easily work together.

8: The second level of interpretation secondly deals with bonded houses. When a same number is in the Birth Diamond more than once, it creates bonds between the houses concerned in a way that when one house is expressed, the other will also be expressed. **Exemple :** same number in houses 2 and 9. Your wealth can be your ability to speak languages, to adapt socially, to grasp opportunities, to travel and also the job you have. A same number can however be expressed differently in each house.

9: Each human soul potentially has all numbers/numbers within him or her, but interpreting the Birth Diamond, only existing numbers are interpreted. What a missing number symbolizes may however be found in that person's astral chart. A person born under the sign of Taurus for example should have number 17, number 2 or eventually number 18 in their Birth Diamond. If it is not the case, what is symbolized by these numbers will still exist in the person but this means that they aren't what the person needs to focus and work on.

10: Finally, the second level of interpretation takes into account pairs of numbers that are called complementary because they add up to a certain number and help to express and manifest what that number symbolizes. The most important number considered is number 22 as it leads to inner freedom. **Complementary numbers 1 and 21 help achieve inner freedom.** Numbers adding to 12, 13, 17 and 21 can also be considered. Using these complementary numbers, with their keywords, requires a good amount of insight and intuition but can be done with practice.

Chapter 4: Interpreting numbers in houses.

The Birth Diamond is made up of various parts:

- The twelve houses which numbered from one to twelve: They are identical to the astrological houses, themselves being the embodiment of the twelve psychological states of being symbolized by the astrological signs.
- At the centre of the Birth Diamond, the Source of Brilliance shows you how to reach your center and how to express the wonderful Diamond that you are so that it shines.
- The hidden facets: They reveal your soul's intention or why you came to earth in this life, your soul's call or cry, your hidden challenge you're your hidden resource and the major contradiction existing in the centre of the subconscious.
- The visible core: It synthesizes the whole of who you through your natural temper, your deep motivation, your key resource, your expression number and you self-realization or fulfillment number.
- Your annual number: It is located at the bottom center of the Birth Diamond. It describes the main influences and opportunities of the year, from birthday to birthday.

How do you analyze a number in a house?

A house is a facet of your soul, a room in your inner temple or village. The number occupying a house describes the energy that fills up the space created by the house. Each house has specific structural characteristics and a specific purpose. That means certain numbers can be expressed much easier and much more naturally in certain houses. Before analyzing a number in a house, it's important to compare what the number symbolizes and wants with the house and its purpose. Are the two similar in energy? Are they going in the same direction or are they really contradictory? In what way?

You can then observe how each number is effectively expressed in each house in the person's real life, and thus how each house/room in the person's inner temple is decorated and handled according the number occupying it. You are then free to choose the best possible way of expressing a given number in its house.

Houses at the heart of the Birth Diamond

Reminder: All calculations are done in base 22. Number 25, for example, becomes 2+5=7. House 1 has been dealt with previously.

NUMBERS IN HOUSE 1: (Your day of birth)

Summary of House 1: It is derived from the fire element and from the astrological sign of Aries. It defines who you are as an embodied human being and what image of yourself do you show to others. It shows your greatest strength and how do you use it, how are you supposed to use it and what are you supposed to do. It represents the male aspect of your personality and the type of man you feel close to if you are a woman.

Names given to House 1: Your sword, your strength, your image, your mask, your business number.

Definition of the house: This house is your sword, your striking power and the masks you put on to express yourself. It's your personality and your personal manner of being here and now. It is thus your natural "business house", the apparent self you bring to life when you express yourself, how you show yourself to the world and what you show others when you express yourself. This house also shows how others perceive you and how you perceive yourself. Do the two match? Its purpose is to spontaneously, in the present moment, express your creative power to do what must be done. The number in this house can be imaged through the corresponding Tarot number.

Calculating the number in house 1: It is obtained from your day of birth reduced to a number equal to or below 22. A person born on the 24th has number 6 in house 1.

Born before sunrise? If you were born before sunrise, you can also check out the number of the previous day and if you day of birth is between the 23rd and the 31rst of the month, you add up the numbers so as to get a new number between 5 and 22. Below are texts for numbers in house 1.

How to interpret a number in House 1:

Your day of birth (number in House 1) reveals the very first part and house of your soul. It reveals your numerological ascendant. The word ascendant comes from astrology and means how you ascend like the sun or in other words how you express yourself in action. A number in house 1 describes your way of being assertive and expressing yourself, your strengths and the image of yourself shown to others. This number is your "persona" or the outside manifestation of your inner identity while the number in house 5 reveals your deep inner identity.

Detailed description of numbers in House 1:

For a person born on the first day of the month you consider Number 1 which is imaged by the Magician or Juggler in House 1:

In order to feel confident, to be assertive, to do what must be done, to be efficient and to feel strong, you need to become one with your body, your instincts, your emotions, your feelings, your energy, your inner child, your playfulness and a practical intelligence. You need to express your creative power, to have fun, and to feel joy in whatever you are doing. You need to set goals, to decide and to act in the real world as as to get results.

You appear to be someone young, lively, natural, spontaneous, motivated enthusiast and full of energy, who likes to do thing in a personal way and who does what you feel like doing. You are smart, clever and practical. You are very good at seeing and handling all facets of a situation and at starting off new endeavors. Are you aware of this? You sometimes seem to lack a bit of maturity but so what, you show that you have all the necessary potential, arguments, know-how, motivation and ability to improvise. And you focus on results. Gifted with creative power, you live in the present moment, act with your instincts and faith, try things out and show bravery, enthusiasm, sportsmanship and entrepreneurship.

You are very good at experiencing and at doing fieldwork, at adapting smartly as the situation requires, at raising your public profile, at being efficient and at succeeding. Your energy, your ability to take quick decisions, your boldness and your ability to overcome obstacles, your frankness, your spontaneity and your commitment are your ways of expressing yourself. You therefore appear to be an active, emotional, audacious and intrepid person. Your constitution is usually strong and filled with energy. This allows you to do a lot of things and to be very independent. A quiet, peaceful, regular and monotonous life doesn't suit you. You prefer experiencing a wide variety of situations, strong commitments and feeling emotions.

You sometimes get the feeling that you only really exist when you're fully in the heat of the present moment, when you are completely dedicated to what you are doing and when you are in contact with the working world. When facing a new situation, your first reactions tend to be spontaneous commitment, enthusiasm and improvisation according to what you feel is required. You tend to be connected with your body, your instincts, your emotions, your perceptions, the energy flowing through you and your practical intelligence. You like to prove your efficiency and are mostly a field player. You prefer doing things alone and doing what you want rather than teamwork.

If you express the dark aspects of number 1, you then tend to be fooled by your mind, your beliefs and the world of matter, your impatience, your impulsiveness and by a lack of awareness, of maturity, perseverance and global vision, not making a clear difference between dreams, fantasy and reality. You can easily get angry when you don't accept situations and people as they are. As you tend to seek immediate results and as you sometimes do things too quickly, you can be better at starting off and at triggering motion than at going right to the end and at finishing. It would help you a lot to be more persistent and to consider taking the required time. When you express the luminous aspects of number 1, you become like a magician living intensively in the present moment. You are also ready, willing and able to take action, to create new situations and to experience new adventures. You are then connected to your body and heart, to clear goals, to what each moment requires, to a very smart and practical intelligence and to an outstanding efficiency. You are then capable of succeeding in whatever you do, to make things work out just like magic and to bring delight to people and places.

For a person born on the second day of the month: Number 2 imaged by the High Priestess in House 1:

In order to feel confident, to be assertive, to do what must be done, to be efficient and to feel strong, you need to experience wellness of body and soul, to feel safe in your own personnal world, to correctly prepare what must be prepared so that events can come to be, to express your feelings, your imagination and your faith, to work on beliefs, souvenirs and the sunconscious, to become free from family secrets, to find the right data or key, to manage data et to experience intimate emotional bonds with people. You appear to be a very interiorized, sensitive, intuitive and deep person who is connected to Mother-Earth. You can be gifted to access whatever data that is required to meet the needs of the present situation. This information can be related to health and wellness, to maternity and motherhood, to psychology or to more administrative data.

This enables you to access and hold the keys to knowledge, data storage and to memory, to be like a guardian of life's memories, to remove the veils of all mysteries, to bring about revelations, to give to others the appropriate keys so that they lives can progress and to help souls blossom. You can appear to be a very motherly type of person or a Grandmother who guards the secrets and traditions that are part of life.

You have a natural ability to show or suggest that you have the required data, that you know a lot of things and that you possess the key to knowledge. You can be very good at finding data and at storing and organizing that data efficiently. Are you aware of this?

You also appear to be a patient and caring person who thinks before acting and who moves forward slowly. You can express a strong emotional intelligence, respect, seriousness, legitimacy and a certain type of authority that may seem a bit severe or bleak to others. When it comes to being assertive, you are highly able to take into account and respect your entire personality and needs, to be relaxed, to recharge your batteries, to live according to your habits and rhythms, to be natural and friendly, to create nice atmospheres where one feels protected from the outside world and a personal world that you protect from any outside influence. You are very good at perceiving the atmosphere of places, at creating strong emotion filled bonds with others, at expressing your emotions, your imagination and your intuition and at managing any emotion expressed in a given situation.

You have a strong need to feel safe and protected and are thus a selective person. Your relationships are carefully chosen according to how they fit into your personal world and to how much wellness you feel with them. You may consider the outside world to be disturbing and thus prefer to create your own personal world and life where your deep sensitivity can express itself and blossom, and your special sensitivity can sometimes intuitively grasp life's architecture and memories, the world's structures, the depths of people's souls, spiritual truths and the laws that govern life and the world.

You may have a natural tendency to feel that there is a huge difference between life's natural laws, nature's laws and the laws of the outside world and it may seem quite obvious that the world just cannot bring wellness, true peace and complete satisfaction. If so, you then organize your life so that the outside world disturbs you as little as possible. You are then very good at separating yourself from the world to a point where you are not easily available because you need to be left alone, quiet and in peace. You sometimes seek a contemplative and meditative life.

If you express the dark aspects of number 2, you then tend to confine yourself to living in a tower, a monastery or into every day habits and rituals where you control as much as possible your sensitivity, your emotions, your relationships and your life. This then prevents you from experiencing fulfilling relationships and others may see you as a shy, cold, severe and distant person which is not at all who you are, as deep inside you, your heart vibrates with unconditional love and with the desire to take care of life and of others. Being more flexible and to allowing life to flow as it comes would greatly help you experience that naturally flowing perfect harmony you are seeking deep within.

You need silence, order and safety but also respect and simplicity in order to feel well, to recharge your batteries and to express your emotions. You also need to have faith in life, to listen to your intuition, to become one with your surroundings and to dream, to have dreams and to access a state of bliss through a spiritual path. You also need to become free from ancestral or past life memories which can have an important impact on your daily life and sometimes prevent you from being truly yourself.

When there is a number 2 in the Birth Diamond, there may be one or more family secrets that need to be unveiled and given back to life, to the past, where they belong, with love and respect, in order to move forward.

You can be very good at seeing the hidden meaning behind events and to see that your life on earth is but a very small part of your eternal life. You thus may have the feeling that you originally come not from Earth but from another world, from a different state of awareness and vibration level or from somewhere else. This can initially make you feel a bit confused until you bring some order into what you perceive and feel. You have the potential ability to see what exists in your memory, in present life, ancestral and past life memories. This can sometimes make you feel that you have lived elsewhere as someone else or it can make you see or feel events that happened in a place when you go there. You can be very sensitive to whatever memories are incorporated in houses and to natural telluric currents flowing all over Earth.

You sometimes have the ability to feel what other people feel, to vibrate on the same wavelength as the person you are connected to, to see a person's astral image or body, his mood, his emotions and his or her inner state of being and to communicate using telepathy. You belong to this special group of people that don't need long explanations, justifications or long speeches as you can intuitively guess what the message is. Everything is for you a question of intuition, perception and feeling. These abilities can allow you to see and relieve the sufferings and misery of body and soul and to take care of others.

Even if you greatly perceive the sounds and vibration of silence and thus value deep silence, you are also very capable of expressing yourself with clear and precise worlds when it is necessary to do so. In short, you are a sensitive, intuitive, committed, devoted, spiritual person, can show compassion, charity and unconditional love and who knows how to make sacrifices. You are like a High Priestess or a Life Magician, like a guardian of life, of its secrets, of its natural flow and of its evolution.

For a person born on the third day of the month: Number 3 imaged by the Empress in House 1:

In order to feel confident, to be assertive, to do what must be done, to be efficient and to feel strong, you need to communicate, to feel that you are listened too, to learn, study, understand, get organized efficiently, play a role in the world, trade, synchronize your thoughts and your actions and control the different parameters existing in your environment. In other words you need to adapt.

You also need to be always on the move, to satisfy your curiosity, to experience social relationships, to feel legitimate, to express your authority and to be like a super mother or assistant that handles it all.

When it come to being assertive, raising your public profile, experiencing life on the field, expressing yourself, being efficient and working within a firm, you are very good at observing, listening, understanding what's going on by connecting the ins and outs of the situation, showing insight, at seeking, finding and processing required information, at communicating, negotiating and trading, at going out to meet people and at creating bonds and at expressing your ideas with authority. You have this special ability to synchronize your feelings, your thoughts, your speech and your actions. This allows you to explore your surroundings, discover what is unknown, shape events by organizing them efficiently, be smart, handle any situation and adapt.

As you highly value curiosity, you like meeting new people, discovering new places and ideas and having fun. Because of your need for motion, you can't stay in the same place for a very long time. You tend to consider life and what you experience as a game whose rules you easily understand and adapt to suit yourself. You are resourceful and expert at finding solutions using whatever is at hand. Your smartness which is sometimes cunning, your dexterity, your ability to see in what way people or things can be useful, your sense of rigor and your demand for quality enables you to play a role in society and adapt to the outside world.

You appear to be someone who show a mix of communication abilities, natural authority, smartness and yet smoothness and elegance. You like showing others that you are quick-minded, that you have a keen eye, that you have a social intelligence, that you know how to communicate clearly, that you pay attention to detail and that you have the energy, the entrepreneurial spirit to do business efficiently, to efficiently handle the matters at stake and to symbolically take care of your empire or of someone else's empire.

You are mostly connected to your thinking mind and to reason rather than instinct and that's how you become aware of who you are and who you are not. This means that initially, you cannot clearly define who you are as you may have a double or multi-facetted personality, with many masks, who spontaneously adapts to whoever you are speaking with.

With time, you can use your mind and intelligence to manage your image and to understand how to go deeper. You can define yourself as an intermediate, as someone who connects people and information, as an organizer, a coordinator, a sales person or as someone who communicates through knowledge, ideas or though commercial transactions. You often look younger than your real age because of your permanent spontaneity, your flexibility and your open mindedness. Your issues may be caused by a tendency to think too much, by a belief that the mind can solve everything, by a need to always understand and control, by an excessive need to move and change and by a tendency to confuse fiction and reality.

The key to your evolution is becoming aware that if your mind is a fantastic and very efficient tool to adapt to the outside world, it can become your worst enemy if it takes up too much space because it impedes you from seeing life deeply, from letting your soul, emotions, feelings express themselves, from accessing spiritual awareness and your deep inner truth, sometimes from being a serious, reliable, truthful and responsible person and all in all in experiencing inner peace. You then need to make the necessary adjustments and to reconnect with your body, heart and soul. You can then become like Mother-Nature and take care of life and others very efficiently and joyfully.

For a person born on the fourth day of the month: Number 4 imaged by the Emperor in House 1:

In order to feel confident, to be assertive, to do what must be done, to be efficient and to feel strong, you need to understand society's rules, to set realistic goals and to work very hard until you get the required results. You need to be well organized, to feel legitimate and confident, to have a recognizd by all social status, to manage a territory or a structure and to either buid your own empire or participate in someone else's empire. You appear to be a well anchored, self-confident, well organized, committed, hard-working, demanding, strong, tough, powerful and persevering person who knows what she wants, who knows how to make it known and who finds the means to achieve her goals so as to find her place in the world and to symbolically build, in her own way, her empire. You have a special ability to see what a person is capable of doing, to be aware of the potential value of things and to see how they can contribute to society or to your own empire.

You express yourself with a natural authority and consider legitimacy but also comfort to be very important. Are you aware that you have strength and abilities of an Emperor and that, in your specific manner, you have built your own empire or helped someone manage their empire?

When it comes to being assertive, you are highly able to structure, organize, plan, authorize or forbid, set limits, give relevant orders, manage complex projects, express a strong sense of duty and to show others that you are capable of mastering a situation and of handling people. You have a certain striking force and a strong personal power. This gives you an ability to achieve, to build or to contribute with great efficiency, to implement and to occupy a territory, to manage it and to govern it. You therefore have a certain stature and appear to be an ambitious, experienced, mature, responsible, stable, reliable, supportive, realistic, practical, strong-willed, strategic and rigorous person.

Your strength lies in being efficient, optimistic, opportunistic and generous, in understanding your social environment with its laws, procedures and culture and in being able to play your role within a group having common goals. You can be very good at expanding your views through travelling, education, culture and sometimes spiritual experiences, at legislating and regulating, at convincing people, at doing business, at representing, counseling, administrating, dispatching, guiding, educating and at fully mastering your trade. You usually need to work within society, to adapt to its laws and social rules, to do something that makes you feel useful and to be a full and dedicated member of your economical and social environment. The outside world or rather the empire you have chosen is your field of experience.

You may be quite a cosmopolitan person and tend to embody higher-class values and lifestyle. You define yourself as someone representing a specific expression of authority through the role you play. You are able to define clear goals according to your positive, optimistic but realistic vision of how things should be, to implement efficient strategies, to make sure they bring about results and to clearly see and take advantage of opportunities when they arrive. You also have a natural ability to feel at ease almost everywhere, to make others feel comfortable and to establish useful social relationships. This highly developed social awareness and your great abilities attract people who protect you and sets of circumstances that allow you to blossom. You may thus seem to be a lucky person.

You can discover who you are by representing an official structure or firm, by spreading a cultural identity or corporate values, through travelling, education or through any job that makes you feel that you are truly part of society. What guides you are not only your instincts and a clear vision but also what you see as obvious, what you feel certain about, facts, logic, common sense and results. Number 4 in House 1 can however sometimes reveal an identity issue if you exclusively define yourself according to the role you play in the world and according to things that are outside yourself. This is because your true identity and your deep inner truth, the one that brings inner peace, can only be found inside yourself through a connection with your heart and with "The Source of all life". If you express the dark aspects of number 4, your consistency and your ability to focus on details can sometimes make you quite quibbling, stubborn and obstinate. Your need to make things work out as you want, to secure your empire and to take care of the members of your clan can turn you into a very severe and harsh person.

Your eventual issues can be caused by materialistic attitudes, by creating dependency based relationships, by seeking excessive comfort, by excessive behavior, by spending too much time at work, by a need to invade and colonize the places where you go, by always having ulterior motives and by systematically needing to define the rules and to control people and events and by a tendency to behave like a dictator. By being aware of your personal power and using it in a positive manner to serve life, by playing a useful role in the world, you give others permission to do the same and live a very fulfilling life.

For a person born on the fifth day of the month: Number 5 imaged by the High Priest in House 1:

In order to feel confident, to be assertive, to do what must be done, to be efficient and to feel strong, you need to be well centered in your heart, to feel legitimate, to get access to the right teachings, the ones that allow you to understand how society works, to find the right job and to give meaning to your life. You need to master data systems to to become an expert in something. You appear to be an outgoing, smoothly communicative, expressive, warm, benevolent, generous, social, self-confident, trustworthy, optimistic and cheerful person who naturally creates a welcoming and open minded atmosphere and thus inspires confidence.

You identify yourself as someone who has faith in life because of an awareness of the connections between sky and earth or between the world of God and the world of human beings, who is highly educated and who has knowledge concerning the human body, the human soul and the laws that govern life, society, data systems and human beings and who is legitimate, open-minded and who expresses a benevolent authority. You appear to feel concerned about people's health, safety and well-being and about the soul's evolution and salvation. You seem to be centered in your heart, well anchored in life, and gifted with a form of cleverness capable of welcoming others and of organizing, giving and spreading knowledge, teachings and even spiritual experiences. You feel at ease almost everywhere, especially in jobs involving human relationships and teamwork and you know how to make others feel at ease.

As you believe everyone has something to teach you or something that you can teach him or her, you highly value social relationships. It's as if you bear within you a timeless power and forces far beyond your own, forces that are backed up by both faith and knowledge. This allows you to accompany, guide and facilitate, to inspire faith and confidence, to relieve or heal the sufferings and misery the human body or soul. You are also able to help each person you meet find meaningful goals and gain access to what is sacred within them. Are you aware of this?

You show others that you have common sense, a broad vision of life and intuition, that are highly capable of organizing, dispatching and administrating and that you can therefore handle complex situations and projects, that you have a strong ethic and a strong sense of duty, that you are able to show gratitude, compassion and forgiveness, that you know how to handle people and that you are ready, willing and able to gather and unite people, to protect them and bless them, to teach them, guide them, educate them and lead them, to adapt to whatever the situation requires and to fully play an official role in the society around you.

You are very good at expanding your views through travelling, education, culture and spiritual experiences, at understanding people and your social environment with all its rules, codes and culture, at incorporating within a group who shares common goals, at legislating and regulating, at and dispatching and at fully mastering your role. You can be very good at doing business but only if it has a meaning to do so.

You often express yourself by referring to cultural, philosophical, medical, religious or spiritual values, by taking into account society's norms, rules, laws and customs and by representing a group, company or the person you work for. The outside world is your field of experience. You may be quite a cosmopolitan person and you sometimes tend to embody higher-class (bourgeois) values and lifestyle. You tend to value comfort and a high standard of living. You sometimes define yourself as someone with a very big heart, as a citizen of the world who is open to exploring foreign lands and meeting foreign people or as someone representing a certain lifestyle, a certain school of thought or a specific expression of moral authority, due to knowledge and expertise, through the role you play. You strangely need a certain amount of disorder to fully express yourself and yet you are very good at managing order.

You special faith often attracts luck and solutions in difficult times. It guides you. This faith is nurtured by religious or spiritual beliefs, by an ability to perceive and understand the secret laws of life and of the universe, by an ability to live harmony with these laws and with your own destiny. You may be quite sensitive to signs and coincidences or to some divine plan guiding you in daily life. You can discover who you are by playing a role in a cultural, religious, spiritual or educational institution. You sometimes consider what you do to be like a mission to which you fully commit with body and heart, as if you were the hand of some collective will or hidden force acting through you. You often need to give a special and more or less sacred meaning to what you do or to events you are involved in. You can therefore become an expert, a benchmark, a model and a reference in your field of action.

Number 5 in House 1 can sometime reveal an identity issue if you exclusively define yourself according to social, cultural or philosophical values, according to the role you play in the world and to things that are outside yourself. This is because your true identity and your deep inner truth, the one that brings inner peace, can only be found inside yourself through a deep inner experience, through the connection with your heart and with "The Source of all life" and through spiritual unity with God.

Your eventual issues can be caused by mental or spiritual confusion due to teachings that are disconnected with reality and with true spiritual requirements, by a tendency to take your social role too seriously, by excessive behavior, by seeking excessive comfort, by creating dependency based relationships, by a need to invade and colonize the places where you go and by ideological or religious fanatism. If you express the dark aspects of number 5, you always have ulterior and sometimes immoral motives and because you believe that you know what is right and good for others, you therefore have the right to define the rules, ideas and beliefs people should comply with, hence tempering with people's freedom. It is therefore very important to make a difference between your social role and your eternal self or identity and to use your knowledge and power to serve life and people. Otherwise, life may bring about painful reminders and appeals to order. When you express the luminous and positive aspects of number 5, you can then experience a very fulfilling life.

For a person born on the sixth day of the month: Number 6 imaged by the Lovers in House 1:

In order to feel confident, to be assertive, to do what must be done, to be efficient and to feel strong, you need beauty, art, colors, harmony, smoothness, joy, pleasure, a loving partner and social relationships. You appear to be someone who is very sensitive to beauty, art, form, colors and shades, to harmony and smoothness, to the vibration of pleasure and joy. You appear to be someone who can both be both centered on his or her own desires and on other people's needs and desires. Your ability to hear your true desires and your artistic abilities enable you to make decisions according to what brings joy, harmony, beauty and pleasure in your life. This allows you to make the right choices, to create form and pleasant social relationships and to turn your life into a work of art. Are you aware of this? Your strength lies in being a kind, gentle, cheerful, joyful, voluptuous, sensual and charming person that expresses herself with grace and elegance. You are very good at connecting with others, at sharing, at being committed and dedicated to the people you like, at finding satisfactory compromises, at using a social, sentimental and artistic intelligence and at being a social, caring, loving, sincere, tolerant, diplomat, pleasant, gracious and attractive person.

When it comes to defining goals and finding the means to achieve them, to being assertive, to raising your public profile, experiencing life on the field, expressing yourself, being efficient or working within a firm, you can be very good at fully using your five senses, connecting things, people and ideas, building strong social bonds, cooperating, showing harmony, attracting what you need, expressing a sense of aesthetics and making things move forward smoothly. You enjoy making the most of the daily joys of life, having a pleasant and harmonious lifestyle, being with kind and beautiful people, leisure activities and spending time creating and consolidating relationships, experiencing love, being in love and offering please to your senses. You tend to flee excesses, conflicts, brutality and confrontation and value non-violence. You can be very efficient when others support you, when your inner balance is at stake, when you work with a partner or within a team, when you feel pleasure and happiness or when you want to create a strong relationship with someone.

If you express the dark aspects of number 6, you always need other people and tend to express yourself though your partner or relationships. This may create an identity problem or a feeling of not living a very fulfilling life. When facing a new situation, your reactions are mostly based on your senses, your feelings and your emotions, on what you like or dislike, of what attracts you or what you find repulsive and on appearance. It would help you to consider causes, facts and meaning. You can be very clever at suggesting that your partner has chosen while in reality, it is you who made and oriented the other's choice according to your own desires. You sometimes find it difficult to say no because of a fear of other people's reactions, of being rejected or aggressed or of disappointing others. You can however react violently when your feelings are hurt or when you feel that what is going on is just not fair. You sometimes have such strong feelings, such a gentleness and kindness that you may find it difficult to express any aggressiveness, to fight for your rights, to be logical and to take the appropriate distance from events. You therefore need to find a balance between the time and energy you dedicate to others and that which you dedicate to yourself and to make sure that your personal happiness doesn't depend exclusively on other people's happiness.

For a person born on the seventh day of the month: Number 7 imaged by the Chariot in House 1:

In order to feel confident, to be assertive, to do what must be done, to be efficient and to feel strong, you need to set clear goals, define the appropriate stragegy/organization and to get results. You need to live a busy life and to be in full control of your life. You need to be quick, efficient, assertive and daring, like a soldier or a general that leads his troops to victory.

You present yourself as a smart, sharp minded, sparkling, well organized, straightforward and philosophical person, who loves to travel or be always on the move and who know how to get results. You are a very quick learner. You appear to be an energetic, motivated, passionate, active, enterprising, dynamic and resourceful person. You express yourself by defining clear goals and by combining intelligence, motion, organization, strategy and legitimacy so as to be efficient and successful, so as to achieve your goals, reach your destination and be victorious.

You have a certain striking force and a strong personal power. You feel passionate about the world. You need life and action. You need to be part of society, to play your role though an official job, to thrive and to blossom. You need to broaden your outlook and expand your vision or your world though travelling, though some philosophical, cultural or spiritual research, by fighting for an ideal, for cultural, entrepreneurial and sometimes military values, for people's or nature's rights or by enforcing the law through a specific form of legal expertise. Your instincts, your fighting spirit and your natural drives strongly influenced by social norms, by a cultural, philosophical, legalistic or spiritual ideal and by a strong awareness of the impact of your actions on the surroundings. This enables you to channel your energy towards positive, noble and socially useful goals and endeavors. You can be very good at buying or selling goods and services, at conquering new lands or new markets and at implementing new norms, rules or laws.

This enables you to find efficient organizational solutions, to realize projects according to a well thought strategy and to implement the appropriate logistics and so to do your job efficiently. One could say that you are like a general leading his troops to battle. You can discover your identity through action, travelling, projects and your entrepreneurial spirit. You are very good at being in control of yourself and of events, at convincing people, at having things go your way, at handling complex situations, at incorporating yourself within organizational structures having common goals or at managing such structures and at bringing, like a coach or a taxi, every person to its destination or every mission to its achievement.

If you express the dark side of number 7, you tend to fooled by your impatience, your impulsiveness and by an excessive eagerness to get results. You then sometimes loose you way, hang on to inappropriate goals, burn the candle at both ends and get exhausted. You can easily get angry when you don't accept situations and people as they are.

If you tend to seek immediate results and do things too quickly, you can be better at starting off and at triggering motion than at going right to the end and at finishing. It would help you a lot to act with joy and peace, to be more persistent and to consider taking the required time.

For a person born on the eighth day of the month: Number 8 imaged by Justice in House 1:

In order to feel confident, to be assertive, to do what must be done, to be efficient and to feel strong, you need order, justice, rightness, harmony, beauty, responsibility and to play a role in society, often within a structure. You seem to be an interiorized, reserved, straight, responsible, serious, strict, rigorous and persistent person who has a deep and intense gaze, who asks herself and others a lot of questions, who looks at people straight in the eyes so as to see the truth, who strongly needs to connect with people and who is very sensitive to balance, imbalance, order and to harmony. Although you may sometimes seem harsh and severe at first sight, you're a very social, balanced and charming person once the ice is broken. You present yourself as someone who believes that there is an underlying invisible order behind life where everything in interconnected and that there is a divine justice where every action has consequences and where each form comes from a content and should express substance. You are therefore highly sensitive to any feelings of fairness or unfairness, justice or injustice, rightness or non rightness and in other words to right or wrong. You are also very sensitive to beauty, art, to the connections between events, things and people, to structure and to form.

You therefore express yourself according to the rules that you feel are right. Are you aware of this? This turns you into someone who feels very concerned about acting in harmony with cosmic laws or with socials rules, about being right and precise and about seeing that things are as they should be when one observes deeply. You can therefore have a strong interest in dedicating yourself to legal activities or in understanding how the human body, the human soul, civilizations, clubs, the current society and more specifically its public administrations works out.

When it comes to defining goals and finding the means to achieve them, to being assertive, to raising your public profile, experiencing life on the field, expressing yourself, being efficient or working within a firm, you can be very good at observing deeply both form and structure, at seeing all the facets of a person, object or situation, at finding compromises and alternative solutions, at weighing the for's and the againts, at selecting, choosing and firmly deciding, at balancing opposites, at restoring order and harmony, at expressing a social intelligence, at creating strong bonds and partnerships with people, at creating or managing clubs, at understanding how society works, at using data systems, norms and rules, at managing contracts and at playing an official role within society.

You can discover your identity through a feeling of harmony, beauty, joy, happiness, grace, through harmonious relationships and partnership, by being a member of a club and by being aware that you are a member of a specific civilization and of something must greater than just yourself. You sensitivity to structure and to form can give you abilities related to legal, artistic or aesthetic activities. If you express the dark side of number 8, you tend to fooled by a need to be perfect and by confusing perfection and doing your best. An excessive need to question, to implement and apply laws and rules, to be right and to control can sometimes weigh you down, create rigid behavior and impede the natural flaw of life and action. You can then be very good at not accepting situations and people as they are and be very unfair with yourself and others. It would then help you a lot to redefine the rules and to reset you inner moral judge.

For a person born on the ninth day of the month: Number 9 imaged by The Hermit in House 1:

In order to feel confident, to be assertive, to do what must be done, to be efficient and to feel strong, you need time, questions, research, simplicity, humbleness, building site like situations and to evolve towards inner peace. You appear to be a deep, interiorized, solitary, reserved, simple, minimalist, quiet, calm, patient, cautious, serious, honest, responsible, mature, persistent, tenacious, relevant, experienced, well organized and practical person. You sometimes appear to be distant and a bit harsh and sometimes wise and mischievous. You think before you act. You like questioning, searching and moving forward along the path that leads to inner peace and to your deep inner truth. You are well aware that there is a hidden order and structure behind reality.

You like working, doing your best and are concerned about quality, long term, durability and safety. You need to express yourself according to principles and to your strong inner judge, through long term goals. You often need to build and to experience building site like situations. Are you aware of this? You present yourself as someone with great work capabilities and an understanding of architecture, as someone with long term goals and a strong sense of duty, as someone who needs to take their time, as someone who knows how to focus, concentrate, show discipline and rigor, take time alone away from the noisy world, experience silence and stillness and meditate. It sometimes seems that you have come a long way, that you have acquired wisdom by incorporating life's lessons, that you are enlightened and that you have the ability to guide lost souls to their ultimate destination, deep within their souls and hearts.

When it comes to defining goals and finding the means to achieve them, to being assertive, to raising your public profile, experiencing life on the field, expressing yourself, being efficient or working within a firm, you can be very good at observing deeply and silently for whatever time necessary, at seeing things deeply and from a distance, at analyzing the history and the causes of the existing situation, at seeing the distance covered so far and that which remains to be covered, at asking relevant questions, at getting to the heart and bottom of the issue, at leaving behind what must be abandoned, at resisting external pressures, at defining simple and clear goals, at referring to principles and eternal laws and at organizing things, at handling projects and long term building sites.

You are very good at defining and planning out each and every step of an endeavor, at making time your ally, at patiently overcoming obstacles along your road, at working with numbers, theories and hypotheses, at experimenting and doing research, at working on structure, architecture or history, at using data systems, plans and technical schemes, at creating order, truth and awareness, at guiding and counseling, at being humble and truthful, at doing your best and at being at peace with yourself. Discovering your identity can occur thanks to personal research, by becoming aware of your family or soul history and or your eternal life, by handling a long term building site, by building a work or art or through meditation.

If you express the dark side of number 9, you may seem shy and sad because you haven't yet learned to see your own worth and value, to love yourself and life enough, to have confidence, to overcome fear, to free yourself from your past, to dare and try your luck and to get out of your isolated world. There may then be a tendency to be insensitive and unconcerned, to find refuge in excessive work, to lack social abilities and joy, to ask too many questions, to be too slow, to be pessimistic and cynical, to miss out opportunities, to need to always be in control and to be selfish and lonely. It's then up to you to express the best of number 9, to change your vision of yourself, of life and of people and to create a meaningful, joyful and happy life that makes you experience true your inner peace.

For a person born on the tenth or twenty eighth day of the month: Number 10 imaged by The Wheel of Fortune/of Destiny House 1:

In order to feel confident, to be assertive, to do what must be done, to be efficient and to feel strong, you need to understand how life, people and things work, to repeat so as to become an expert and to adapt. You appear to be a smart person that has great practical abilities, a strong sense of service, a strong sensitivity to cycles and numbers and great abilities to analyze, criticize and filter, to process data, to focus on details and limits but also on health issues, cleanliness and hygiene, to organize, trade and to adapt. Are you aware of this? You present yourself as someone modest and discreet and yet smart, skilful, astute, clever, crafty, ingenious, practical, resourceful and as regular as clockwork, with an orderly mind and a methodical spirit, as someone who loves using numbers and working with great precision, with a strategy and with a sense of perfection, as someone who has quantified targets and a strong ability to focus, as someone who has a strong willingness to serve and a strong sense of duty and as someone who feels very concerned about the environment and nature and about health and hygiene.

You often love plants and animals. Your very special connection with time allows you to see and understand time cycles, repeated schemes and history. You often need to be in constant motion and to show others that you have a strategy and the know-hows to implement it. You have a strong marketing, commercial or technical intelligence, a strong ability to do things with your hands, to process data, handle numbers, communicate negotiate, try your luck and adapt.

This allows you to understand how to best use the resources in your environment, to understand how things work, how to make life flow and to put things into pieces and rebuilt them in a better way, either by copying or either by innovating and improving. You can be very good at copying what already exists so as to reproduce it in great numbers, at creating something new from something old but also at getting out of repeated schemes so as to evolve, create your own life and a totally different life cycle or in other words, to make the wheel of destiny turn the right way. You appear to be quite lucky but this is because you have given yourself the means to be so, because you take matters in your own hands and do what must be done and because you are able to find, create and use appropriate and efficient tools, handle time, manage projects and adapt smartly. And you are very good and expressing these qualities when it comes to defining goals and finding the means to achieve them, being assertive, raising your public profile, experiencing life on the field, expressing yourself, being efficient or working within a firm. This allows you to find your way in the world of matter and to master it. Discovering your identity can occur through your awareness of what moves and what stays still, though rhythms, numbers and cycles, through vibration, tools and through the intelligence of life. If you express the dark side of number 10, you then have a tendency to over think, overanalyze and overcritisize and to believe that this is a normal state of being whereas you can only find happiness and discover who you are by being intensively present and by being connected to your body and centered in your heart. It would therefore help you a lot to become the master of your very efficient brain and not its slave in order to stop being stuck in repeated schemes and to get access the more authentic and intuitive parts of yourself.

For a person born on the eleventh or twenty ninth day of the month: Number 11 imaged by Strength in House 1:

In order to feel confident, to be assertive, to do what must be done, to be efficient and to feel strong, you need to be centered in your heart, to love what you do and to do what you love, to do what you want, to use your creative power and to become the best version of yourself by setting goals, getting organized efficiently and by succeeding. You appear to be a worthy, hardworking, frank, sincere, efficient, reliable solid, strong, calm and yet very observant, passionate and vibrant person who has a big heart, a strong will power, lots of energy and who lives intensively in the present moment.

You sometimes look like a wild cat ready to pounce. You are usually well centered in your body and heart and yet strongly connected to others. This allows you to be both very good at incorporating into a team and working by yourself in total autonomy. You present yourself as someone who is very sensitive to self-image and to any power based behavior and who is highly concerned with self control of animal instincts, preferably with harmony and unencumbered.

What is really important for you is to express yourself according to what you value, according to an ideal and to what you consider as essential, to be clearly aware of who you are and to have a clear vision of every person you are related too, of the situation you're in and of your environment. And you tend to trust your instincts. You also need landmarks, to see where you stand and where you are heading and to be well organized. Are you aware of this? You are very good at making your resources and you ideal or goals match and meet and at using your will power to achieve your clearly defined goals. If you can show great generosity to those who go your way, you have a tendency to resolutely and firmly state what you believe is the absolute truth and have difficulty accepting being hindered or contradicted, making mistakes, failing or when things don't go the way you want. You can become aware of who you are by being intensively aware in the present moment, through an ideal, values, goals, action, commitment, and achievements, by asserting your strength and by expressing you will power and your creative power, sometimes by struggling to promote a company by being efficient and competitive but also by becoming the best version of yourself, by becoming a radiating center, a brilliant person, a source of strength, awareness and love.

When it comes to defining goals and finding the means to achieve them, to being assertive, to raising your public profile, experiencing life on the field, expressing yourself, being efficient or working within a firm you have the need and the ability to be fully centered in your body and heart, to feel that special state of calmness where how to be and what to do becomes clear and to connect yourself with the creative power of love and with "The Source of all life". You need landmarks, relevant goals that make things progress, an efficient organization, to find appropriate resources and solutions and to succeed. You then have great insight, a clear vision and a keen sense of what is obvious and of what is required at each moment. You are a hard working and dedicated person.

This gives you a good amount of self confidence, bravery, a fantastic ability to summarize, an ability to manage and handle people, self control and to the master of your life according to how you see and want. You are very good at making connections between matter and spirit, at doing your best, at finding a balance between expressing power and love or human values, at bringing about change, at improving what needs to be improved, at living a harmonious sex-life, at bringing about more awareness and autonomy and at using your strength to serve life. This usually allows you to be a very successful person.

If you express the dark side of number 11, you then have a tendency to have a materialistic or flawed vision of life and of yourself, to be self centered, disconnected from people and selfish and so to live in a lonely world, be very stubborn and rigid, to be excessively proud, to nurture a superiority or inferiority complex because you lack self confidence, to give your power to other people who then decide how you should be or what you should do or to always try to control and dominate others in a way that creates power based relationships, stress and tension. You are sometimes very impatient and to get angry when things don't go your way! It would help you a lot to see that life loves you and that you are worthy, to see that you deserve to be happy and successful because you are a child created by "The Source of all life", to learn to just be here and now, to accept people and situations as they are, to accept that some things take time, to let things flow as life wants them to, to focus on the love in your heart on feelings of joy, harmony, stillness, peace or bliss, on your abilities and on successful strategies, to stop struggling, creating conflict, focusing on duality and feeling cut off from other people, to change non-adapted beliefs, to connect with people within your heart so as to create harmonious relationships, to become autonomous and self sufficient, to express your uniqueness, your truth, your power, your light and what your heart tells you, to become the best version of yourself and to live as a creative, free and happy person.

For a person born on the twelfth day of the month: Number 12 imaged by Strength in House 1:

In order to feel confident, to be assertive, to do what must be done, to be efficient and to feel strong, you need to go from a state of suffering to a state of bliss or enchantment, to become free from ancestral or past life memories, to relieve people's suffering and to satisfy societie's needs.

You present yourself as a radar like, highly sensitive and intuitive person who knows how to let go and let things flow, as someone who knows how to be without expectations, who accepts situations and people as they are and who knows how to be like a little drop of water, by playing a role in your community, in the ocean of life, as someone who has faith, a spiritual vision of life that makes you see what is beyond everyday reality and sometimes experience transcendence and as someone who has knowledge coming from ancestors or past lives or knowledge of how to unknot situations and bring relief to the sufferings and misery of people's bodies or souls. Your amazing sensitivity can sometimes enable you to tune into collective consciousness and to bring back information from there. Are you aware of this?

When it comes to defining goals and finding the means to achieve them, to being assertive, to raising your public profile, experiencing life on the field, expressing yourself, being efficient or working within a firm you have the need and the ability to connect with people, to become one with the existing atmosphere and the people around you, to slip in like a fish in the flow of events, to express yourself according to your feelings and intuition, to be inspired but also to see things from a distance beyond matter, to give an appropriate meaning to the current situation and to dedicate yourself with love to what the situation requires.

You can be very good at waiting for the right moment to act, at showing charity, compassion, devotion, forgiveness and unconditional love, at taking spiritual laws into account, at being aware of what is sacred, at calling upon your ancestor's or past lives' abilities but also at becoming free from them, at reversing those inadequate points of views and beliefs that prevent you from moving forward, at making things flow and at bringing joy, delight and magic wherever who are. You sometimes have the ability to act by taking into account invisible data and subtle details that others just don't see, according to what you deeply feel or to a very special and personal logic. When you do this, you can turn what seems impossible into an implemented achievement that matches your goals and express a very special efficiency.

If you know how to go with the flow of events, follow others, live on a day to day basis and just let things happen without interfering, you are also very going at considering society, its models, norms and religions, from a distance and at living according to your own truth, dreams, intuition and feelings, especially during hard times.

You sometimes need to explore different paths before finding your way and you sometimes need to be guided, taken in charge and reassured. You can become aware of who you are by expressing your great sensitivity, by using your faith and its magical powers, through meditation or spiritual practices, by living according to spiritual truths, by playing a role in a large community or international firm, by bringing relief to others and by expressing devotion, charity, self-sacrifice and love. You can therefore thrive in any activity related to medical or paramedical care, religion, spiritual counseling, image and sound, data systems and social care. You can balance and increase the efficiency of this number by developing an ability to analyze and discriminate, by using a technical intelligence, by processing data with accuracy, by being well organized on a daily basis and though courses in self-growth.

If you express the dark side of number 12, you may seem confused, chaotic, lost, incoherent, strange, complicated or stuck with repeated ancestral or past life patterns that need to be deactivated. You then sometimes have a tendency to go underground, indulge in secrecy, lack of clarity, wishful thinking and illusions, nurture suffering, always complain and be pessimistic, flee reality by being into dream worlds and to place yourself in very complicated, tangled, messy and knotted situations. You sometimes lack energy, motivation, appropriate organization and practical abilities, tend to count on fate to decide what should be done, let others assist you rather than be in charge of your life or follow unhealthy religious or spiritual belief patterns. It's then up to you to undertake the necessary work so as to express the best of number 12 and gradually become the best version of yourself.

For a person born on the thirteenth day of the month: Number 13 imaged by the unnamed card or Death in House 1:

If you were born on the very special thirteenth day of the month, you may have experienced some on the following situations or carry difficult ancestral or past life memories. Someone very close to you may have died suddenly or have very serious problems. You may have a very strong connection with people living in the afterlife and be able to perceive this part of reality. You may have experienced a disaster, a trauma, a painful divorce, a disruption or breakdown. You may be structured in a way that there are only very thin screens, within you, between the world of matter and the world of invisible and subtle energies.

This then allows you to see, feel, and reveal what is invisible and more specifically the invisible structure of matter and the structure of motion, a bit like an X-ray device. You may also have chosen to implement great changes within yourself or within other people in this lifetime. How you express your personality and create your life then depends on how you manage what has just been said. You are however asked to become aware that your soul is eternal and that your life will continue when your physical body ceases to exist. This can be quite challenging!

You present yourself as someone who is profound, mysterious and secret, who has a great magnetic strength and a strong personal power, as an authentic, intense, fascinating and spellbinding person, as someone with a deep and penetrating eye and as someone who's extreme sensitivity can access the depths of invisible realities, of people and of humanity. You are very good at experiencing complete fusion with your environment, at seeing behind appearance, at feeling what is not said, at perceiving hidden emotions, hidden tensions, risks, flaws, issues, power struggles, dangers and what is at stake. You have the ability to grasp what is causing the present situation, to decode symbols and signs, to resolve enigmas, to access data located in the genetic code, to reveal to each person what her issues are, to go to the bottom of the pit, to unlock the mysteries of life and death, to explore the afterlife through "out of body experiences", to see ghosts or invisible people and to gradually transform yourself so as to implement your deepest inner truth and live according to an awareness of eternity. Are you aware of this?

When it comes to defining goals and finding the means to achieve them, to being assertive, to raising your public profile, experiencing life on the field, expressing yourself, being efficient or working within a firm you have the need and the ability to clearly name things, to perceive and handle your subconscious drives and existing invisible structures, to master your sexual and subtle energy but also how things join, fit and get set in motion, to trust your flair and feelings, to act according to your personal logic and to very subtle details that only you can see, to focus and channel energy where is required, to make great efforts to make things move and to get to the point.

You are very good at resisting to external pressures, at solving problems and at overcoming crisis, at handling fear, at letting go of the past, at severing links with people and the past, at ending what must be brought to an end, at accepting loss, at going beyond wounds and traumas, at eliminating physical or psychological toxins, at showing others what is unknown to them, at revealing change bringing initiation techniques, at transforming people and events, at creating new products from raw materials, at fighting for what you want with great intensity and at quickly regenerating after a tiresome experience like a phoenix becoming reborn from its ashes. This can make you efficient in a very special way, as if you were able to change the field of what is impossible so that it matches your deepest will, your goals and your achievements. You can be very good at seeing people, society and life from a great distance and at becoming free from educational or environmental beliefs, opinions, norms, culture, pressure or desires. You prefer to create you own identity, your own ways and your own destiny. Because you value intensity and authenticity, you can sometimes be harsh and despiteful with people who live and focus on fiction, who are not at 100%, who compromise and live mediocre lives, who are lazy or who play games with themselves and others.

If you express the dark side of number 13, you may seem to be a complicated, anxious, anguished, tormented, tortured, unhealthy or toxic person. You may be stuck with psychological or physical toxins that need to be cleaned, in bad habits that need to be ended, in destructive patterns that need to be unlocked, in unhealthy past life schemes that need to be dissolved and in excesses that need to be balanced. You may have an excessive need to break with the past and to change people and events, to create tension, drama, tragedy or crisis, to live underground and to be at war with yourself and the world. Your issues may then be caused by ignorance and blindness, by a tendency to focus exclusively on problems, negativity, imperfection, pain and suffering, by a tendency to reject and exclude and by refusing to live happily and to be alive. It's then up to you to undertake the necessary work so as to gradually become the best version of yourself.

You can increase the power and efficiency of number 13 with number 9, i.e. by accepting to learn and evolve by seeing that this can only happen through change, by asking the right questions, by seeing things in a long-term perspective, by looking deep within and experiencing silence, by meditating and going beyond emptiness, by naming what needs to be named, by seeking quality, honesty and inner peace, by moving forward on the path that leads to your deep inner truth, by letting yourself be guided by your inner light, by learning how to build and handle building sites, by becoming aware of how reality and life are structured and by living a life according to spiritual principles. Meditation and walking can be very beneficial.

For a person born on the fourteenth day of the month: Number 14 imaged by Temperance or the Angel in House 1:

In order to feel confident, to be assertive, to do what must be done, to be efficient and to feel strong, you need to feel connected to the universe and to humanity, to promote human values, to use a special psychological or technological intelligence to fix what needs to be fixed, to find solutions, to do things within a group, to be part of a network, to somehow create a better world and to adapt to modern life. You present yourself as someone who is natural and balanced, unusual, angel-like and unique, who is contradictory and paradoxical, very kind and smooth and yet very energic and dynamic, calm and yet quick witted and relevant, who greatly values freedom, sincerity, connecting with people, brotherhood, helping others and human values, who is gifted with a strong psychological, technological, logical and intuitive intelligence, as someone who can understand concepts, diagrams and plans, find solutions, show the way and bring messages with a great truth, benevolence and purity of heart and as someone who can handle complex projects. Are you aware of this?

When it comes to defining goals and finding the means to achieve them, to being assertive, to raising your public profile, experiencing life on the field, expressing yourself, being efficient or working within a firm, you are very good at setting aside your family, educational or social background so as to express your uniqueness, at being fully aware of space, time and what the situation requires, at connecting with the universe, life energy and with people, at being in a vibrating state of calm and joy, at handling and processing data, at communicating clearly by synchronizing yourself with others, at working within a network or a team and at managing transitional type situations.

You can also be very good at seeing and creating coincidences and synchronicities, at exerting your free will, at being fully self-sufficient and free from any economic or emotional dependence, at helping, fixing and healing, at bringing hope, serenity and balance, at implementing progress, at mastering technology, media and networks, at promoting human values, at making things flow, at taking time for leisure activities, at serving with kindness and efficiency, at facing the unexpected, at adapting to modern life, at expressing the angel that lives within you and at living freely and happily. Are you aware that others sometimes see you as an angel? You can become aware of who you are by playing a role in a group or network, by helping others and by becoming aware that you are made of love. You can increase the strength and efficiency on number 14 through number 8, by creating truth, order and justice, by taking the law of balance into account, through a beautiful love relationship, by promoting balance, by choosing and deciding according to what you feel is right, by understanding the laws and rules of the society you live in, by living in harmony with cosmic laws and society's laws and by playing an active role within a club, an administration or within society.

If you express the dark side of number 14, you then sometimes seem to come from another planet or to be an unpredictable, insensitive, over thinking, non-assertive, artificial, asexual, dreamy, lazy, excessively nervous or on the contrary completely apathetic person who lives in a world of utopia or according to personal concepts, programs, illusions, ideologies or to the needs and wants of society.

Being multidimensional, you can connect yourself to various realities and people at the same time but you sometimes give the impression that you are not really here and now. Your issues may be caused by a tendency to be disconnected with your body's needs and desires and with the world of matter, by a tendency to abandon others because you are afraid of being abandoned, by the excessive need to save others, by a tendency to spend too much time with your friends or with the group where you belong and by neglecting your personal/family well being, by a tendency to lack energy, realism and authority and to be dependent on other people and to confuse true freedom with the illusion of ghost of freedom. It is then up to you to undertake the necessary work so as to express the positive aspects of number 14.

For a person born on the fifteenth day of the month: Number 15 imaged by passion or the devil in House 1:

In order to feel confident, to be assertive, to do what must be done, to be efficient and to feel strong, you need to feel passion in what you do and to do what makes you feel passion, to take into account the dark side of life and people, to handle crisis, people with problems or safety issues, to overcome your wounds, traumas and fears, to put love and light where there is darkness and misery, to earn money and spend it, sometimes to work with metal, to have a satisflying sexual life, to express your personnal power by serving life and to be in full control of your life.

You present yourself as someone who has lots of energy, a great fighting spirit and a strong survival instinct, as a magnetic, passionate, intense, daring, intrepid and fearless, very lucid, quite secret and mysterious, authentic, intriguing, exiting and spellbinding person who can sometimes be cheeky, bold, mischievous, naughty and manipulative. You carry within you strong emotions that burn like the flames of a volcano. This gives you an extreme sensitivity, a strong personal power that can seduce and influence and a deep and penetrating eye that can see or feel what lies within the subconscious, what exists behind appearance, what is not said, hidden emotions or tensions, risks, flaws, issues, power struggles, dangers and whatever is at stake. When you want something or when you make a decision, your deepest will and your instincts express themselves. This makes you feel your needs, wants and decisions so intensively that you just must make them come true, for the better or the worst and with you, one never really knows what is going to happen and how things will turn out. Are you aware of this?

When it comes to defining goals and finding the means to achieve them, to being assertive, to raising your public profile, experiencing life on the field, expressing yourself, being efficient or working within a firm you also have the need and the ability to take every parameter into account and especially the invisible ones, to access hidden data, to decode symbols and signs, to solve enigmas, to find the needle in the haystack, to see the flaws, dark zones or risks and then bring about changes, to reveal to each person what her issues, flaws or fears are, to act according to very subtle details that only you can see, to focus and channel energy where is required, to master your sexual and subtle energy, to make incredible efforts to make things move your way and to get results.

You can be very good at exploring the dark side of human nature, at provoking others, at seeing and handling the saboteur which potentially exists in every human being, at controlling your emotions, at overcoming your fears, wounds or traumas, at resolving issues, conflicts, problems and crisis, at eliminating physical or psychological toxins and pollution, at fully expressing your instincts, your impulses and your passion, at creating suspense or intense emotions, at living a passionate but harmonious sex-life, at resisting to any external pressure, at trusting your flair, at facing danger, at being aggressive and at fighting to make events go your way or to make the situation safe.

You can be very good at chaining, at unleashing and at breaking free, at creating bonds and at breaking them, at quickly regenerating after a tiresome experience like a phoenix becoming reborn from its ashes, at expressing a highly efficient strategic intelligence, at showing great tenacity, at implementing change, at creating new products from raw materials, at working with metal, at earning money, at expressing your personal power to take the situation in charge, at mastering the world of matter and at teaching others what is unknown to them. You usually tend to reject models and you don't grant much credit to appearance and to social or cultural values. You are sometimes very individualistic and like to go your own way without being indebted to anyone. Your inner tension and aggressiveness and your need of intensity can sometimes generate a difficult character and relationship issues.

If you express the dark side of number 15, you may them seem to be a complicated, anxious, anguished, tormented, tortured, unhealthy or toxic person. You may be stuck with psychological or physical toxins that need to be cleaned (greed, possessiveness, jealousy, lust for power and obsessions), in bad habits that need to be ended, in destructive patterns that need to be unlocked, in unhealthy behavior that needs to be changed and in excesses that need to be balanced.

You may have an excessive need to create tension, drama, misery, tragedy or crisis, to live underground and to be at war with yourself and the world. Your issues may then be caused by ignorance and blindness, by a tendency to focus exclusively on problems, negativity, imperfection, pain and suffering, by a tendency to reject and exclude and by refusing to live happily and harmoniously. This can then create very stressful and gloomy situations.

An excessive or destructive aggressiveness always ends up turning against yourself as live makes you pay whatever misery you cause. It's then up to you to undertake the necessary work so as to gradually become the best version of yourself. When you learn to master the dark side of yourself, to make peace with yourself and to love yourself, you can then become a very powerful and fascinating person who can use his or her power to reveal mysteries, change people and make this world a better and safer place to live. You then use your power to serve life. You can increase the efficiency of number 15 through number 7, i.e. by honestly recognizing your potential, worthiness and value, by giving yourself permission to become the best version of yourself, by defining clear goals and a clear direction that enables you to channel your energy and passion, through a job or activity that makes you feel passion and by handling complex projects, issues and situations.

For a person born on the sixteenth day of the month: Number 16 imaged by The Tower in House 1:

In order to feel confident, to be assertive, to do what must be done, to be efficient and to feel strong, you need to act freely, to be enthusiast, to work on structures or on complex data systems, to implement changes in structure though organization and awareness and to manage housing issues, builing sites or complex projects. You sometimes need to go deep within yourself and to be isolated from the outside world in order to connect with the universe, find God, connect to the light within your heart and to understand the will of God and do what is required by Necessity. At other times, you need to rebel, to express yourself, to breack down the walls and any chains hindering your inner freedom and to explode like a dynamite stick so that things change the way they need to by bringing out a new vision. You also need to use a special psychological or technological intelligence to fix what needs to be fixed, to find solutions, to do things within a group, to be part of a network, to somehow create a better world and to adapt to the modern world and its complex data systems.

You present yourself as someone who is contradictory and paradoxical, who can sometimes be very silent, calm, solitary, interiorized, attached to tradition, focused, highly structured, well organized, always questioning and thinking and regularly confined in a tower because of a more or less conscious need to connect with God and at other times as someone who greatly values freedom of action and expressing one's uniqueness, who can be able to suddenly increase inner tension and be very energic, dynamic, electrical, impatient, quick witted, relevant, surprising, unpredictable, chocking, stressed, modern and like a dynamite stick ready to explode. You know how to be intensively aware of the present moment and yet to be inwardly unattached at the risk of seeming to be insensitive and unconcerned. You seem to greatly value sincerity and connecting with people, to be gifted with a strong psychological, technological, logical and intuitive intelligence and to understand structure, architecture, concepts, ideologies, diagrams, numbers languages and plans. Are you aware of this?

When it comes to defining goals and finding the means to achieve them, to being assertive, to raising your public profile, experiencing life on the field, expressing yourself, being efficient or working within a firm you have the need and the ability to be isolated from external turmoil, to see things from a distance, to look within and connect with the universal underlying order of life, to access spiritual truths, to be in a vibrant state of calm and joy, to be optimistic and positive, to show enthusiasm, to see the promising aspects of a person or situation and the best version of people and situations, to live in harmony with cosmic order, to concentrate, to take "Necessity into account, to bring hope and find solutions, to structure and organize in the best possible way, to process data and to handle complex projects. You can be very good at being suddenly inspired, at expressing yourself with great power according to your intuition, your uniqueness and your very structured beliefs, at seeing and creating coincidences and synchronicities, at making God a part of your life, at processing data or at handling networks, at working on structure or light and at changing the structure of things, at breaking down walls and chains and at overcoming obstacles, at becoming free from rigid structures, myths, illusions, educational, family or social schemes and influences and from the past, at exerting your free will, at using speech to liberate what was confined, at being fully self-sufficient and free from any economic or emotional dependence, at making things explode or burn, at upsetting, creating havoc and turning things upside down, at revolutionizing and healing the existing order or whatever requires change or fixing, at transforming people and events, at implementing awareness and at bringing about a new vision.

You can also be very good at handling building sites, at implementing progress, at discovering, inventing, innovating and reforming, at mastering modern technology, at guiding and counseling others by showing the way, at adapting to the unexpected and unforecasted and at adapting to modern life. Your need for freedom and change makes you seek and like what is unexpected and unforcasted. Although you can be quite individualistic and like to be different, you can best become aware of who you are and express yourself by working within a group, an international firm or a club, by playing a role in creating a better world, by satisfying collective needs, by helping yourself and others become free from slavery brought about by past memories, physical tension, excess, imbalance, fear, ego, rigid structures, constraints, tyranny, routine and banality.

You show great persistence in your undertakings and once the course is set, you know how to motivate yourself, do your best and act with great obstinacy until you get the results you want and until you master the situation. You rarely allow events or people's opinions to change your course of action and are very good at overcoming obstacles and at taking your life in hand. You tend to believe that the heavens will help you if you help yourself and rarely believe in pure chance. Quite often, your undertakings are backed up by support from friends, by coincidences or by people you meet. You however take full responsibility for what happens to you and tend to believe that people get what they deserve because it is they who create their own life. This can make you harsh and demanding.

You can increase the efficiency of number 16 through number 6, by expressing what you feel, by making choices that express your true desires, by seeking harmony, smoothness, wellness and balance, by connecting with your heart and letting the power of love flow through you, by creating harmonious relationships with others, by dedicating yourself to a project. If you express the dark side of number 16, you may them seem to be a person who lives blinded in a world of utopia or according to personal concepts, programs, illusions, ideologies or to the needs and wants of society and to be confined in a virtual world of thoughts and ideas or in a prison. You may seem to be unpredictable, insensitive, over thinking, rigid, self-centered, selfish, artificial, asexual, excessively nervous, stressed, explosive, chocking and rebel towards authority and society. Your issues may be caused by a tendency to be disconnected with your body's needs and desires and with the world of matter, by a tendency to abandon others because you are afraid of being abandoned or by an excessive need to save others.

You issues may also be caused by technical, psychological, language or communication problems, by a tendency to spend too much time with your friends or with the group where you belong and by neglecting your personal/family well being, by a tendency to be like a thunderstorm that devastates everything on its way, by an excessive need to control yourself and other people, by a difficulty to let life flow and let go and by a tendency to confuse true freedom with an illusion of freedom.

For a person born on the seventeenth day of the month: Number 17 imaged by The Star in House 1:

In order to feel confident, to be assertive, to do what must be done, to be efficient and to feel strong, you need to feel close to nature, manage resources or artistic abilities, to take care of the bodie's wellness and beauty, to work with wemen, to feel joy and to create a happy and prosperous life for yourself and others. You present yourself as a kind, smiling, smooth, friendly, caring, cheerful, joyful, pleasant, welcoming, open-minded, tolerant, sincere, intuitive, highly sensitive and charming person with a mischievous and playful aspect, as a person who is alive, deeply connected with nature, sensitive to the natural order that supports life and well embodied in the world of matter, who fully inhabits his/her physical body and therefore listens to and takes into account what the body says, who is sensual, kinesthetic, voluptuous and sometimes fairy like. You are very sensitive to beauty, harmony, colors, shades and to how forms vibrate. You show or suggest that you are capable of inspiring, awakening joy and happiness, attracting abundance and bringing delight, good vibes and hope in the hearts of people. All of this allows your personality to express itself with grace and elegance. You can be very good at seeing and listening to your true desires, to other people's desires and at setting your course according to what brings you joy and pleasure, at making the right choices, at connecting with people, at sharing, at making harmonious compromises, at seeing what resources are available and needed, at managing resources, at serving with devotion using a social, artistic, aesthetic, financial, legal or kinesthetic intelligence and at making your life a work of art. Are you aware of this?

When it comes to defining goals and finding the means to achieve them, to being assertive, to raising your public profile, experiencing life on the field, expressing yourself, being efficient or working within a firm you have the need and the ability to use your senses, to feel well with your body and the female parts of yourself, to see the positive aspects of female values, to be ok with pleasure, to undertake leisure type activities that make you feel joy and pleasure, to find and preserve balance and harmony, to give as much as you can, to commit yourself to others and to show charity, compassion, forgiveness and unconditional love.

You can be very good at having faith in life, at producing, at creating wealth, abundance, harmony and beauty, at smartly managing supplies and resources, at building a network of social relationships, at attracting, seducing, organizing and preserving what you need, at making things flow smoothly, at enjoying simple things of daily life, at playing a role in society, at creating a happy life and at bringing a touch of delight, grace and magic wherever you go. You can increase the strength and efficiency of number 17 through number 5, by being aware, by learning to see that you are protected and blessed by life, by seeing the meaning of events, by finding and incorporation appropriate teachings, by being legitimate or seeing that what is happening is legitimate, by being aware of what is sacred in your life, by listening to your heart, by showing rigor, discipline and generosity and by giving the best of yourself.

If you express the dark side of number 17, you may them seem to be submitted and down on your knees, naïve, incoherent, very slow, dilettante, ignorant, enslaved by fear or an excessive need of physical pleasure, relationships or money, to focus too much on relationships, appearance, beauty and form and to be excessively emotional or relaxed. It may be difficult for you to make energy flow within your body and you may then lack energy, bravery and enthusiasm. When facing a new situation, you tend to react with your feelings, emotions and senses, according to appearance and what the situation seems to be and you sometimes blindly obey what you are attracted too and what seduces you. Your need for peace and harmony makes you flee excess, conflict, violence and confrontation. It's not always easy for you to say no if you fear other people's reactions or if you are afraid to disappoint or to be rejected.

Because you have such strong feelings when you express yourself and become assertive, you sometimes find it difficult to see things from a distance, to struggle for your rights, to overcome obstacles, to reason logically or to be organized in a logical manner. On the contrary, you can be very assertive and highly efficient when you feel loved and supported, when harmony and balance are at stake, when you do things with a partner or with people, when you create relationships or when you feel joy and pleasure.

It would then help you a lot to find a balance between the time and energy you dedicate to others and that which you dedicate to yourself and to make sure that your joy and happiness doesn't exclusively depend on other people's joy and happiness.

For a person born on the eighteenth day of the month: Number 18 imaged by The Moon in House 1:

In order to feel confident, to be assertive, to do what must be done, to be efficient and to feel strong, you need to experience wellness and fluidity, to work with water, to feel nourished or to nourish others, to express your emotions, to be natural and to avoid overheating, to express your imagination and your inner child, to tell stories, to live your dreams, to be aware of how you feel, to create strong emotional bonds with others and to take care of yourself and of others like a caring mother. You present yourself as a natural, sympathetic, welcoming, highly sensitive, very intuitive, emotional, changing, sometimes anxious, imaginative, dreamy, intimistic and poetic person who is full of life, attached to tradition and to the past, to family, home and well-being and who lives in a very personal world. Are you aware of this?

When it comes to defining goals and finding the means to achieve them, to being assertive, to raising your public profile, experiencing life on the field, expressing yourself, being efficient or working within a firm you have the need and the ability to be relaxed, to listen, perceive and be receptive to people, to the existing atmosphere and to what is happening, to move along with the flow, to express your imagination and your emotions, to handle and manage your fears and concerns, to respect your natural rhythms, to avoid excesses or overheating, to create pleasant atmospheres where everyone feels well, to make sure that you feel well and safe, to recharge your batteries and help others do so, to create strong emotional bonds with people and to preserve your inner balance.

You can be very good at nourishing yourself correctly in all sectors and at helping others to do so, at using your imagination and your faith to create events, at being inspired, at memorizing, and telling tales, at taking the past into account, at perpetuating tradition, at expressing your inner child, at creating a private life or family life that you protect from whatever does not belong to it, at creating and protecting life, at making things flow, at being a mother or at expressing motherly love, at taking care of others and of your home, at housing people, at giving birth, at seeing your dreams and at making them come true, at living according to your dreams and at living in a state of joy and abundance. You tend to become aware of who you are through your past, your origins, your family, your native land, your emotions and your feelings and are not always clearly aware of who you are as an individual person.

Because of your many emotions and your strong imagination, going out of your personal world and undertaking the necessary efforts to find your place in the outside world can sometimes be a little difficult as you tend to consider reality as a hard place to live in. Music, drawing and family support can be of great help to express yourself. You can also be very good at being a mirror to others, at being cute, at touching people's hearts and at making people behave tenderly towards you and forgive your occasional absent-mindedness. You can increase the strength and efficiency of number 18 through number 4, by defining clear goals and by implementing the appropriate and efficient organization so as to achieve them, by learning how to use logic, by finding your place in the world for example by taking care of children, of people's safety and wellness, through jobs related to housing, house building, nourishment, water, liquids, protection, music, biology and life. It is often through your ability to nourish, to take care of others, to handle resources or money, to create wellness and to implement recharging atmospheres that you can give the best of yourself.

If you express the dark side of number 18, you may them seem to be emotionally stressed and unwell, concerned and bothered, unstable and lunatic, lazy, apathetic, fearful and panicky anytime something new upsets your tranquility. You seem to be living in the past, in your family's world, in a world of dreams or in a state of semi-consciousness, to be confusing fiction and reality, to be excessively relaxed, emotional, naïve, child-like, slow, incoherent, ignorant, submitted and full of illusions. You may then lack energy, enthusiasm, bravery and autonomy. You may find it difficult to nourish yourself correctly, excessively seek nourishment or physical pleasure and nurture dependency based relationships. It is important for you to find a balance between the time and energy you dedicate to others or to your family and that which you dedicate to yourself and to make sure that your personal wellbeing doesn't depend exclusively on other people. It's up to you to undertake the necessary work so as to express the best of number 18 and become the best version of yourself.

For a person born on the nineteenth day of the month: Number 19 imaged by The Sun in House 1:

In order to feel confident, to be assertive, to do what must be done, to be efficient and to feel strong, you need to be centered in your heart, to do what you love and to love what you do, to play a major role wherever you are, to be seen, recognized and values, to become the best version of yourself, to live according to your ideal, to set clear goals, to get organized efficiently and to succeed, to create a happy life for yourself, to be brilliant, to become famous and to radiate like the sun. You present yourself as a warm, cheerful, joyful, positive, luminous, clear and loving person, as someone with a big heart and a strong will power, as someone who has an ideal and who lives according to successful models, as someone who knows how to define clear goals and how to find the means and organizational solutions to achieve them, as someone who can be a source of light, heat, energy, awareness and love, as someone who needs sunshine, as someone with a big heart and as someone who is available to share, create partnerships, educate and manage. Are you aware of this?

It is very important for you to know who you are or to clearly define yourself, to have a clear vision of the situation, of the people within it and your environment. What you do helps you find landmarks and become more aware of who you are and you usually become more aware of who you are through the joy in your heart, through awareness, though action, self-expression or theater, by using your creative power and through a strong love relationship with a partner, and with children. You can be very good at making your ideal and your resources match and at finding a great deal of energy to carry out what you want. This gives you self-confidence; a natural authority and a conquering spirit who creates his/her own life. When you are here, it is often widely known. You like being at the center of events, being visible, getting up on stage, being in charge, managing, being recognized and admired. You like comparing yourself to others to see how great you are but you are not very sensitive to other people's opinions. You are mostly concerned by your achievements and by your personal and visible success. You are often fond of art and culture and of positive thinking.

When it comes to defining goals and finding the means to achieve them, to being assertive, to raising your public profile, experiencing life on the field, expressing yourself, being efficient or working within a firm you have the need and the ability to be fully centered in your heart, to listen to what it says and to know what you want. You also have the ability and the need to be optimistic, to see the positive aspects of people, to find clear landmarks, to call upon principles, to balance male and female energy, to build special brotherhood type or love relationships, to take care of your image and reputation, to express your authority and beliefs, to be opportunistic and realistic, to make sure things go your way and to help whenever possible

You also need to be and feel noble and honorable, to attract and gather things or people around a central point, to do your best with great devotion, to be your own master, to be self-sufficient, to succeed, to be the best version of yourself, to experience God and full awareness and shine like the sun. You can increase the strength and efficiency of number 19 through number 3, by learning to listen, by communicating clearly, by being smart and well coordinated and by adapting to what the situation requires.

If you express the dark side of number 19, you can sometimes lack clear vision, tend to nurture a flawed vision, ideal and goals or excessively focus on appearance, image and reputation. You are sometimes excessively proud, arrogant, self-centered, selfish, rigid, oversensitive, theatrical and megalomaniac. Because of a feeling of excessive self-importance, you sometimes believe that all is due to you and you then express a superiority complex and behave like a dictator who wants to define all the rules and control everything. Your intentions can sometimes be to easily seen. It's up to you to undertake the necessary work so as to express the best of number 19 and be the best version of yourself.

For a person born on the twentieth day of the month: Number 20 imaged by Judgment or Resurrection in House 1:

In order to feel confident, to be assertive, to do what must be done, to be efficient and to feel strong, you need to overcome the impact of ancestral or past life memories, to give yourself and others a second chance, to live a meaningfull life and to reveal messages, though speech, sound, music, images or vibrations, that bring about change, awareness, a higher vision, rebirth, healing of body and soul and inner freedom. You sometimes need to manage complex projects involving very advanced technologies.

You present yourself as a smart, very intelligent, vibrant, dynamic, positive, enthusiast, highly sensitive, inspired, relevant and powerful person who lives in the present moment with a generous heart. When it comes to defining goals and finding the means to achieve them, to being assertive, to raising your public profile, experiencing life on the field, expressing yourself, being efficient or working within a firm you have the need and the ability to be connected with the depths of your subconscious and soul, to encompass reality in all its dimensions, to listen to your intuition and life's messages, to perceive invisible energies and vibrations, to become aware, to have faith and prey and to communicate in a very clear, eloquent and relevant manner. Revealing what you feel needs to be revealed to that people can thrive, blossom and fulfill is important to you.

You can be very good at bringing about a new vision and at being ahead of your time, at spreading knowledge, at being a spokesman, at awakening others, at passing on messages though books, websites, conferences or teachings, at adapting to the unknown and to unpredictable events, at renewing yourself, at seeing the meaning of events, at bringing hope, at shaking and upsetting what needs to be changed, at implementing change, at healing body or soul through speech, vibration, touch, sound or quantic therapy, at helping others rise from their ashes, resurrect in a new life form and have a second chance, at vibrating in unity with music, at adopting a higher vision and an awareness of sacredness, at preparing, at processing data and at being organized in a highly efficient manner. This allows you to handle and manage complex data systems, complex projects or complex cutting edge technologies and to adapt to modern life.

You can increase the strength and efficiency of number 20 through number 2, by learning to veil or unveil the secrets that lie in your subconscious, by purifying your personal, ancestral and past life memories, by learning to relax and recharge your batteries, by nourishing yourself correctly at all levels, by taking care of yourself, by connecting with joy and Mother-Earth, by letting things flow, by handling your emotions, by learning to remain silent when it is right to do so, by learning patience, by being aware of the consequences of what you say to others, by expressing a right speech, by opening up your heart so as to speak with your heart, by finding the keys that allow you to progress and move forward and by expressing motherly love.

If you express the dark side of number 20, you may then seem to be quite ill-adapted to your world and environment, confined in your own grave, living as if you were dead and not really embodied in this world, stuck in ancestral or past life memories, unable to thrive and blossom. You may tend to believe that you are the only one who knows the truth, make errors in judgment, spread false information, confuse fiction and reality, tell lies and spread propaganda, always judge and criticize others according to your own very limited vision, make others suffocate or feel stifled and muffled, fuel conflict, make others feel guilty or nurture your own guilt, manipulate people and enslave them in a Machiavellian manner and create misery and despair. You can sometimes be quite excessive, always be in a hurry and burn the candle by both ends which can lead to burnout. It's up to you to undertake the necessary work so as to express the best of number 20 and be the best version of yourself.

For a person born on the twenty-first day of the month: Number 21 imaged by The World in House 1:

In order to feel confident, to be assertive, to do what must be done, to be efficient and to feel strong, you need to explore the world and space, to understand how life, society and spiritual evolution works, to be part of a larger group, to express your power, to play a role in the world, to travel or to be connected with foreigners, to blossom, to thrive, to experience self-realization, to become the best version of yourself, to live a happy life, to turn your life into a work of art and to serve life wherever your skils are needed.

You present yourself as a warm heated, cheerful, broad-minded, humanistic, confident, optimistic, opportunistic, highly resourceful, multitasked, multidimensional, universal, highly social, cosmopolitan, mundane person who understands the laws, rules and cultures of the world and who is ready willing and able to serve the world by playing a specific role in it. When it comes to defining goals and finding the means to achieve them, to being assertive, to raising your public profile, experiencing life on the field, expressing yourself, being efficient or working within a firm you have the need and the ability to express a great will power and creative power, bravery, persistency, precision and a global intelligence that can encompass the body, motion, the soul, human relationships, philosophy, law, sociology, psychology, engineering, art, space and spirituality.

You can be very good at having a global view of the situation and its many facets, at deeply understanding who the world, business, legal matters and people work, at feeling at ease everywhere, at balancing male and female behavior and skills.

You can also be very good at expressing your authority with elegance, at being very well organized, at handling complex projects, at dedicating yourself to your task at 100%, at playing a role within a team, a club or a large international firm, at working with foreign people, at gathering people from all over the world and at managing them, at teaching, at exploring the world, at having an international scope, at doing business, at achieving your goals, at creating wealth and abundance, at adapting to today's modern and global world and at being amazingly successful.

You can also be very good at coordinating resources and people, at creating high quality works of art, at synthesizing, at harvesting and reaping the fruit of your labor, at living in harmony with the flow of evolution, at creating a happy and fulfilling life, at dancing your life and at making it a piece of art, at bringing delight to people and places and sometimes at guiding others. You can seem to be quite a lucky person. You can increase the strength and efficiency of number 21 though number 1, by expressing your inner child, by smartly managing your energy, motivations and enthusiasm, by being open to adventure and newness, by taking care of yourself confidence, by using your creative power and by living in the present moment.

If you express the dark side of number 21, you may then seem to be disconnected with your heart, with common sense and with your deep inner truth, unbalanced regarding male and female behavior and skills, socially isolated, confined in your own world or completely suffocated by your duties, responsibilities, work, and your role, excessively focused on work life and neglecting your personal needs and family life, indulging in self-importance and exaggeration and thus lacking an ability to question and change, always calculating, wanting to control and manipulating even though you show an angel like appearance. You may seem to be pretentious, self centered, megalomaniac, snob, artificial, false, virtual, utopian, invasive and colonialist. It's up to you to undertake the necessary work so as to express the best of number 21 and be the best version of yourself.

For a person born on the twenty-second day of the month: Number 22 imaged by The Fool or Genius in House 1:

In order to feel confident, to be assertive, to do what must be done, to be efficient and to feel strong, you need to live or to avoid living according to past lives or ancestors, to express your uniqueness, to be a genious, to feel free, to take care of people who have difficulty to adapt and to bring the future into the present times. You present yourself as a special, unique, atypical, highly sensitive, imaginative, poetic, natural, flexible, multi-tasked, nomadic, spontaneous, relaxed, cheerful and joyful person, who lives in the present moment on a day to day basis, who is full of ideas, who is always on the move and who is totally open to whatever is possible.

When it comes to defining goals and finding the means to achieve them, to being assertive, to raising your public profile, experiencing life on the field, expressing yourself, being efficient or working within a firm you have the need and the ability to have sufficient space, to live unconfined in any system or structure, to become free from any past influences or memories and to feel free, to think as you want and do what you want, to move beyond family, educational and social structures, to get out of the box and open up new paths, to express your own personal truth and specific beliefs and to live in a state of grace, as a free, joyful and happy person.

You can be very good at being inspired and connected with cosmic influences and with the flows of love that spread across the universe, at finding amazing solutions that no one though off, at being unclassifiable, at being extremely relevant, and working with form with great talent, at seeing what is invisible, the future and what people feel and think, at being a pioneer, at making the most of your resources and at living with very little, at packing up your rucksack and going out on adventure to explore new lands, at going beyond limits and at being timeless. You can also be very good at expressing your creative power, at showing a very strong sense of humor, at bringing delight to people and places, at dissolving knots and at breaking chains so as to free whatever needs to be freed, at adapting very smartly, at being a genius in your field, at being an artist of life or at turning your life into a work of art and sometimes at being a prophet that can show others the way to start a new life and to access their supreme inner truth, bliss and total freedom.

If you express the dark side of number 22, you may then seem to be lost in the meanders of ancestral memories or past life memories, to be unbalanced, confined in permanent inner chatter, strange, disconnected from reality and from any structure, from your identity and from relevant goals and clear landmarks, to be unaware that you are turning around in circles doing the same mistakes, to live in an artificial or virtual world of ideas, concepts, dreams and illusions, to be like a maverick or a wandering and meaningless soul living a meaningless life, to be ignorant, confused, absent-minded, incoherent, immature, chaotic, irresponsible, unpredictable, irrational, depressed, very stubborn, depressed and more or less crazy. It's up to you to undertake the necessary work and therapy so as to express the best of number 22 and be the best version of yourself.

What each birth number could show, as a title, if it had a personal business number:

Number 1: Business owner, craftsman, jack of all trades or smart guy.
Number 2: Seer, keeper of knowledge and secrets, midwife of body and soul.
Number 3: Mother Nature, mother, communications officer, sales person or assistant.
Number 4: Empire builder, CEO or Politician.
Number 5: Educator, Political advisor, counselor, guide, expert or Doctor of body and soul.
Number 6: Artist of Life, lover, public relations officer or making choices specialist »
Number 7: Certified Coach, taxi driver, general or contractor.
Number 8: Justice, expert in social relationships, Guardian of Civilizations, civil servant and order specialist.
Number 9: Lamplighter, Building Site Manager, Organizer, architect, hermit, truth seeker, wise person or Guide.
Number 10: Watchmaker, Technician or Health Advisor, accountant or master of numbers.
Number 11: Creator, coach, Jedi Master or Big Hearted Person»
Number 12: Mystic, Nurse, caretaker or Priest
Number 13: Master of subtle energy and change, gold seeker, safety officer, X-ray technician or Yogi.
Number 14: Therapist, Angel, Psychologist, Computer Specialist, Network Specialist.
Number 15: Passionate Plotter, Financial Manager or blacksmith.
Number 16: Structure specialist, freedom builder, healer, Electrician, computer specialist or Radio/TV speaker.
Number 17: « Happy person, fairy, messenger of joy, love and abundance.
Number 18: Wonderful Mother, Nanny, nourishment provider or Ambassador of Emotions and Well-being.
Number 19: Source of love, heat and light, model, creator or happy person
Number 20: Judge, shaman, ferryman of souls, messenger of the Gods or Hi-tech officer.
Number 21: World citizen, dancer, engineer or businessman.
Number 22: Idiot, lost soul, genius, forever new happy person or free electron.

HOUSE 2: It is made up from the earth element and from the astrological sign of Taurus.

Names of the House: Wealth house, main resource house, pleasure house, joy house and abundance house.

Definition of the House: House 2 is where your wealth is and how you experience embodiment. This house shows one of the major resources on which you can call upon in order to move forward in life. These resources being natural, you are not always aware of them. What are your assets, your natural skills, and the treasure you dig into when you need to move on? What resources do you call upon to handle your potential abilities, to make them grow and to make a profit from them? What do you do when you seek pleasure? What makes you evolve more easily? What makes you happy? What helps you achieve your life mission? The answers can be found with the number in house 2.

When you consciously use and express the qualities of the number in house 2 to meet your challenges, to evolve, to progress and to accomplish your life mission, you enable yourself to give the best of yourself to life. When you don't use these natural talents, it is quite likely that they will use you in a more or less constructive manner! You then don't' get very far! You don't really progress and you feel frustrated and shameful as you have, with very little effort, the ability to express the best of this number.

Calculating the number in this house: It is obtained by adding the day of birth reduced to base 22 and the month of birth. Someone born on December 25th has number 7+12=19 in house 2.

Numbers in House 2:

The number in house 2 reveals your inner wealth, your natural resources, the ones you can always count on to live your life in the world of matter and to get results. It also reveals how to get access to joy, to happiness and to pleasure. The number in house 2 is mostly expressed during the first part of your life, and to be more specific until you are 36 years old minus the value of your house 10 number reduced to a number between 1 and 9).

Example: Number 17 in House 2:

The Star is in a house where it can fully express all its potential. It is symbolically "at Home". So, while being physically here and now, you are also connected to the stars! You are naturally able to feel well with female values, with female body or with wemen, to see the positive aspects of feminine values, to feel beautiful, to see beauty in everyone, to embellish and decorate, to express artistic talents, good tastes and a sense of harmony, to show a certain purity of heart, to hear and take into account your true desires, to manage your energy, to bring peace and hope, to have faith in life, to give, share and forgive, to promote truth, to experience leisure activities and to create joy, happiness and abundance in your life and in other people's life.

You are particularly able to live a balanced life, to connect with others and to create strong bonds with them, to build social or family relationships, to express a relational intelligence, to create a happy couple, to express harmony, sweetness and kindness, to attract, to please others, to be liked, to cooperate and to participate actively in life.

There may be, within you, a link between love life, senses, pleasure, the feeling of being happy on one hand and money, resources, wealth and possessions on the other hand. Your wealth can be connected to your marriage, to your love life, to a club to which you belong or to social relationships. You can also get rich by using your ability to create relationships, through activities connected with the body, with beauty, with nature, fashion, decoration, pleasure, art, singing, conditioning, production or any activity symbolically connected with planet Venus. Whatever pleasure and joy you feel motivate you to express your wealth. These skills are talents that you can and should express to evolve and accomplish your life mission.

Examples of some famous people born with number 17 in House 2: Antoine de Saint Exupéry, Kate Moss, Axelle Red, Albert Einstein, Krisnamurti, Maurice Carême, Nicolas Tesla and Marcel Proust.

HOUSE 3: It is made from the air element and from the astrological sign of Gemini.

Names of the House: The mind, adaptation, communication, motion or trade house.

Definition of the House : House 3 enables you to experience communication with the surrounding world thought words and contacts and to adapt to the surroundings thought movement, exchanges, dialogue, information, intelligence, know-how's, craft skills and trade. Being adapted in the world is the purpose of this house. This requires using your brain, intelligence, communications abilities and setting yourself in motion.

Calculating the number in the house: It is done by adding the month of birth and the year of birth. A person born during the month June (sixth month of the year) of year 2011 will have number 6+2+0+1+1= 10 in House 3.

Numbers in House 3:

This number shows how you communicate and behave with your surroundings, with the people you meet, with district merchants, neighbors, colleagues, buddies or brothers and sisters. It describes how you move around and how you adapt to whatever comes up. You use this number to encounter people or ideas, to get information, to discover new things, to exchange goods or ideas, to go from one place to another, to learn and to trade. During a lifetime, this number is particularly important from the ages of twelve to 24 and then after the time corresponding to your motivation number (see motivation number further down).

Example: Number 19 (The Sun) in House 3:

Understanding life, studies, knowledge, contacts, trade, written or oral communication, movement are not only of major interest to you, and thus important energy expenditure activities, but also means to raise your profile, boost your visibility and enhance your self-esteem. As soon as something arouses your curiosity, as soon as it become necessary to find information, to understand, to argue, to defend your interests, to adapt, to explore the surroundings, to communicate or to trade so as to adapt, you are particularly able to find your marks, to be very clear, to manage your image and your reputation, to embody your ideal, your values and your principles, to define specific goals and to use all of your will power to reach them. You are also particularly able to use your creative power, to do your very best, to take care and control the situation, to succeed and even to glow and shine like the sun. You adapt because you spend the required energy in order to do so.

When you communicate and adapt, or in order to do so, you need to be clear and synthetic, to be a source of love, awareness, energy and heat, to call upon your divine self, to be a positive, warm-hearted, generous, happy and luminous person full of energy and vitality. You also need to speak with your heart, to create very strong bonds with others, to play a central part, to have well defined goals, to show whatever is in your heart and to help others find the right place for themselves and to give the best of themselves.

When you consider someone to be important, you consider him or her to be a part of yourself and you take care of him or her as you do for yourself. This gives you a special talent to touch and win other people's hearts and minds.

Examples of some famous people born with the Sun in House 3: Eric Emmanuel Schmitt (28/03/1960), Marion Zimmer Bradley (03/06/1930), Georges Gurdjieff (13/01/1872).

HOUSE 4: It is made from the water element and from the astrological sign of Crab or Cancer.

Names of the House: Origins, family mall, parents' project, going from unwellness to wellbeing, home and emotional bonds house.

Definition of the House: House 4 shows the genealogical legacy that comes from your parent's more or less conscious wishes and desires concerning their child i.e. you at conception and birth. This house describes a psychological and genetic package transferred to you by your parents. In these malls, there are very often more or less highly impacting "cumbersome objects" that create a psychological and energetic knot or tension. The result is the existence of beliefs and psychological schemes that must be changed in order to move ahead on your path. The main knot is house 4 is the root of the problems encountered in house 6. In order to become a totally free and happy person you must learn to experience in a balanced and positive manner the number in House 4.

To do this, you can call upon the values, qualities and tendencies of the complementary number. (Number 4 + complementary number=22).

If the complementary number exists in the birth Diamond, it will greatly help to unknot, transform and reverse the difficult trend into a positive one. When the number in house 4 is freely, naturally and happily expressed, you then have powerful natural available innate skills that you can count on to succeed in life and to give the best of yourself to life. When you unknot the number in house 4, you also unknot the house occupied by the complementary number (if it exists in the Birth Diamond).

Calculating the number in the house: It is obtained by adding the numbers in houses 6+7+9.

Numbers in House 4:

They reveal what you carry that actually belongs to your parents. They describe a legacy that must be transformed so that it becomes not a burden but an asset who can then contribute to building efficient foundations.

Example: Number 8 (Justice in House4):

Because of what you carry from your parents, you are extremely sensitive to the existence of an invisible order hidden behind life on Earth and to anything that is not in harmony with this cosmic order. Embedded in your cells and in your flesh is a need for truth, order, rightness and justice. But you more than likely also carry a strong memory of injustice. You may have come to earth to restore balance, to repair an injustice or to actively participate in civilization. This number brings you potential skills to handle information, administrative data and data systems, to get rid of any burdens in your life, to be very demanding so as to create high quality deeds, to overcome conflicts and restore harmony, to be in line with cosmic laws and human laws, to be fair and to see that things are fair, to accept your part of responsibilities, to see the different facets of any given situation. You have a strong potential ability to weigh the "fors" and the "againsts", to balance opposites, to create truth, order and justice, to firmly choose and decide, to structure events according to a certain rhythm, to promote public welfare, to understand how a civilization functions and to actively participate in clubs and in civilization.

These skills however, are also the cause of your problems and sufferings, in the sense that it's difficult for you to express them with peace and joy, in a positive manner, until you free yourself from your parent's heritage. Maybe you are always afraid of not being in harmony with cosmic law, of being caught up by "Law", of being declared guilty, of being punished by justice, of being reduced to an object and of being exploited.

Maybe you transfer your inner severity, your sharpness and your ability to firmly decide to others, but then you complain that others are too severe, harsh, sharp and firm with you. These problems create obstacles in your life and hinder your growth and your self-realization. A deep change is necessary for you to find freedom and happiness. It would be very helpful if you changed your beliefs and attitudes towards justice and to get over "justice wound" handed over by your parents.

Lise Bourbeau's book "The five wounds" can help you with this task. What can also help is to experiment the skills and tendencies of the complementary number, in this case number 14, "The Angel" and to pay a special attention to the house occupied by the complementary number if it exists in your Birth Diamond. If the complementary number isn't in the Birth Diamond, it will help to connect with people who have and express that number in their Birth Diamond.

When you are able to evolve from an unconscious expression of the Justice number to a conscious expression thanks to the adequate work on yourself, you gradually move from a state of unwellness to a state of wellness and balance. You can then powerfully use the skills of this number to succeed, to accomplish your mission on earth and to become more aware. Doing so, you can become like a mirror that reflects and reveals the different aspects of reality, what is right and the cosmic order that creates civilizations.

Examples of people with number 8 in house 4: Charles Darwin (12/02/1809), Lewis Caroll (27/01/1832), Sri Aurobindo (15/08/1872), Georges Gurdjieff (13/01/1872), Bô Yin Râ (25/11/1876).

HOUSE 5: It is made from the fire element and from the astrological sign of Leo.

Names of the House: The heart, the way of expressing love, becoming aware of deep identity and major deep need house.

Definition of the House: House 5 is the source of love, energy and vitality buried deep inside you. It describes your spiritual identity, what you really are deep down, what the light within you wants, a main potential to reveal, the qualifications that enable you to express your specific talents, to succeed in life, to blossom, to give the best of yourselves and to shine like the sun. House 5 is the house that reveals your creative power and your joy. And when that occurs, you become playful and become able to create your own life. Becoming fully aware of the number in house 5 is vital to find your essence but also to allow yourself express the divine child within you and discover and experience your power of love and your magnificence.

Calculating the number house 5: This can be done by adding the numbers in Houses 2 and 7. If you want to go deeper, you can also learn more about house 5 by adding numbers in Houses 1 and 9.

Numbers in House 5:

The number in house 5 allows you to express your inner light which reveals who you are really are in your deepest self i.e. Love. It enables you to express your creative power, to experiment different leisure activities, to feel love for life and to move towards the center of yourself.

Example: Number 16 (The Tower) in House 5:

The particular connection you have with both the earth and the sky gives you a very keen understanding of structures, technology and of the human soul. It turns you into a very special and paradoxical person. You are at the same time very fond of freedom and very autonomous and yet very obstinate, with well defined concepts and ideals. Deep inside you, you have the need and the ability to work with data structures, to handle modern technology, modern means of communication and languages, to embody human intelligence and a keen awareness of human psychology, to be highly disciplined, to invent, discover and innovate and to embrace an ideology, human values or spirituality.

You are very organized. You need to acquire and preserve a certain freedom of action while being quite open to the unexpected and to turnarounds of events. You are very good at withdrawing into silence or inside your personal ivory tower in order to express your potential, in organizing your creative power by managing it as if it were a complex project and in insisting, with an incredible work power until your well defined goals are reached. You have a strong project management skill.

One of your facets, however, may be like a dynamite stick. This specific facet brings you a high inner voltage and a stormy temper. It strongly enables you to free yourself from confinements, to freely express your creative power and your speaking abilities, to canalize a powerful energy flow, to look into the future, to find clever solutions, to break down impeding walls, to reform so as to improve things, to be positive and optimistic, to see the promising aspects of a situation, to generate hope around you, to express your specificity and your convictions, to upset, revolutionize and even demolish what must be and sometime to make a situation that must no longer be explode as if by "handling lightning".

You have the ability to free yourself from the limitations of the thinking mind, to experience intense moments of awareness, to speak without exploding, to split things apart, to adopt a new vision of yourself or of the situation, to bring about a new vision capable of liberating others, to experience divine inspirations or to include God in your life. You tend to express these tendencies as soon as you need to find your marks, when you handle your reputation, embody your ideal, your values and your principles, define goals, use your will power and your creative power, when you become committed and give the best of yourself, when you impose your authority, control a situation, succeed, glow, shine, accomplish yourself or when love is at stake.

Your love life may be quite unusual. You may be with a very special and multidimensional partner or you may experiment relationships that come and go suddenly in an unexpected manner. You are not easily satisfied because you always need new situations, progress or because you always need to go further or to get closer to God. Your need to refuse monotony enables you to experience exiting relationships that are full of life and of unexpected events and that are finally a source of greater freedom. You are prone to love at first sight and you tend to prefer to live common law than to marry because of your strong need for freedom.

These different experiences are all opportunities to be explored so as to evolve and accomplish your life mission. What can also help you to express the full potential of The Tower is to experiment the skills and the tendencies of the complementary number, in this case number 6, (The Lovers) and to pay a special attention to the house where the complementary number is located is it exists in your Birth Diamond. If the complementary number isn't in the Birth Diamond, it will help to bond with people who express the Lover in their Birth Diamond. You can increase your freedom and go deeper in the "House of God" if you take into account what you feel in your body, if you learn to make choices that match your true desires, if you express love and kindness, if you create harmonious relationships with others, if you become committed to a project or a relationship and if you nurture joy, harmony, happiness and well being.

If you have the Tower in house 5, then you automatically have the Lover in house 6 because the number in house 5 and the number in house 6 add up to twenty two. And because house 6 is where problems arise, the number in house 6 is not one that is naturally and harmoniously expressed. It is important to see if the Lover is in any other houses than house 6 and if so in which house. If the house occupied by the Lover is "difficult" (Houses 4, 7, 8 and a part of axis 3-9) it will be more difficult to fully express your deep self than if the Lover is in a more easy house (Houses 1, 2, 9 and 11) when you can more easily solve the existing house 6 problem and thus express all the potential of the number in house 5 i.e. your solar essence, your power of love.

Examples: William Herschel (15/11/1738), Mahatma Gandhi (02/10/1869), Pierre Numberin (02/07/1922).

HOUSE 6: It is made from the earth element and from the sign of Virgo.

Names of the house: Technical intelligence, recurring problems (due to a childhood, genealogical or soul memories), the traumatic cycle and expertise house.

Definition of the House: House 6 contains both a raw memory with a specific wound and a powerful thinking process. This brings about recurring problems when this memory is not defused and when solutions are seeking only though thinking. In this house, a traumatic cycle goes on and on until it is transformed into a cycle of love and service.

You will see how the number in this house is expressed by observing the negative thoughts and beliefs that you are always repeating in your mind and that need to be purified, cleaned up and changed, in connection with the number. House 6 describes a path towards health and purity, a building site that must be opened so as to clean up old memories and so as to bring about changes in your vision of things and your behavior, in connection with the number. If the necessary building site or cleaning process is not taken into account and if you continue nourishing the problems connected with the number in this house, you don't make any progress and you will remain stuck in recurring schemes and situations of failure. But if the necessary work is done with success, House 6 becomes a house of intelligence, of expertise and of safety. It becomes a foundation and a technical tool that can be used for growth. Numbers in Houses 2 and 5 can help you work on your House 6.

Calculating the number in the house: 22 – House 5. There are 22 numbers in the tarot deck and this makes up a whole. The number in house 6 is the perfect complementary number to enable the number in house 5 to shine and to experience certain wholeness.

Numbers in House 6:

The number in House 6 reveals the special tool you can master to adapt to the real world and to serve the world. But either the tool masters you, which initially tends to happen or either, when the adequate work is done, you master the tool. If your technical intelligence controls you, then that creates recurring problems. When you master the number in House 6, you then become an expert at expressing the ins and outs of that number.

Comment: Numbers in houses 5 and 6 are always complementary numbers i.e. they always add up to 22.

Example: Number 1 in House 6:

You quite likely have difficulties to get started, to wake up in the morning, to motivate yourself, to dare, to know what to do, to take initiatives, to improvise, to become embodied in life and action, to be born, to express all of your potential abilities, to become aware of the tools you have, to understand how to use or to coordinate your different tools. Why is this?

Well, mainly because instead of being here and now with all of yourself and with your whole body, you focus on thinking and you seem to believe that your ability to think and your mind will fetch all the solutions. Here thinking is not the solution but the cause of the recurring problems because it impedes you from "feeling" things and from having a self confidence that allows you to see what is obvious. These recurring difficulties impede your growth until they are dealt with. You possibly have experienced a difficult childhood. You possibly need to learn that adventure, all that is new and that the fact of not having adequate tools enables one to develop a fantastic ability to improvise with whatever is at hand, to bounce back and to find smart solutions, to embody an openness of mind and to acquire a powerful faith in yourself and in life.

You can overcome the recurring issue of the Number 1 (Magician) with the Magician's complementary number, number 21, (The World) i.e. by being centered in your heart, by seeing things from a much larger point of view, by organizing and synthesizing your various experiences and by embodying them in the world, in society with a greater awareness.

You can then become highly able to be in the present moment, to act according to instinct and to adapt efficiently to any immediate necessity, to gather your energy, to assert your points of view, to be punchy, brave, high-spirited, fearless, enthusiast, enterprising, efficient and performing when you adapt to the real world using various tools and techniques, communicate, trade, serve, organize data, create safety for yourself or others, deal with health and hygiene issues or when you use data systems. You can then become an expert in understanding how things work, in craftwork, in starting new things, in coordinating tools and potentials and in making a business run efficiently. These qualifications can greatly help you to find a place and to blossom in the world (your number in house 5).

Examples: Thérèse de Lisieux (02/01/1873), Antoine de Saint-Exupéry (29/06/1900), Gérard de Nerval (22/05/1808), Charles Baudelaire (09/04/1821), Albert Einstein (14/03/1879).

HOUSE 7: It is made from the air element and from the astrological sign of Libra.

Names of the House: The antipode, how you bond with others, the main challenge, the inner storm to soothe house.

Definition of the House: In house 7, you are required to become open to the person you meet, to others and to civilization. This implies cutting yourself off from your center and finding a new center somewhere between yourself and the other person. In this house can be found your antipode, your complementary opposite and your main challenge, creating bonds with someone else other than yourself. You must here confront first with yourself, with your inner enemies and then with other people.

So, the number in this house tends to be expressed in an excessive manner or to be rejected and not expressed at all, or rather expressed in its negative aspects. In order not to express the negative side of the number, you must change the vision you have of the number in house 7 and the beliefs connected to it. Only then can you express the number in a positive manner. This requires a new awareness, work on yourself and to use skills which you are not accustomed to use. A certain amount of energy is needed to face this challenge because you are facing the least natural part of yourself. If you do not face this challenge, if you continue to stick to your difficulties, if you keep nourishing your troubles and putting aside the obstacles, you do not evolve because you are not expressing your potential and the resources in house 2 to their full abilities.

When the challenge is successfully overcomed, then the number in House 7 becomes a very strong asset, a source of strength, a catalyst, a ladder and a springboard that can only be used in a state of full awareness so as to give the best of yourself to life, express your wealth and accomplish your destiny. The number in House 7 can then become fully mastered and the challenge then becomes a treasure in which you can dig into to experience self realization.

Calculating the number in the house: House 8 – House 9 or House 9 – House 8.

Numbers in House 7:

The number in house seven reveals an initial imbalance, your antipode and a part of you that you tend to dislike and reject. In house 7, you uncenter yourself to connect to the person facing you. Something must be done to recover your wholeness. Effort is required to recover lost harmony. This is a major challenge and remains so until the "House1-House7 axis" has not being reunited to your whole self. A key here is to seek for the secondary benefit of house 7's challenge! What skills did you chose to develop thought the challenge corresponding to the number.

The number in house 7 also shows what attracts you in other people and the qualities you seek in others because you consider that they are missing in you until you have not reunited the number in house 7 to yourself. This means that you tend to attract a partner who will push you to consciously develop the qualities and tendencies corresponding to the number in house 7. You also tend to blame your partner for expressing or showing you the dark side of the number in house 7.

Beyond the difficult and challenging aspect of the number in house 7, this number describes your way of encountering others and of creating relationships. When the number in House 7 is well integrated within the soul, it describes how the relational intelligence is expressed.

Example: Number 3 (The Empress) in House 7:

You may have experienced a communications problem in your childhood. It is possible that things were not said, that you always had the feeling of not being listened too or that there was always a mismatch and a discrepancy between what was said and reality as it was perceived. This may have influenced the quality of your breathing and thus the exchanges between you and the outside world. You may have encountered problems in listening, in hearing, in handling your communication, in choosing the right words, in saying what needs to be said, in synchronizing your thoughts, your words and your actions, in taking a distance from your thinking mind, in putting things into shape, in expressing your authority and in smartly adapting to your environment. These issues may have enabled to develop means of communicating that are far beyond words.

In order to adapt and communicate efficiently, you must listen to your heart, access your inner joy, become aware of your worth and of the sun that shines within you so as to discover the universal language that springs from the heart. When that happens, your abilities and needs to adapt, to share information and to communicate are expressed in full awareness in social life, club activities, relationships and partnership life. Number 3 in house 7 can turn you into a communication specialist. You are highly interested in people. People stimulate your curiosity, surprise you, intrigue you, amuse you and in a way fascinate you. This pushes you to meet many people and to create many relationships.

You love discovering other people, analyzing them and discovering yourself thought their eyes and though the way they look at you. You are very opportunistic when it comes to relating with others. Your relationships with others may mostly be based on sharing information or on commercial or financial interests rather than on purely sentimental and emotional bonds. The more an unknown person can help you make things run smoothly, the more that person is intellectually or commercially stimulating and the more you feel attracted to him or her. You rarely experience enmity because you communicate in a smart, fair and diplomatic manner, cleverly balancing authority with elegance and smoothing any issues and differences that may occur. Your difficult beginnings, concerning language and communication, can become powerful speaking skills, a strong ability to discriminate and handle form, an efficient relational intelligence and a special talent to give the right information at the right time to the right person, whatever the type of communication used.

Examples of famous people with the Empress in house 7: Jean de la Fontaine (08/07/1621), Ludwig Van Beethoven (16/12/1770), Albert Camus (07/11/1913), Paul Claudel (06/08/1868), Eugène Delacroix (26/04/1798).

HOUSE 8: It is made from the water element and from the astrological sign of Scorpio.

Names of the House: Initiation to the mysteries of life, your treasure quest and the secret passage towards your eternity house.

Definition of the House: This house shows the hidden and unknown part of you, what is innate and not yet clearly conscious, what seems to be missing yet is there, knocking at the door deep inside you and yet that tends to be ignored. This part of you is idealized and erected into a quest so that you can go searching for it and find it. It is the secret passage between you and the light within you.

Why search outside of yourself with obstinacy for something that is within you? The situation here is like that of a person searching for her glasses until she realizes that they are on her nose. House 8 is a spiritual and energetic pathway towards yourself, towards your wholeness and towards recognizing who you really are. Each month of the year holds two astrological signs. For people born during the first two thirds of the month (days 1-21-astrological sign A), it is the excesses of their astrological sign that impedes them from finding out who they are and from getting access to their inner treasure.

For people born during the last third of the month (21-31-Astrological sign B) it is on the contrary the excess of the number in house 12 that impedes them from becoming aware of whom they really are in connection with their astrological sign. A tendency to express the number in an excessive manner prevents you from expressing your astrological sun sign. The solution often comes through a balancing with the opposite sign, by learning to express both your astrological sign and its opposite.

People born in January or July: Aries-Libra
People born in February or August: Taurus-Scorpio
People born in March or September: Gemini-Sagittarius
People born in April or October: Cancer-Capricorn
People born in May or November: Leo-Aquarius
People born in June or December: Virgo- Pisces

Calculating the number in the house: This number is obtained from your month of birth. If you are born in December, then number 12 is in house 8.

Numbers in House 8:

The number in house 8 is the nucleus at the center of your heart, the hidden treasure that you seek during your entire life outside of yourself until you finally find it inside you, what is overshadowed and so the pathway or stairway that leads to your deepest self. House 8 is the only house where there are no numbers above number 12. Number twelve symbolizes transcendence, spirituality and a gateway to infinity which allows you to experience your supreme truth and to permanently break the bonds of karma. Experiencing this mystic transcendence requires becoming aware of the subtle invisible energies of life and of life beyond the physical world. When you get access to this treasure, you become reunited, you reveal your truth to yourself and you then become able to express the number in house 8 in a very intensive, authentic and efficient manner.

Example: Number 2 (The High Priestess) in house 8: (People born in February).

Either you have the feeling that most of what exists in life is hidden and needs to be explored/revealed or either you have the feeling that there are no mysteries at all when something does need to be revealed. You may also have the feeling of not knowing anything, of not being connected to your intuition, of not being legitimate or well organized, of not being able to be a mother or a grandmother for yourself or for others, of not being able to recover or of not really feeling well for some unknown reason. Your quest then starts by exploring the invisible realities behind all visible life, whether these realities are located in the scope of matter, soul or spirit.

Sign of Aquarius: A tendency to always be processing concepts and projects, to live a virtual life or to always want to control things with the mind impedes the free movement of energy within you, to take practical action or to be efficient. Too much agitation and dispersion, a tendency to be totally absorbed by the outside world and by people impedes you from becoming aware of your deep inner truth and from accessing your inner light. When you give so much importance to your mind, to your technical qualities, your psychological skills or to your friends, the risk is that you then fail to experience the connection with the mysteries of life, with the supreme knowledge. That impedes you becoming aware of who you really are and from discovering your inner treasures.

Advice to succeed in your quest, balance your excesses and compensate what is missing:

Define practical and personal goals and organize your paperwork efficiently. Practice meditation. Meet people born under the sign of Leo. Grant your intuition all the attention it deserves.
Pay attention to your dreams and use them to explore mysteries and symbols. Explore the invisible realities behind visible life. Learn to center yourself in your heart and to express your creative power. Read books about quantum physics and apply for programs in personal development.

Sign of Pisces : Too many mysteries, intuitions, deceptions, information, genealogical or past life memories, or a tendency to hide the truth to yourself impedes you from becoming aware of who you really are and from getting access to your inner treasures.

Advice to succeed in your quest, balance your excesses and compensate what is missing:
Structure all information by taking notes, by sorting things out between what can be revealed and what should remain hidden, by analyzing situations in a logical manner and by using checklists. Meet people born under the sign of Virgo. Read books about quantum physics and apply for programs in personal development.

Sublimated: When you are aware of your quest and the treasure it holds, you consciously need to experience well being and serenity. In order to do this, you need intensity, authenticity, passion, transformation and ritual experiences. You need to discover the secrets of life and you need a certain amount of mystery. Otherwise, you feel dissatisfied. You have a very keen intuition and are very sensitive to the world of life beyond, to the secret forces of nature, to what lies behind the apparent scenery, to the unsaid, to mysteries and enigmas of life and to the many questions and issues that life holds. This number enables you to be a keeper of knowledge. That knowledge can helps one become free, experiment what is sacred, become aware of the collective span of humanity and master specific technologies that help humanity progress, both at a psychological and material level. You chose to be born with number 2 (a High Priestess) in house 8 to become aware of secrets within your family, to experience change and personal growth, to awaken to spiritual truths, to reveal secrets to people, to use a secret knowledge to heal body and soul and to bring an important contribution to the group to which you belong.

Examples of famous people born in February: Rudolf Steiner (25/02/1861), Jules Vernes (08/02/1828), Galileo (15/02/1564), Nicolas Copernicus (19/02/1473), Charles Darwin (12/02/1809), Thomas Edison (11/02/1847).

HOUSE 9: It is made from the fire element and from the astrological sign of Sagittarius.

Names of the House: Social inclusion, great journeys of body and mind, playing one's part in the world house.

Definition of the House: House 9 firstly represents the concerns of the mind and the filter though which you see the world and with which you do your best to find your place and adapt to the world. It is where you maneuver between your unconscious self and your conscious self so as to find a place to work in the world. House 9 helps you go from house 4 (parent's hopes for you) to house 10 (your personal life project). It tends to manifest in the following way inside you: "I strongly believe that I must (the needs are shown by the number in house 9) in order to let go of parent's hopes and desires and to live my own personal life. The desire to experience, almost instinctively, what is symbolized by the number in House 9 is very strong. There is also a strong fear of being unadapted or unfulfilled if this number is not expressed.

Secondly, house 9 brings a package of qualifications and skills that can and should be used to adapt to the outside world. The number in house 9 represents one of the major resources on which you can count on to find the right job, to play your part in the world and to accomplish your life mission. The number in house 9 enables you to handle languages, both spoken and symbolic, to communicate with all members of society, to picture things and life through concepts, judgments and generalizations.

It shows how you give a meaning to life and how you assimilate your different experiences. It enables you to experiment culture, exploring space, philosophy, religions and all intellectual frames like laws, economic schemes, norms, rules and whatever knowledge is necessary for you to do your work. House 9 also tells you how you react when you move away from your native background or from your familiar environment and also how you go beyond your known limits to broaden your scope of action, seek new adventures so as to embody your ideals, find prosperity and satisfy your quest for fulfillment.

You may sometimes find it hard to recognize yourself in the house 9 number which may seem strange or far away from your natural way of being. However, this number gives you an authority and power so that you can play a part in the economic life of your country. Finally, house 9 describes the superior abilities of the thinking mind, studies, spiritual research in the outside world, expansion, the ability to guide or to be guided and the ability to make laws.

Calculating the number in this house: The number in house 9 is obtained from the year of birth. Example: 2011 = 2+0+1+1=4.

Numbers in House 9:

The number in house 9 describes how you handle space, how you adapt to the outside world and how who play your part in the economy of your country. It describes how you expand, how you study, how you travel, how you negotiate and how you do your business. The number in house 9 can be expressed in three different ways, in an instinctual, adventurous and travel frenzy manner, in an official or business manner or in a more philosophical and spiritual manner.

Example: Number 5 (The high Priest) in House 9:

Expressed instinctively, the High priest will push you forward to find, take on and incorporate courses and teachings, to learn a maximum of more or less useful things, to travel, to learn foreign languages, to do business, to trade or to know all about the philosophies and religions existing on the planet. You are also very good at finding people who protect you, who bless you, who help you gain a greater self confidence, and more faith, who act as soul or body doctors, who bring teachings to you or who help you give a greater meaning to your life. It is by playing a role in public affairs that you can broaden your views and experience expansion and fulfillment.

This can be done through trade, travelling and business, through transmitting moral, religious, metaphysical, cultural or ethical values, through medical or welfare activities or through the world of teaching and education. You possess a certain spiritual strength, a certain span and a mix of benevolence, speaking abilities and authority. You have a natural ability to find a role to play in society, to handle space, to do your job, to participate in group activities with common goals, to understand the codes/the culture of your surroundings, to assert your authority, to negotiate, do business, to be optimistic, opportunist and generous, to make laws/rules, to organize, manage and distribute, to advice and educate, to create comfortable situations, to travel or to be in the right place at the right time.

You also have an ability to feel blessed by the gods and protected by life, to make connections between heaven and earth, to be legitimate, to acquire, assimilate and transmit an expertise or teachings with human or moral values, to accept the education system, to embody a legal or spiritual authority, to live a meaningful life where sacredness exists, to nurture gratitude, intuition and common sense and to express rigor and discipline, with benevolence and a kind authority, both towards yourself and others.

You may experience the opportunity to be a moral authority who can give meaning to life, which can help others develop their self confidence, their faith and their sense of sacredness, who can help people give the best of themselves and who can commit themselves whole-heartedly to serve life. These virtues can greatly help your evolution. Number 5's complementary number is number 17 (The Star). (5+17=22). You can increase the fluidity and efficiency of number 5 by remembering to take your personal needs into account whatever your social position may be, by being able to see beauty in everyone yourself included, by listening to your true desires, by knowing who to please yourself, by giving and forgiving, by expressing harmony, purity, truth and by living with a joyful and happy heart.

Comment: Here, the values/meaning of the number are very similar to the values/purpose of the house. This makes it much more possible to embody and fulfill the needs of both the house and the number.

Examples: Edgar Cayce (18/03/1877), Krisnamurti (12/05/1895), Jean Giono (30/03/1895).

HOUSE 10: It is made from the earth element and from the astrological sign of Capricorn.

Names of the House: The life path, the life lesson, destiny management house.

Definition of the House: This house describes how you walk along your path and how you build your life so as to fulfill your life mission and whatever you have come to Earth to do. It describes your global growth direction and the main teaching or life lesson that you have come to learn in this lifetime. What drives this house is ambition, the need to be recognized by others thanks to a social status, organization abilities, determination, integrity, an ability to see things in the long term, seriousness and the ability to act as a responsible and autonomous adult. Concerning inner growth, this house shows the path to wisdom, the necessary works that needs to be done on the self and the manner in which the inner cathedral or temple can be built. House 10 allows clarifying the expression number and the life axis.

Calculating the number in this house: It is found by adding the day, the month and the year.

Method 1: 27/12/1963 = 2+7+1+2+1+9+6+3 = 31=4
Method 2: 27/12/1963 = 27+12+1963 = 2002 = 4

When the two methods do not give the same result, there is a second message and a necessary adjustment to realign the person concerned with his or her life axis.

Numbers in House 10:

The number in house 10 enables you to experience a chosen career, autonomy, destiny, structures and to reap the benefits of all the work previously accomplished. It supplies information concerning major career experiences, work upgrades, social success and achievements. It enables you to organize your destiny, to take order, schemes and structures into account, to evolve and to reach a symbolic mountain peak. It shows the major life lesson you have come to experiment and your achievements.
This number can be seen as an inner building site and a steep slope that needs to be climbed. It requires effort, work, organization and long term commitment.

Example: Number 9 (The Hermit) in House 10:

Your achievements possibilities, your life lesson, your path or life mission are connected with your ability to be simple, humble, truthful, to walk towards your deep inner truth, to isolate yourself from unwanted influences, to check things up, to look inwards and meditate, to look back and see how far you've gone, to ask the right questions, to handle long term projects, to manage time efficiently, to manage building sites, to do research, to enlighten the world with wisdom, to work on structures and to build a masterpiece.

Examples of jobs related to number 9: Guide, spiritual guide, monk, adviser, consultant, speleologist, geologist, investigations journalist, architect, pharmacist, archivist, public documentalist, trades dedicated to lighting up places or people, historian, building activities, farmer, herbalist, shepherd, research engineer, explorer, laboratory assistant or soul doctor.

Comment: The meaning of number 9 is very similar to the purpose/values of house 10. This makes it much more possible to embody and fulfill the needs of both the house and the number.

Example: Mother Amma: (27/09/1953).

HOUSE 11: It is made from the air element and from the astrological sign of Aquarius.

Names of the house: The key to freedom, adapting to modern life, the compulsory solution house.

Definition of the House: This house is the key to your freedom and to your accomplishment. It shows what you must experience, go through over and over again and the skills that must be used so as to express your full potential, to move on and make progress, to achieve your life mission and to become free from whatever is holding you back. The number in this house is not naturally expressed. Conscious effort and organization are required. It is the eye of the needle and the key that opens the door of the Birth Diamond. It you don't use that key, your Diamond just doesn't shine doesn't vibrate and you miss the best of yourself. It's like a bridge you have to cross, a compulsory solution and the door you must go through to access your deep identity (house 5).

The number in house 11 shows how you react in a group and how you handle modern life, progress and newness. It connects you with the universe. It gives you a power so that you can act for the common good and so that you can play a role in making humanity progress, though handling more or less complex projects and through an ability to find psychological or technological solutions. While the number in house 10 places you in front of your responsibilities, the number in house 11 helps you become aware of that "Necessity" which comes from humanities' spiritual laws of evolution. It shows your ideal picture of society and humanity. It enables you to feel a multidimensional openness to the unknown.

Calculating the number in this house: This number is found by adding the numbers in Houses 1, 8, 9 and 10.

Numbers in House 11:

House 11 calls for collective force, network activities and group power and for obvious and needed solutions so that progress can take place and so that inner freedom can increase. The number in house 11 is the key which you don't spontaneously tend to use even thought you have full ability to do so. You just have to dare, to supply the required energy and to get to work. You quickly find out that when you do use this number as a key to find solutions, using group energy and networks if necessary, then all doors open up.

Example: Number 12 (The Hanged Man) in House 11:

Comment: This number is quite the opposite of the purpose and values of the house. So at first sight, it doesn't seem to be simple to express and fulfill the needs of the house and to express this number in this house in a positive manner. House 11 has the ability to release the positive aspects of the number it houses. You must identify the key you have chosen to embody in connection to the hanged Man, understand why you have chosen that specific key in your birth Diamond and then use it. With the hanged Man in house 11, you are very sensitive to humanities sufferings and misery. You are also very impacted by memories that can be collective, genealogical or soul memories. You may have a very strong faith; religious beliefs and an ability to feel the currents of unconditional love that subtly flow through the universe. This enables you to become aware of the multiple dimensions of life's immensity, of the power of God and of the eternity of life where each human being is just a droplet in the ocean of humanity.

To experience the full benefit of this number, it is required that you consider life from a spiritual point of view, that you learn to see the meaning of things and the connections between the "inside" and the "outside", that you learn to wait, that you embody spiritual values or that you become devoted to a cause or an organization. It is also required that you develop faith, that you learn to forgive, that you learn not to feel abandoned by life, that you play a role in relieving the sufferings and misery of the world, that you help people find Jesus Christ (sacredness, embodied light, faith, unconditional love) within themselves and that you learn to let go and accept people and situations as they are.

In your life, solutions often come up when you reverse the beliefs that impede you from evolving, when you change your points of view if they are unadapted, when you flee if it is necessary, when you show compassion and unconditional love, when you let go of unadapted past life or family memories, when you deal with your genealogical tree so as use the skills that your ancestors have given you but also so as to give back to them the burdens that belong to them and not to you, when you call upon the power of love or when you play a role in a collective organization. You can then become highly skilled at using the magical power of faith, that very one which can lift even mountains. You have a real possibility, with number 12 in House 11, to do the necessary work to free yourself from past memories so as to live your own life and to express not only the positive aspects of number 12 but also those of its complementary number, number 10(the Wheel of Fortune).

If there is a number 10 (Wheel of Fortune) in your Birth Diamond, the house where it is located will help you find solutions and move towards greater freedom. If there is no number 10 in the Birth Diamond, it would help having relationships with people who have that number in their Birth Diamonds, and who therefore know how to make "The Wheel of life" turn the right way. By using the number 12 key and the complementary number 10 key, you give yourself the means to express the best of yourself and to move forward towards accomplishing your life mission.

Examples: Degas (19/07/1834), Thomas Edisson (11/02/1847), General De Gaulle (22/11/1890), Frederic Nietzsche (15/10/1844).

HOUSE 12: It is made up from the water element and from the astrological sign of Pisces.

Names of the House: Transcendence or suffering, ancestor's gate, the guiding lighthouse, the end of the story house.

Definition of the House: Because house 12 is connected to individual or collective genealogical or soul memories, it can, at first symbolize suffering. Beyond this potentially difficult facet, it mostly reveals the ultimate goal of your destiny and of yourself as an unlimited being. It then becomes the gateway to your experience of transcendence and the furthest destination you can reach when you use all your resources, when you discover your treasures in house 8 and when you accomplish your life mission.

Just like a long term goal or a lighthouse used a benchmark, house 12 enables you to look into the future and to see the picture of yourself in a state of self realization, bliss and communion with God. House 12 is your mean to reach your deep truth and to heal what must be within yourself. Finally, house 12 is your epitaph, the picture and heritage that you will leave to future generations.

House 12 symbolizes your ability to go beyond your known limits, the necessary sacrifices needed to evolve, the ability to take into account and handle hypersensitivity and the collective unconscious. It shows your eternal soul, your soul's past lives, your last judgment or the judgment you have on yourself, your faith in the future, your dreams of evasion, your search for transcendence, your religious or mystical aspirations and your ability to play your part in collective experiences.

Calculating the number in this house: It is found by adding the numbers houses 2 + 8 + 10.

Numbers in House 12:

In this house, you are highly sensitive to the world's sufferings and misery with the risk of believing that they are unavoidable. The number in this house is thus sometimes connected to feelings of suffering, to necessary sacrifices and to a spiritual path leading to healing. The number in house 12 can help you travel from suffering and from living someone else's life to joy, bliss and living your own life by using your resources, by experimenting your deep truth and by expressing the best of yourself.

It shows what your long term goal is. It reveals your lighthouse, the benchmark enabling you to picture the best of yourself in the future or yourself as a droplet of water returning to the ocean of divinity. It also shows how you write the end of your story. The number in house 12 invites you to experiment new states of consciousness. In order to do this, you must learn to see things from far away, experience deconditioning from real life experiences and from the influence of the outside world, get access to and perceive images, symbols, legends, archetypes, collective emotions and experience spiritual truths with a keen sense of sacredness.

The number in house 12 invites you to go beyond ego and the small thinking mind, to become more aware spiritually so as to access higher planes, without denying or neglecting real life experience in the world of matter.

Example: Number 12 (Death) in House 12:

Your long term goal, the best you can make of your life, the way you can experience transcendence and heal, what you will leave behind you to future generations, the way you can develop your faith, your sense of forgiveness and your unconditional love are all connected to your ability to see behind the scenes, to transform yourself and others, to mourn your loved ones and past experiences, to cut all links with the past, to end what must be, to sweep away what so longer is, to get to the heart of the matter and to handle crisis and conflicts. They are also connected to an ability to recover from wounds and traumas, to make sure all is safe, to handle any anguish, to hear, listen to and handle unconscious drives, compulsions and impulses, to explore the worlds of life beyond though out of body experiences, to be clearly aware of your eternal identity and of the name of things, to find and experience your deepest truth and to embody your eternal life within. What you leave behind can greatly change people's vision of reality.

Example: Carlos Castaneda (25/12/1925).

THE SOURCE OF BRILLIANCE HOUSE

Definition of the House: This house is located at the center of the Diamond. This is the house that enables you to make your light shine, to glow, to give the best of yourself and to accomplish your mission on earth. The house is strongly connected to your life path and your life axis.

Calculating the number in this house: It is found by adding the numbers in houses 2 and 10.

Source of Brilliance numbers:

This number is your "Sun gate". It allows you to make an optimal use of your resources, to overcome your challenges and your contradiction, to express the best of yourself, to access the Diamond in the center of your heart and to be the star that you really are. He more you express the positive aspects of this number and the more you will shine and accomplish your mission on earth.

Example: Number 15 (The Devil) as Source of Brilliance number.

Comment: At first sight, this number doesn't seem to be very well suited and compatible with the house! Expressing the needs of the house may not be simple. However, it is possible to express the positive aspects of the number and to consider that in order to shine, it is required to know how to handle one shadows, one's sex appeal, one's personal power and one's ability to master the world of matter.

To express your full potential, to optimize your resources, to solve your challenges and your contradiction, to be aligned with your life axis, to achieve self realization and to shine the best of what you are, you need to develop your lucidity and your personal power, to become aware of what lies behind the apparent scenery and more specifically that there are shadows or dark zones with visible effects existing in the invisible realms of reality. At an individual level, this dark side manifests as the saboteur, who's role is to destroy what no longer needs to be. It also reveals a material power which you can generate abundance.

To incorporate number 15 as a Source of Brilliance, you need to explore and manage the dark side of your human nature and the saboteur who exists in each person, to master suspense and emotions, to become aware of power struggles existing in all situations, to transcend anguish and fear, to control your energy, your instincts, yours impulses, your sexual drives and your passion, to trust your nose and your instinct, to be daring, assertive and combative, to take risks and have no fear of danger, to break anything that chains you up, to take advantage of other people's weaknesses and flaws and to use your fearful strategic intelligence to master the world of matter. You will shine by using your great power and your incredible lucidity to serve life.

You then become a magnetic, passionate, instinctive, intensive, energic, courageous, fearless and bold person who has a strong ability to seduce and influence people. You are able to take into account every detail and especially those that are hidden. Your lucidity enables you to reveal, to each person, their flaws, their dark sides and the cause of their problems. It also enables you to take advantage of any existing opportunities or flaws in a situation and to find a needle in a haystack.

You know perfectly well how to operate intuitively, instinctively and according to your drives and impulses. You have a fearsome strategic intelligence backed up by a great persistence. You also know how to be offensive, how to induce suspense and strong emotions and how to fight with obstinacy until you get what you want. Your need to control things sometimes makes you become obsessional and possessive.

When you incorporate the dark side of your human nature in a positive manner, you then become a passionate person who is able to use invisible energy flows to create abundance in the material world and to access your light within. You are then able to reveal and breakdown all malfunctions. You are able to solve the mysteries of life and death so as to allow the light of deep awareness to appear. This enables you to bring deep changes wherever you are.

Exemples: William Roengten (27/03/1845), Keanu Reeves (02/09/1964), Rafael Nadal (03/06/1986), Elie Saab (04/07/1964).

Houses that make up the Birth Diamond's foundations

These houses are the foundation on which your structure can evolve. They are made up of your hidden facets i.e. parts of you that are initially hidden until they become conscious and of "The Visible Core" that summarizes your skills, schemes, resources and behavior that are always available for use in your life.

THE SOUL INTENTION HOUSE: An ideal of Self-realization

Long before being born on earth, you had a certain need, an ideal, an intention and a goal concerning what life you wanted on Earth. The « Soul Intention number answers the question « What do I want to achieve during my life on Earth and how can I do it?" it shows a deep and often unconscious need. Hearing the soul's intention enables you to connect with your deep self and to grow towards you self-realization.

Calculating the number in this house: It is found by adding the numbers in houses 8, 9 and 10.

Example: Number 8 (Justice) as Soul Intention Number:

Deep within yourself, you have a memory, an ideal, an intention and a need to live a balanced life, to balance what is unbalanced, to express a psychological, artistic, social or legal intelligence, to experience harmony, equity, truth and order, to respect law and justice, to create bonds with others and clubs and to contribute to civilization. You also need to understand the order behind life and to be aware of how you are somehow responsible in creating your life.

THE SOUL CALL HOUSE:

Definition of the house: Deep inside your soul, there is a call, a cry that echoes as a deep need. This house answers the question "What does your soul want?"

Calculating the number in this house: It is obtained by adding the vowels of your first name and family name.

Example: Lilli Anna: 9+9+1+1=20

1	2	3	4	5	6	7	8	9
A	B	C	D	E	F	G	H	I
J	K	L	M	N	O	P	Q	R
S	T	U	V	W	X	Y	Z	

Soul Call numbers:

This number describes a deep and often unconscious need that may be connected to soul memories, whereas the expression number describes a conscious need.

The number in this house enables you to become aware of this deep inner call, of this cry and of this need. When it is listened too and fulfilled, you experience a greater inner freedom.

Example: Number 20 (Judgment) as soul call number

Deep inside you, echoing like a soul call, there is a need and an ability to listen to yourself without criticism or judgment, to listen to your intuition, to others or to the messages given by life, to see and accept coincidences and unforcasted events, to reveal yourself what you have within, to incorporate the creative power of faith, to have a new vision of things, to renew yourself and to experience rebirth. There is also a need to vibrate in unity with music and colors, to inform, communicate and share information, to give important hope bringing messages, to use and understand modern technologies and to manage complex projects, all this in order to bring more freedom, to trigger deep changes, to bring hope and meaning, to allow each person to have a second chance, to heal with speech and energy and to promote people's awareness. Your soul is asking you to discover and experience the power of resurrection! What is symbolized by this number are opportunities that you should embody so as to accomplish your life mission and facilitate your evolution. This can also be done with the complementary number, number 2 (the High Priestess), by connecting yourself with Mother Earth, by nourishing yourself wisely in all areas, by handling your emotions and by choosing with great care what should be shown and what should be veiled, checking the impact of what you say and being opened to the flow of life.

THE HIDDEN RESSOURCE HOUSE

This resource is like a seed you bring with you when you are born. It is a gift of life. Like any seed, it needs the right soil, water and sunshine to be able to grow. This number brings you certain abilities that lie deep within you. They need to be revealed and used. When so, growth occurs.

Calculating the number in the house: This number is obtained by adding the last two numbers of the full year of birth. **Example:** 1998 = 9+8=17.

Hidden resource numbers:

This number brings about a set of skills that are complementary to the resources in houses 1, 2, 3, 9 and 10. These skills need to be used to change the seed into a beautiful, fulfilled and happy tree.

THE HIDDEN CHALLENGE HOUSE

Definition of the house: This challenge or difficulty is much less important and visible than the challenge in house 7 or than the recurring difficulty of house 6 but it can be like a spine in the foot that it is wise to remove so as to move with more fluidity and freedom.

Calculating the number in this house: Number in House 1 – number in House 9 or number in House 9 – number in House 1.

Hidden challenge numbers:

This number reveals a specific problem which is very often hidden. You have lived with it for so long that you no longer see it. Becoming aware of it and transforming it makes you move on with greater freedom.

Example: Number 18 (The Moon) as hidden challenge number

It may sometimes be difficult for you to show your emotions, to overcome confusion, worries and anguish, to listen to your intuition, to handle daily life, to build a family, to be a mother or to act like one, to recover after a hard day's work in a cozy home, to feel well at home or with yourself, to use your ability to "feel" and your emotional intelligence, to express your inner child, your imagination and your creative power, to create strong emotional bonds with others, to tell stories that stimulate peoples imagination, to live your dreams or to keep alive and perpetuate traditions. You may have a tendency to live with illusions, dependencies, lies, anguish, subjectivity and inner confusion. These are then obstacles that hinder the achievement of your life mission and your evolution.

You can overcome the hidden challenge by developing the skills and values of the complementary number, in this case number 4 (the Emperor) (because 4+18=22). Number 4 can help you experience logic and organization, an ability to define limits, structure and channel your emotions towards playing a part in economic life, in a job connected with, for example, well being, food, children, family or relations with the general public.

THE CONTRADICTION HOUSE

Definition of this house: Just as our universe is made up of many many galaxies, the human soul is made up of many different forces. Certain galaxies can have two suns at their center, two double interconnected stars. In the same manner, the contradiction house can hold two numbers, one being in base 22 and it's little sister being in base 9. One therefore first considers the number obtained by adding the numbers in houses 6 and 7 and then it is also advisable to look at the sister number.

Numbers in base 9 and their equivalent in base 22								
1	2	3	4	5	6	7	8	9
10	11	12	13	14	15	16	17	18
19	20	21	22					

Hidden deep inside you is a conflict-causing contradiction which is at the same time your strength and your weakness, your wealth and your challenge, something that attracts you like a magnet and yet deeply disturbs you. The contradiction number show a state of being, which is at first a state of unwellness, that you personally create in your life. This state of mind and the skills that you can show, strange as it might seem, are a powerful force at the center of your soul.

Your contradiction initially manifests as an inner conflict which hinders your growth and which is one of the main causes of your difficulty to move on towards a better life. It forces you to challenge yourself, to change your vision of the number in this house and to do work on yourself so as to change the structure of what you are, in connection with the number. If the challenge is not overcomed, if you continue to "feed" your contradiction, you make very little progress and you stay stuck in the problems connected with the contradiction number. This recurring conflict is quite often projected on others and then manifests as relationship issues. In a second phase, your contradiction number describes the available solutions to overcome your inner conflict and it can give you the keys to open the closed door so that you can move on to a better life.

When the background problem connected with this number is solved, your contradiction then becomes a very great strength, a stepping stone, a catalyser that can help you achieve self realization. The number hence opens a door to a new life.

To overcome your contradiction, you can use the positive aspects of the number but you can also use the existing resources in houses 1, 2, 5 and 11.

You can also call upon the experiences of the houses where there are complementary numbers to those in Houses 1, 2, 5 and 11, if these complementary numbers exist in the Birth Diamond.

Reminder: Number considered + complementary number = 22.

If the contradiction's complementary number is not found in the Birth Diamond, people who have that complementary number in their Birth Diamond can help you solve the challenge that is part of your contradiction.

Calculating the number in the house: This number is found by adding the numbers in houses 6 and 7.

Contradiction numbers:

This number reveals a major contradiction hidden within you. It is at the same time a powerful resource but also a major challenge to accept, to recognize, to admit, to love and to use this resource. What are you always complaining about in your life or about yourself? What do you always criticize others about? What do you strongly want, and yet don't want, or rather you prefer that is not known? The answer to these questions, in connection with your contradiction number, often helps to reveal your contradiction. You can shape your contradiction into a powerful growth lever when you become aware of the aspects of the number that are difficult for you and that creates conflicts, when you search for and embody he higher aspects of the number and also of the complementary number and when you use your different resources, mainly those in houses 1, 2 5 and 11.

Example: Number 10 (The Wheel of Fortune) as contradiction number.

You have a strong ability to understand the meaning of your destiny, to understand the chains of events that create history and the mechanisms of life, as if you had an inner clock tuned to eternity. You have within you real abilities to innovate and to get out of recurring schemes, to invent new things from scrap or to improve what is, to experiment tools and techniques that bring progress to life, to use a keen intelligence, a strong sense of humor and commercial abilities to adapt, to be a smart life mechanic, to understand how things work, to know how to try your luck and take advantage of opportunities, to take matters into your own hands, to start all over when necessary, to make the wheel of life turn, to handle information and data systems and to serve life in a practical manner.

But either you refuse, at first, to express these skills, either you express them so much that they hinder your evolution or either you tend to consider that these skills are not worth very much and so you use them from time to time, when it suits you, while often complaining about them. Can you see that these recurring difficulties hinder your evolution?
Your tendency to repeat can however help you become an expert, high analytical powers and an ability to master tools and techniques that can help adapt to real life and progress.

To your life, to experience inner freedom or a new life and to express the best of yourself, you can use and practice the following skills:

- Understanding the deep meaning of your destiny and of historical events.
- get out of recurring schemes, innovate and live your own life.
- invent new things from old things or improve what is.
- Experiment tools and techniques that help life move on.
- use your intelligence, your smartness, your financial management and sales abilities to adapt.
- understand how things work and be a life mechanic.
- try your luck, see and seize opportunities.
- take things in charge, make the wheel turn and start all over again when necessary.
- learn to say "so what" if people laugh at you" and use your sense of humor

You can also overcome the challenge brought about by number 10 (the Wheel) by using the complementary number, number 12 (The hanged man), i.e. by learning to relax, by getting out of the permanent thinking going on in your head, by opening up to your intuition, by inverting your beliefs and points of view, by working on your genealogical tree and on the recurring schemes in your life.
You can then become an expert in tools, techniques and data systems that help people move on and that enable the wheel of life to turn the right way.

Examples: Nicolas Copernicus (19/02/1473), Fidel Castro (13/08/1926), Edgar Cayce (18/03/1877), Jean Cocteau (05/07/1889), Padre Pio (25/05/1887).

ANNUAL NUMBER HOUSE

Definition of the house: The annual number describes a series of experiences that are available for you to experiment during the year, from birthday to birthday, as well as available energies that can be expressed. When whatever is symbolized by this number is experienced in a state of awareness and in an eagerness to grow, these experiences can help you move closer to your deep inner truth, become freer and help you express the full potential of your Birth Diamond.

This number deserves a special attention when:

It already exists once or more than once in the Birth Diamond. The energies of the annual number then tune up with the house where an identical number is located. It's complementary number exists in the Birth Diamond. The annual number is the Moon or the Sun which have a very particular influence. The Moon tends to amplify inner life or private life and put outer life to the background while the sun does the opposite.

Calculating the number in the house: This number is found by adding the number in house 2 and the universal numerological year.

Example : If we are in 2031 (2+0+3+1=6), a person having number 17 in House 2 will have the High Priest as annual number. (17+6=23=5). You will note that in this case, the annual number is the complementary number of the House two numbers (17+5=22). This suggests a possibility to express what makes up one's wealth in a new, different and more efficient manner during this year.

Annual numbers:

The annual number reveals a new array of experiences that can occur during the year and new energies and trends that are available for you to express. If the annual number or it's complementary exists in the birth Diamond, then the house concerned will be highlighted during the year and you will have the opportunity or the obligation to focus on that specific part of your Birth Diamond.

Extra data: If you add the current month with your annual year number, in base 9 or in base 22, you obtain indications of a given month's atmosphere.

Example: Number 6 (The Lovers) as annual number:

Your will experience, this coming year, the opportunity and the need to listen to your true desires and to act according to them, to connect with others, to meet new people and to build new partnerships, to share, to serve, to use a relational intelligence or artistic abilities, to experience greater commitment in your love relationship, to create new bonds, to make important choices, to enhance harmony, diplomacy and social life, to love, to feel in love and to express your feeling of joy and happiness. These various opportunities should be used to accomplish your life mission and to help you grow further towards your deepest truth.

This year, you can also increase and complement the opportunities brought by the Lovers by freeing yourself from any confinements, by canalizing your energy, by being open to new and unexpected events, by using modern technologies, by learning to experience a new vision of life and of yourself, by learning to look inwards so as to experience sparks of awareness and by including spiritual values in your life.

NATURAL TEMPER HOUSE

Definition of this house: The natural temper is one of the more or less conscious aspects of your dominant psychological characteristics. It lies between your way of asserting (house 1), your roots (house 4) and your deep identity (house 5). It usually brings new resources but it can sometimes create problems depending on the number concerned. Basically, it describes your natural tendencies, the way you are when you are spontaneous, well and happy, a bit like the moon in an astral chart.
Calculating the number in the house: This number is found by adding the numbers in houses 1, 8, 8 again and 9.

Natural temper numbers:

This number describes how you are when you are natural, how you recover, what you need to feel well and how you express the contents of your subconscious. The complementary number, if it exists in the Birth Diamond, can help increase your well-being.

Example: Number 11(Strength) as natural temper number:

You have a natural tendency to be well centered in your body and heart, to be self confident, to be brave and to be willing to fight till victory is obtained, to make connections between spirit and matter, to trust your intuition and your instincts, to express in a natural and harmonious manner your sexual needs, to vibrate with love and to express the power of love, to strike a balance between power and love, to use your strength with great efficiency and to control and master what you want to thanks to your powerful will and the power of love. As you are naturally autonomous and yet very skilled at connecting with others, you can both work alone by creating your own activity or within in a group or a team.

These skills are qualities that you can become aware of and use to nourish your evolution. If your wounds are not healed or if your natural temper is not harmoniously expressed, then you may have a tendency to act like a selfish wild lion, to create conflicts wherever you go and to be violent because of unaccepted and misunderstood past events. Acceptance and reconnection to the heart is then necessary.

DEEP MOTIVATION HOUSE

Definition of the house: This house brings you a set of skills and qualifications that deeply belong to you and that are specifically there to help you accomplish your life mission by coordinating all the skills in your birth Diamond. The number in this house describes your deep drive or motivation to accomplish your destiny. It is an organizational strength. You use these coordination abilities when you accomplish your life mission to do what you have come on earth to do. It is by using these skills in the world that you can make them grow. The different houses in the Birth Diamond aren't very well coordinated if you do not use the motivation number.

Calculating the number in the house: This number is found by adding the numbers in houses 1, 5 and 8.

Deep motivation numbers:

This number reveals the main motivations that you can call upon to accomplish what you have come to do on Earth, to accomplish your life mission and to progress towards your eternity. It is one of the major resources that you can call upon, with the numbers in houses 1,2,5,9 and 10, to create, coordinate and manage your true life project.

It shows and nourishes your motivation. It helps you to get organized in time so as to move on.

Example: Number 7 (The Chariot) as motivation number:

You have a strong ability to motivate yourself, to take initiatives, to give yourself permission and to organize the means to obtain victory, by applying efficient solutions and management strategies, to do your job efficiently, to plan for the future, to put operational projects into place, to control your energy, to handle situations, to find your marks in space, to go where it is necessary to go, to use your strength and your technical intelligence, to take the necessary action, to handle transport equipment, to drive, to find your way around, to find your personal pathway, to reach your destination and to be like a general conducting his troops to the battlefield. It is necessary and wise to use these skills to be on your right path and to accomplish what you have come on Earth to do. What motivates you is handling things and organizing complex projects. You can also increase number 7's power by using its complementary number, number 15, by living a fulfilling sexual life and what you feel passion for, by managing the dark side of yourself smartly and by using your personal power to serve life.

THE KEY RESSOURCE HOUSE

Definition of the house: This Resource is the deep background wealth that is your foundation, your dominant psychological characteristics. It is a major asset and lever that can and should be used to transform yourself so as to experience rebirth. Using it can greatly help you move towards more freedom and accomplishment.

Calculating the number in this house: This number is found by adding the numbers in houses 2, 10 and 11.

Key Resource numbers:

This number brings a set of skills that are complementary to the resources in houses 2, 3 and 9. These skills tend to be used and can be used to play ones role in society and to coordinate all other resources so as to adapt to the world.

If you look deep inside you, you will see that you have practical skills to connect with the universe, with people or with information, to call upon a psychological or technological intelligence to find solutions and bring about progress, to promote human values, to help yourself and others, to call upon spiritual values, to master technologies, to cross from one state of being to another, to remain free from any addiction, to work within a group or a network, to grant yourself a time for leisure activities, to experience temperance, serenity and progress, to express the angel within you and to live free and happy. These skills you can use to play your role in society, to transform yourself, to accomplish your life mission and to enhance your evolution.

You can also do this by using number 14's complementary number, number 8 (Justice), by actively playing a role in civilization or society, by understanding it's rules and processes, by learning to handle information, by creating truth, order and justice and by living in harmony with both cosmic laws, human laws and yourself.

EXPRESSION HOUSE

Definition of the house: It describes how you are when you express yourself and shows one of your major psychological characteristics. It also shows what specific energy you have come to embody and your conscious needs. It's always interesting to compare the expression number with the soul call number and the natural temper number as by this one can see how the conscious and unconscious selves interact and match.

Calculating the number in the house: It is obtained by adding the numerical values of all the letters in your first and family names.

Expression numbers:

This number describes your character, your way of expressing yourself and what you need to express yourself. It also shows what psychological tendencies you have come to express and that you should express in your life to achieve self realization. Expression number tends to work together with the number in house 1 and also with the number in house 9. It describes a general psychological atmosphere in which the number in house 1 tends to be expressed so it's important to compare the two and see how they get along. If the complementary number exists in the Birth Diamond, the number and the experiences corresponding to the house will facilitate one's expression.

Example: Number 22 (The Fool) as expression number:

When you express yourself, you have a need for and a tendency to:

- be without structures, borders or limits; be unclassifiable and outside existing norms.
- be always on the move, be ready to pack your luggage and hit the road, go out on adventurous paths to explore new territories.
- go beyond known paths, experience your own truth and assert your specificity by being unique.
- have total freedom of speech and movement, feel free, enlightened, trendsetting, futuristic and at the forefront of things.
- express the genius within yourself and your creative power, break the bonds of karma, and bring about liberation and a new start.
- live freely and happily.

These abilities and skills should be expressed to enhance your evolution.

SELF-REALIZATION HOUSE

Definition of this house: When you express who you are (first and family name) and when you follow your life path (house 10), then self realization occurs. This house is your "highway to heaven". It describes the atmosphere, the energy and the skills that you must develop and use so as to accomplish your life mission, your destiny and so as to experience self realization. It describes in a very synthetical manner the general direction that your life should take in order for you to become completely free and happy.

It shows what you do with who you are. It reveals the tree with its fruits. It reveals why you have chosen to embody in the specific space and time where you are. This number is also sometimes called the life mission number or the personal legend number. It enables you to reach the source of brilliance in the center of the birth diamond and to shine like a Diamond created by "The Source of all life" with the power of love.

Calculating the number in this house: It is obtained by adding the value of the expression number and house 10.

Self Realization numbers:

This number is unique and very special as it is the only number that combines both your name, with the letters that make up your identity and the numbers of your birth date. It summarizes the reason and the meaning of your presence on Earth.

Example: Number 21 (The World) as Self-Realization number:

What you have come to do on Earth and the general trend that your life should take are connected with your ability to explore the world, to play your part in the world, to take action in economic activities, to gather men and to go beyond frontiers, to work with foreign people and countries, to accept what comes from abroad, to teaching or dance, to adapt to societies' rules and regulations, to reap the fruits of your labor, to experience victory and official recognition and to develop a universal and international scope.

Your evolution is also connected with an ability to summarize, to undertake successful studies and projects, to be an open minded, warm hearted, stable, prosperous, organized person, to expand your sphere of action and broaden your inner and outer horizons, to be at ease everywhere, to realize your ambitions and to guide others in the world. You have come to earth to finish something. With the Magician as complementary number to the World, you can also succeed by listening to your inner child, by being in the present moment, and by using your personal abilities in connection with your own specific goals.

Chapter 5: Interpreting numbers existing two, three or four times in the Birth Diamond.

A same number can be found twice, three and more rarely four, five or six times in a specific Birth Diamond[©]. A house becomes more important when it hosts a number which also exists in another house. It becomes three times more important if it hosts a number that occupies two other houses in the Birth Diamond. This rule can help establish a certain hierarchy within the houses. Interpretation is then done according to what the numbers two, three or four symbolize. Let's look at this in detail.

Numbers that are in the Birth Diamond twice:

Number two both symbolizes duality and complementarities. At first, it tends to symbolize a difficulty that needs to be dealt with and that needs readjusting, negotiation and doing some work on one's self. One then needs duality to express the number. This duality tends to be expressed in two different manners. Either one tends to consider that the number is bad, upsetting, unpleasant and difficult or either one tends to have an excessive and compulsory need to express the number and to have a tendency to force things. A key is to observe the secondary profit that is obtained or that is believed to be obtained by entertaining and nourishing the existing duality or excess.

Number 2 is symbolically similar to the second number of the tarot deck, the High Priestess, the keeper of secrets that she hides or unveils. This means that in order to express the positive aspects of a number existing twice in the Birth Diamond, an increased awareness is necessary in connection with the number. It is through awareness and by changing the direction of one's attention and intentions that one can transform duality into an asset. Duality exists in the first place so that one can express the number with total awareness in all its aspects. The initial duality can then become a conscious complementarity.

A number existing in two houses creates a bond between the two houses. The characteristics of this bond depend on the characteristics of the two houses concerned and on how the two houses are expressed in the person's real life. The initial duality tends to manifest in the houses occupied by the same two numbers.

If the two houses concerned tend naturally to be harmonious (Houses 1, 2, 3 , 5, Key Resource and Self-Realization)   or if they have at least one harmonious aspect (Houses 9, 10, 11 and 12), the effects of the initial duality tend to be lessened to the benefit of complementarity but there is then less awareness.

If the houses concerned are those that carry all the difficult aspects of the Birth Diamond (Houses 4, 6, 7, 8, 12 and the Hidden Challenge) there is then a stronger duality but also an increased awareness. If a harmonious house and a difficult house are involved, the situation is then more complicated. Either one suddenly faces a difficulty when one expresses a skill or either certain skills cannot be expressed because they are blocked by the difficult house. Personal growth and work on one's self then enables one to free the jammed skills and then to call upon the harmonious house to balance the difficult one.

When a same number exists twice in the Birth Diamond, the two houses and the life experiences symbolized by these houses can then help each other to become aware of the initial duality and to express the number consciously and in the best possible manner.

Example: Two number ones in the Birth Diamond

You probably feel either a compulsory and excessive need to or a refusal and recurring difficulties to:

- make energy move inside you and to feel full of energy
- take initiatives and improvise
- motivate yourself, dare and be confident
- know what to do and how to do it
- start things, wake up in the morning and being born
- Be embodied in life and action
- Be aware of the tools at hand, knowing how to use them and coordinating them to achieve a goal

There may sometimes be a specific issue during birth. These difficulties require work on one's self so as to express the number in full awareness and in a positive manner. You can overcome the duality of Number 1 (the Magician) with its complementary number which is 21, (the World), by defining clear goals, by learning to get well organized, by summarizing your different experiences and by incorporating them in the world, in society and this in a conscious manner.

Connecting two houses:

Two harmonious houses: House 1 and House 11:

In order to feel confident, to be assertive, to do what must be done, to be efficient and to feel strong, you need freedom of action and to use your psychological and technological intelligence to fix what needs to be fixed, to find solutions and to adapt to modern life. You may have special abilities for fixing things or people, to create netwoks or to experience group activities.

Two disharmonious houses: House 4 and House 7:

When a same number is these two houses, your antipode, that part of you that you tend to reject or that you tend to see in a negative way, the beliefs that limit you, your inner enemies and the major challenge that you have to deal with are all connected to your genealogical heritage and what has being transmitted to you by your parents. It's quite possible that you are either reacting to your parent's problematic schemes, hence your refusal to express your number in House 7, or reproducing them. It is quite likely that you have chosen these specific parents so as to settle a karmic difficulty. Your major challenge may be to transform your genealogical heritage so that it becomes not a burden but your major asset, and so that you can express your specificity. You can then use your heritage to recover and incorporate your antipode, to overcome your major challenge and to develop your relational intelligence. There can be a close bond between couple life and family.

Harmonious and disharmonious houses: House 2 and House 6:

In this case, the inner wealth, the natural resources, the qualities, the skills and the assets are connected to the technical intelligence, to a need for health and hygiene but also to that part of the self that thinks all the time instead of acting in the present moment, to the traumatic cycle, to difficult memories, to a specific wound that turns around in circles and brings recurring difficulties and failure schemes until it is healed and until the awareness switches from the traumatic cycle to the cycle of love (House 5). This combination can at first limit self expression until work on one's self is done, because as soon as one tries to express their inner wealth, they fall into your traumatic cycle. But it is possible here you use one's wealth and resources to overcome the so human tendency to be stuck in the thinking mind, in the wounds and in recurring failure schemes. In order to this, one can upon the luminous facets of the number, upon the complementary number and upon the other resources within the Birth Diamond.

You can phrase this the following way: In order to feel joy and happiness, to earn money and to create a happy life on earth, it is necessary to repeat something so as to become an expert so as to serve efficiently. This makes the wheel of your life turn around the right way. It is also necessary for you to technically understand how to feel joy, happiness, how to earn money and create prosperity.

House 8 and House 9:

Your subconscious, your inner quest and the treasure that you are seeking are connected to the outside world, to enlarging your scope and to your work life. It can at first not be very simple to find your place in the world, but your hidden wealth and inner quest can be found within your official work and your ability to explore the world and its philosophies or though cultural beliefs. It may be necessary to go on an inner quest to find your work resources or your place in the world. When this is done and when you use the personal power to serve the world, it can then be done with a great inspiration, passion, authenticity and efficiency.

Year House with other houses: House 12 and Year House:

One can interpret this combination as follows. This number is in House 12 and in your year house. You may feel less concerned than usual by world affairs this year! You may have the possibility or the obligation to let go, to take care of what makes you suffer or of your ancestors, to recover your faith, to incorporate spiritual values in your life, to bring relief to people's suffering and misery, to finish something, to move towards the ultimate goal of your destiny and to experience transcendence, enchantment and unity with God.

Numbers that are in the Birth Diamond three times:

Number three is the result of a complementarity action between conscious and unconscious, between Spirit, Soul and physical Body or Holy Spirit. It symbolizes communication, movement and coordinated action. It is symbolically connected to the third number of the tart deck, the Empress, who gives a form to things by using creative power, authority and relational intelligence. When a number exists three times in the birth Diamond, one then has the need, the possibility and natural abilities to express that number in all of its aspects, on all realms, through a coordinated movement, with authority, mastery and elegance. Three same numbers then bring the gift of trinity. They are a wonderful gift that can bring great luck and an asset that can be expressed with both a great fluidity and efficiency. There may however be less awareness than when a number exists twice in the Birth diamond. Harmony is greater if the houses concerned are harmonious and the positive impact of a number existing three times may initially be lessened if the houses are the difficult ones. A number existing three times creates bonds between the three houses concerned. These houses can be expressed together in a coordinated manner. It is interesting to observe that same numbers can be expressed in three totally different ways in each house.

Example: Three number sixes (lovers) in the Birth Diamond.

You have a natural and strong ability to:

- listen to your true desires, make the right choices and dedicate yourself to others
- express your feelings and your joy
- love and bring happiness to yourself and others
- use your relational intelligence and your artistic abilities
- connect with people, experiment bonds and couple life, share and serve life, express harmony and be a social person

The positive impact of number 6 can also be increased with its complementary 22 partner number, in this case number 16 (House of God or Tower) by:

- learning to be centered in your inner temple and to experiment inner life so as to increase awareness.
- learning to canalize and direct your energy,
- experimenting a new vision of things, of life and of yourself
- being open to the unexpected and to newness
- using modern technologies
- incorporating spiritual values in your life
- feeing yourself from whatever is confining you
- and by submitting your relations, your couple, your abilities to express form, your desires and your joy to your "path towards God", to your spiritual evolution.

Numbers that are in the Birth Diamond four times:

Number four symbolizes the structures of life and materializing things in a given space-time environment. It is connected to the fourth Tarot number, the Emperor, who enables one to express authority, personal power and powerful organizational abilities in order to, symbolically speaking, build and manage an empire, one's own or the empire of someone else. A same number existing four times in the Birth Diamond enables one to express that number in the material, mental, soul and spiritual realms.

It can reveal a great power to express the number but also an excess of something that impedes something else from being expressed. The challenge is then to use a real gift so that it doesn't take over one's entire life and so that it doesn't impede one from living a balanced life. Birth Diamonds where there are four identical numbers are quite rare. Only certain numbers can be found four times or more. These numbers are 5, 6, 7, 8, 9, 10 and 11.

Special years: A person that has a same number three times in his or her Birth Diamond will experience a special year when the Year Number is the same as the one already existing three times. The year is then strongly impacted by that number and by the houses concerned.

Example: Four number fours (The Chariot) in a Birth Diamond.

Because this number exists four times in your Birth Diamond, you probably have an excessive tendency to:

- give permission to yourself or to others
- prepare expeditions, move to different places, travel around and reach different destinations
- motivate yourself; take action and fight so as to obtain victory
- find the means to reach a goal and to be efficient
- focus on a destination, on a mission or on what needs to be done
- control your energy
- use your thinking mind, your technical abilities and your sticking power
- To be symbolically like a general leading his troops to the battlefield

Even if you can be a highly efficient expert within a company, your excesses can seriously upset certain parts of your life, lock you up in recurring problems and limiting schemes and block certain parts of your life, thus impeding complete self realization, the accomplishment of your life mission and your evolution.

You can overcome the excesses of number 7 (the Chariot) by using its complementary number, number 15 (the Devil), by learning to:

- manage with more awareness the impulses and drives of your subconscious
- live a blossoming sexual and financial life
- live according to what you feel passion for without being consumed by your passion
- accept the dark part of yourself and handle your shadows
- use your strong personal power to serve life

The main problems with having four number fours (Chariots) is matching work life obligations with the possibility to do what one feels passion for, respecting speed limits, having enough time for private or love life and taking proper care of one's health.

Chapter 6: Practice through examples.

Example 1: Marion Zimmer Bradley: American writer

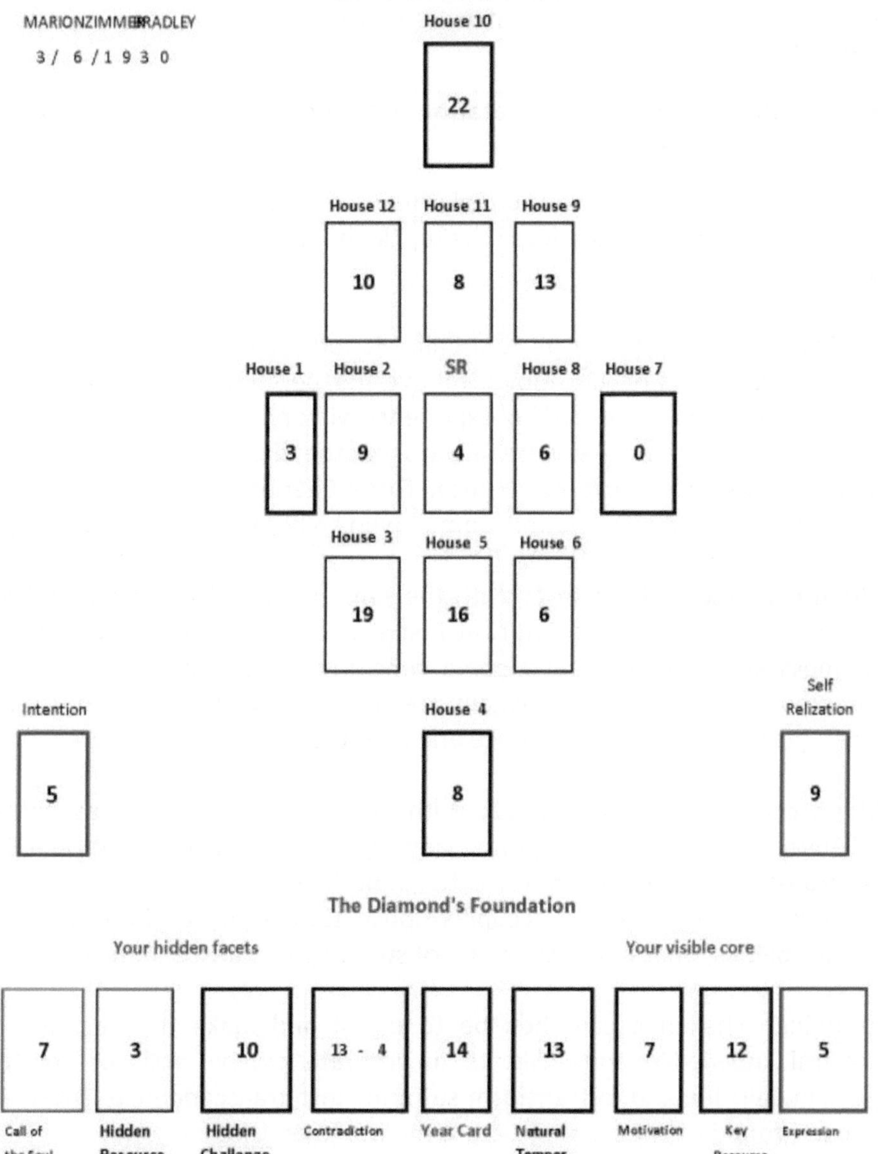

MZB is a Sci-Fi, fantasy and detective novelist. She wrote the Avalon novels (Lady of the lake and Mists of Avalon), the Darkover Landfall series and the Unity novels. The characters in her novels show amazingly well the different facets of her Birth Diamond. Let's check out the different houses and let's have a look at the numbers that exist more than once in Marion's Birth Diamond.

You can either start the interpretation with the Diamond's foundation or with the Diamond 'core.

Soul Intention: Marion's soul deeply needs to experience soul and body medicine, teachings, blessings, being legitimate and broadening her awareness.

Soul Call: With the Chariot as Soul Call, Marion's soul feels a need and an ability to be always on the move, to give her permission, to be active, to reach well defined goals and to experience victory. Her father worked on trains and her characters were always on the move. This number also occupies House 7 and Life Key House. Three Chariots make Marion a very active, dynamic and high spirited woman who knows where she wants to go.

Hidden resource and house 1: With the same number in House 1 and the hidden resource house, Marion is at first sight a very secret person. Words and messages need to spend some time inside her mind before being expressed in a very fluid and elegant manner. She has the ability to use the hidden resources of her intelligence and adaptability.

Hidden challenge and House 12: With The Wheel of Fortune as hidden challenge, how can one incorporate and digest past experiences? How can one transform repeating cycles into something new? This is a hidden challenge. This number also occupies House 12, the house of ancestors, of psychic abilities, of ecstatic music and of suffering or transcendence.

Her hidden challenge can then be to digest and make the best use of ancestral knowledge and skills, to incorporate psychic skills or spiritual values in daily life and to transform suffering into transcendence. These are the background themes that structure the Darkover Landfall series.

The Wheel is strengthened by the Magician as expression number (number 10 is the higher version of number 1). Some of Marion's ancestors came from Scotland and others were Native American Indians. Both cultures strongly exist in Marion's novels.

Contradiction: The Unnamed Number or Death also occupies House 9. This allows this number to be expressed in the world (House 9). Marion Zimmer Bradley wrote under four different names in addition to her official name! Mystery, anguish, death, violence, inner transformation and seeking one's real identity were very strong themes in the characters of her novels.

The Darkover Landfall and Unity Novels are founded on the idea of totally eliminating one's past to start an entirely new life from scratch, after a loss of identity and after a major disaster requires a large scale reconstruction. Marion had very strong inner impulses and was often stressed between allowing these drives to exist and a need for justice and harmony. This number also symbolizes the shamanic culture and the occult powers expressed in the characters of her novels.

Natural Temper: With number 18 (the moon) as natural temper number, Marion is full of life, imagination and sensitivity. She has a highly imaginative vision of life and loves stories. She feels strongly connected with family values. Music, which plays an important role in many of her novels, makes her vibrate. Her daughter is a musician.

Key Resource: With number 12 (the hanged man) as key Resource, Marion's imagination is connected to the collective unconscious and to her ancestral memories. She has the ability to access the worlds of dreams, of magic, of sacredness and of fantasy. The key resources of the characters in the Darkover Landfall novels are actually telepathic abilities and different skills like extracting minerals with magical psychic powers.

Expression: Marion expresses herself with benevolence and in a clear, instructive and pedagogical manner. She is very sensitive to titles and to the meaning of things.

Self-realization: With the Hermit in Self-Realization House, Marion came to Earth to deliver messages and teachings, to experience long term projects and to help people experience wisdom, sacredness, depth, magic and faith, regardless of religious beliefs. She knew very young what she wanted to do and how to get organized so as to get results. MZB fulfilled her destiny by walking along the inner path leading to her deep inner truth and by building a cathedral, a work of art, and her novels.

House 1: With number 3 (the Empress) in House 1, Marion looks like a smart, brainy, determined and intelligent woman.

House 2: Number 9 (The Hermit) in house 2 enables Marion to need very little to live, to look inwards, to concentrate, to harmoniously manage her need to be alone and to see things in the long term. Some of the characters in her novels lived a very simple life. Others lived in cold, massive, barren and somewhat austere castles. Some dedicated their lives to seeking and finding their deepest truth, in monasteries or elsewhere.

House 3: With number 19 (the Sun) in house 3, love plays a central part in her novels. Her writing style is warm, luminous, clear and passionate. She studied art and theatre at Hardin-Simmons University in Texas.

House 4 and 11: Number 8 (Justice). Marion's parents were very strict and often away from home. We wrote mainly to recover and entertain a feeling of balance. The themes of civilization, cultural choc and the pressure, felt by individuals, coming from the requirements and laws of civilization, underlie the Darkover landfall and Unity series. A number in house 4 is often rejected or not well considered. Marion has highly sensitive to how, in the name of civilization, local cultures could be destroyed. The fact that this number 8 is both in Houses 4 and 11 enables and gives a drive to become free from the past and from a strong feeling of injustice.

House 5: Who is Marion deep down? With the House of God or The Tower in House 5, Marion is sometimes a person locked up in her tower, just like many of the characters in the Darkover Landfall series but also a person seeking God, above all religious beliefs. Marion is deeply inspired, revolutionary and liberating.

House 6 and 8: The Lovers are in Houses 6 and 8. Marion's quest is a quest for happiness, joy, softness and harmony. These are also Marion's recurring difficulties as she very often feels a lack of kindness, tenderness and affection. She compensates by being hyperactive and by writing. The themes symbolized by the Lovers, desire, joy and couple life were quite complicated in Marion's life. She had to face deviant sexual interests. House 6 also concerns daily work life and with the Lovers in that house, it is often possible to combine work and love, as it was the case for Marion.

House 7: This house is the antipode house, the house of all that is in opposition with how one sees one's self, the house showing a main challenge and also how one creates relationships with others. The Chariot is in House 7. This sometimes tends to make one behave a general leading troops to the battlefield! It symbolizes here Marion's masculine part which was a problem for her, just as were the numerous changes of dwelling places due to her father's job. Marion used the Chariots energy to fight for wemen's rights.

House 10: The Fool in House 10 invites Marion to express her uniqueness and the genius within her, to go beyond known structures and know paths and to work on the theme of freedom. These themes are strongly expressed by certain characters in hers novels.

House 12: The Wheel of Fortune enables Marion, through a keen technical intelligence and fantastic writing skills, to transcend her sufferings. She left behind a remarkable series of books that helped many people take a positive step and turn a page in their lives.

Source of Brilliance: Marion shines, glows and gives the best of herself by building up her empire through a very well structured work.

Example 2: Elodie Gossuin-Lachérie: Television speaker, fashion designer, French local politician and ex-top model.

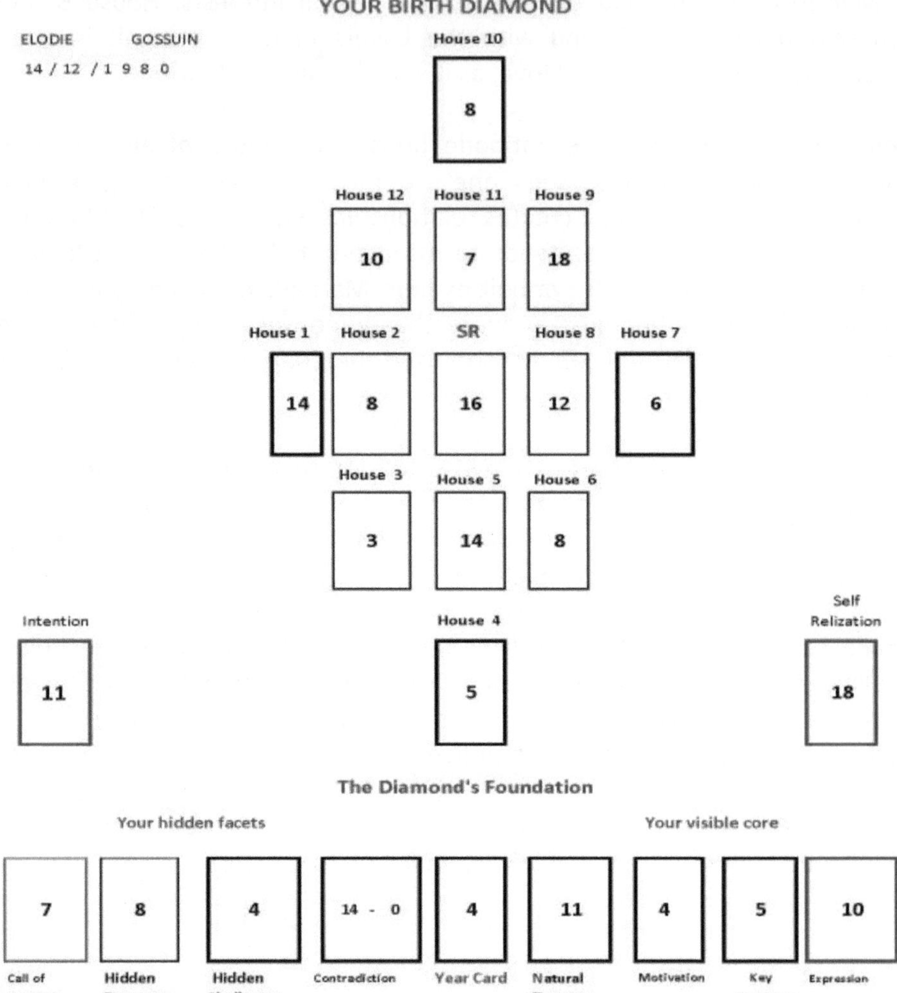

EGL, one of French people's favorite celebrities, is an amazing lady not only for her beauty, but also for her intelligence, her big heart, her righteousness and both her personal and political commitment to life in bringing well-being and progress to the French society. With Elodie's official birth date which is 15/12/1980, let's have a look at the different houses and at the numbers that exist more than once in Elodie's Birth Diamond.

144

The Diamond's foundation:

Soul Intention: Elodie needs here to take into account her ancestors, to arouse her awareness beyond the material aspects of life, to make people dream, to have faith and to experience transcendence.

Soul Call: With the Chariot as Soul Call, Elodie's soul feels both the need and the ability to motivate herself and others, to act, to do a lot of things, to be always on the move, to give herself permission, to reach well defined goals, to be efficient and to experience victory. This number also occupies House 6. This makes Elodie a very active person and also shows that if moving around all the time is not always pleasant for Elodie, she was able to become an expert in driving race cars!

Hidden resource: Elodie's hidden resources are a powerful sense of justice and balance, social intelligence and an ability to understand social structures and to organize information. It is by playing a role within a club and within society that Elodie can express her hidden resources.

Hidden challenge, House 3 and 12: How can one be listened too? How can one find the right words, adapt, synchronize thoughts, words and action and coordinate everything so that life may go on. These are the themes of the Empress. This number is in House 3, house which concerns communication and adapting to the surrounding world. The Empress is quite at ease in House 3. The fact that the number exists three times in Elodie's Diamond makes the needs of the number extremely important. Elodie is curious, needs to be well informed, gives a particular care to her communication and to the way she says what she says. House 12 makes one very sensitive to ancestral memories but also to the misery and sufferings of humanity and of youth. It creates a need to dream and make others dream, to give a meaning to life and to experience bliss and transcendence.

Contradiction: The Unnamed number or Death gives Elodie a very strong need to be authentic, to see beyond apparent scenery so as to experience the essence of beings and situations, to experience transformation and to live a life which she feels is in agreement with her deepest truth. It also helped Elodie become aware of her "second self" and of her astral body.

Her contradiction might be that Elodie has such an inner wealth that the different parts of herself all want to be expressed intensively so that it's not always obvious or easy to choose and also that although she has a very strong need for peace, relaxation and harmony, she always needs to keep her eyes open and to maintain a certain inner tension. This number also helped Elodie to experience a sweeping change of course in her life and to what she believes is right without being influenced by whatever people may say. She wanted to be a pediatric nurse. She became a top model, a radio and TV presenter, a local politician and the manager of the cosmetic firm she created. She played an active role in the TV series "the farm" and many people criticized her for that, not seeing the funds she was able to raise to help suffering children.

Natural Temper and House 8: The number existing in both houses connects the two houses and makes them work together. One can thus say the Elodie has a natural "House 8" temper or personality and also a "Hanged Man" personality. Like all people born in December, twelfth month, Elodie has the hanged Man in House 8, house symbolizing the quest of one's treasures. House 8 can sometimes be extreme or be connected to events which hinder the expression of the number in house 8.

People born under the sign of Sagittarius are sometimes so committed to the outside world and to their businesses, or so much in a hyperactive thinking state that it's not easy for them to relax, to experience a thoughtless serenity, sacredness, spirituality, transcendence, bliss and the suffering soul who craves to return to its divine source. This can make it difficult to take a distance from work life, to let go, to handle genealogical memories, to surrender to unconditional love, to have faith and to listen to one's secrets needs. The quest of people born under the sign of Sagittarius becomes a mystic quest aiming at going beyond genealogical or past life memories, a quest for meaning and a generous commitment towards the good of the community.

Elodie's quest may well be a quest to create a society where there is no suffering. With the hanged Man, Elodie is very sensitive to human misery and sufferings as well as to events that have a collective emotional impact. She has wanted, for a very long time, to become a nurse so as to help relieve people's sufferings.

She intensively dedicated time to clubs helping disabled children and adults. Number 12 (The Hanged) man also enables Elodie to express a strong ability to have faith, to let go, to pray, to turn her beliefs upside down, to listen to her intuition, to relieve people's sufferings and to experience unconditional love.

House 9 and Source of Brilliance: There are two Moon number in Elodie's Birth Diamond. The two houses concerned become important and are connected by the Moon number. With the Moon, Elodie is full of life, imagination and sensitivity. She is a very natural, close to people, kind and nice person who arouses immediate feelings of sympathy. She is strongly connected to family, children, past and to well-being and works with different clubs dedicated to bringing well-being to deprived children. She shines glows and sparkles through her feminine values and through her naturalness.

Key resource, House 2, House 10 and House 11: It may seem strange to see the hermit four times in Elodie's Birth Diamond! And yet! This means that the four houses concerned become very important in Elodie's life. The Hermit is a building site architect and master. He is very good at organizing, at being serious, wise and at undertaking responsibilities. He also symbolizes he grandparents, who played an extremely important part in Elodie's life. This number turns Elodie into a person which a high sense of morale and responsibility. It gives Elodie an enormous work power, an ability to adapt to organized structures and large organizations, to handle building sites and yet to remain simple and do her best with honesty and determination.

Motivation House and House 7 : Number 2 (The lovers) as motivation and as house 7 number gives Elodie beauty, sex appeal, tolerance, a strong sense of harmony, an ability to quickly weigh the "for's" and the "against", to listen to her true desires and to make what seem to be the "right" choices. Number 6 (The Lover) as motivation number means that it is by expressing joy, pleasure, relational intelligence, charisma, feelings and artistic abilities and also by experiencing marriage that one can fulfill and satisfy one's motivations. But number 6 is also in House 7, a house symbolizing the antipode, what we perceive as opposite to ourselves, as our major challenge.

House 7 also shows how we relate to others. Number 6 in this house strengthens Elodie's abilities to express beauty, relational intelligence, sociability and harmony, to connect with others while listening to her own desires and to choose. It also shows that being beautiful and refusing to be diplomatic when things must be said is not always easy. Elodie had to fight against human mediocrity, jealousy and numerous criticisms. She often had to prove that she is more than just a pretty woman but also an intelligent, efficient, responsible and great hearted person.

Expression: Elodie expresses herself in a smart and practical manner. She likes numbers and she likes to master the technical aspects of all files, endeavors and situations.

Self-realization: With (number 19) the Sun as Self-realization number, Elodie has come to earth to be a success model, to express the best of herself, to embody the luminous and generous power of the Sun, to be a living testimony of the power of love, to express her creative power and to manage people. She also had twins just like the ones showed on the Sun Tarot Number.

The Diamond's core:

House 1 and House 5: Number 15 (The Devil) in House 1 gives Elodie a magnetic, intense, energic, daring and lucid personality with a strong power of seduction and a strong ability to handle the world of matter and money. She gives the perception of a woman with a strong personal authority.

She is aware of the dark side of human nature and of the saboteur who exists in each person but with the lovers in House 7, Elodie's lucidity is expressed with tolerance, intelligence and sensitivity. Who is Elodie deep inside? Number 15, which symbolizes mastering matter, turns Elodie into a woman of full of passion and commitment. He is able to take into account every parameter of a given situation and especially the ones that aren't visible because she is strongly aware that there is a backstage and hidden power struggles in every situation.

She is able to go beyond her fears, to control her energy, her impulses and her emotions, to trust her instinct, to dare and challenge, to face danger, to break anything that tries to chain her up, to express a smart strategic intelligence and to fight with a great determination until she controls the situation and until her goals are reached. Elodie expresses the full strength of feminity and uses her power, her lucidity and her fighting spirit to serve life.

House 4 : Number 4 (The Emperor) in House 4 enabled Elodie to grow up with a strongly bonded and structured family where she was able to develop a logical and well organized mind, an understanding of how to build an empire, abilities to manage the world of matter and motivation to search for the right path. The number in House 4 often has a difficult aspect and Elodie is very sensitive to any abuse of masculine authority (the dark side of the Emperor), of power or of rigid structures that impede life to flow.

House 6: In Elodie's Birth Diamond, number 7 (the Chariot) occupies the Soul Call house and also House 6. House 6 creates technical intelligence, care for health and well-being issues but also recurring difficulties when one uses the mind too much and thinks too much. With this number, Elodie feels attracted to health matters, to science, to travelling and to organize the logistics of events, just as does a general leading troops to a battlefield (what he Chariot symbolizes). The difficult part of the number is probably experienced through a difficulty in handling everything at the same time, which is what many modern active wemen have to do, in France and elsewhere.

House 10: The hermit in House 10 invites Elodie to express simplicity, to walk along a path towards her deep inner truth, to isolate herself when necessary, to look inwards, to ask the right questions, to handle building sites and projects, to experiment, to search, to enlighten the world with wisdom, to work on structure or within a structured organization and to build something. The Hermit is "at home" in tenth House where its needs and abilities can fully be expressed. This position shows Elodie's commitment in politics in the counties' government.
When a same number is both in House 2 and House 10, it enables a person to use its entire wealth to develop, grow, build an interesting career and go towards self-realization.

Born before sunrise: Elodie's Birth Diamond reveals a very important rule. Official administrative day starts at midnight but the real terrestrial day starts when the Sun rises above horizon, at dawn. A person born between midnight and rising sun time, which is usually between 5am and 7am, is strongly affected by the numerical vibration of "the day before". In that particular case, it's very important to look at the person's Birth diamond established the day before her official date of birth. This second Birth Diamond brings a new and important complementary vision, where up to 15 houses out of the total 22 can change. Let's see this now.

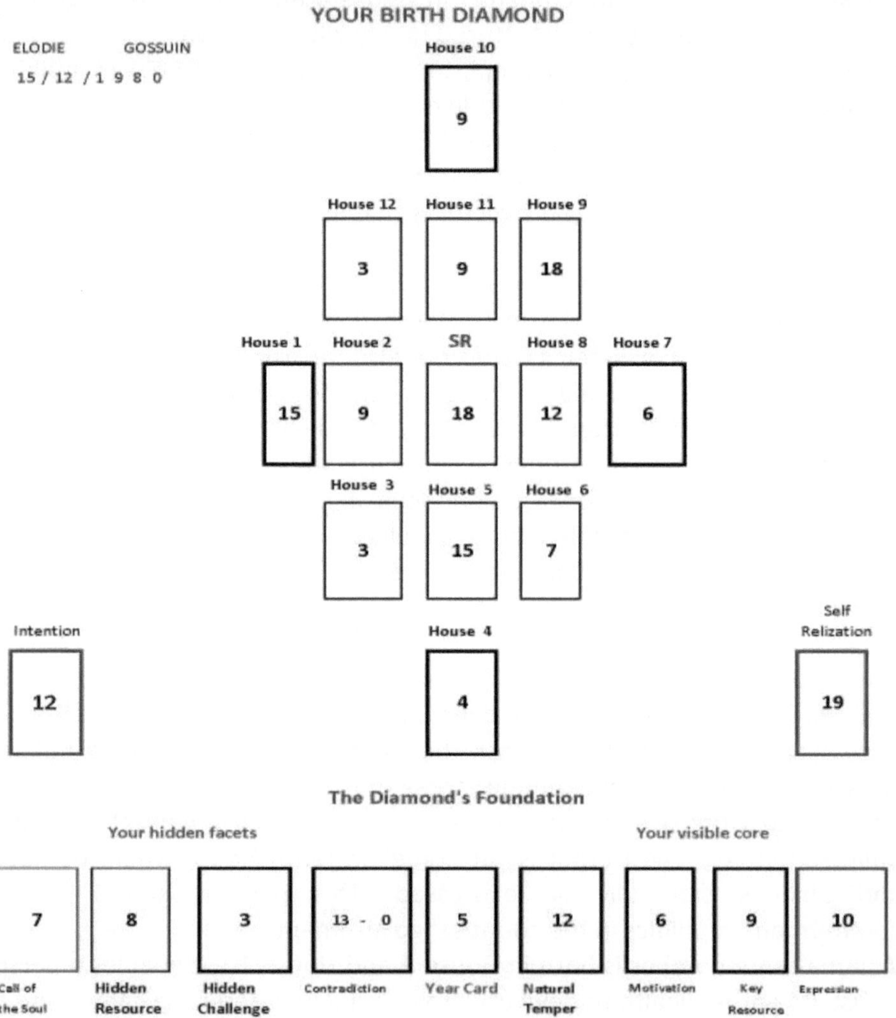

House 1, House 5 and Contradiction: When there is the same number in House 1 and in House 5, a person appears as she is deeply. When this same number is also in the Contradiction House, this creates a situation where one has some trouble handlings one's image and finding out what one really wants deep down. The fact that there are three same numbers nevertheless creates a positive drive and an understanding which enables a person to adapt. This is what happened to Elodie.

The three angels (number 14) give Elodie an ability and a need to go from one state of being to another, to connect with people and information, to communicate by using moderns tools and technologies, to see each person as a member of humanity beyond individual form, to appease and cushion, to become free from any addiction, to use a psychological or technological intelligence to find solutions, to promote human values, to work within a team or within a network, to be connected to the forces of progress flowing through the universe and to bring hope. The Angel is aware that beyond the world of matter is a world and a state of being where each person can express his or her uniqueness and live freely and happily.

House 2, House 6 and House 10: The number representing Justice (Number 8) bonds the houses of inner wealth (house 2), of technical intelligence (house 6) and of the life path (house 10). House 6 is where we think all the time so with Justice in house 6, one tends to always be thinking about what is fair or unfair, right or not right, in harmony with the laws of civilization or not. This can create a bit stress but the fact that there are three numbers and not two or four enables avoiding excesses and allows to be positive and to express the best of the number. Justice is the complementary number of the Angel (8+14=22). Having three complementary pairs means that these two numbers are the most important in Elodie's Birth Diamond.

Number 8 (Justice) gives Elodie a powerful need and ability to handle information and administrative data, to be in harmony with both human and cosmic law, to be fair or to see that things are fair, to accept and handle responsibilities, to create truth, justice and order, to firmly decide, to promote public interests and public welfare with the help of rules and regulations, to understand what is required to make a civilization work efficiently, to become a member of a club or party or in an organized structure and to play a part in civilization.

Key Resource and House 4: Number 5 is imaged by "The High priest", doctor of soul and body, who seeks to give a meaning to life, to connect heaven and earth, to teach, to protect and to bless connects the two houses of family heritage and key resource. The few years of medical studies and the values given to her by her family are certainly connected to this number.

House 11: When we take the 14th as birth day, the Chariot occupies Soul Call House and House 11, which symbolizes necessary solutions, whereas it occupied Soul Call house and House 6 with 15/12/1980 as birth date. This number shows that for Elodie, progress arises when she gives herself permission to live what she wants, when she sets well defined goals and gets organized to reach them, when she fights to obtain victory, when she travels as much as is necessary, when she works in the corporate world, and when she is, from a symbolic point of view, like a general leading his troops to the battlefield.

House 12 : The Wheel of Fortune in House 12 shows that Elodie's long term life goal, as well as her means to experience bliss and transcendence and also what she will leave behind is connected to a ability to understand how life, history, finance and trade works, to an ability to innovate and to become free from recurring schemes so as to live one's own life, to invent new from old, to use and experiment different tools and techniques to help life move on, to use intelligence and sales skills, to know when and how to try her luck, to handle situations, to know how to start all over if necessary and to act so that luck may come across the way and make the wheel of life turn.

Source of Brilliance: The Tower or House of God shows that Elodie can shine, glow and help people to shine when she helps others get out of their confinements, when she makes others become more aware, when she allows a new vision to come about, when she breaks down existing structures so as to build differently, when she adapts to the unexpected and the unknown, when she upsets and creates the adequate shock to bring about the necessary progress and when she uses modern technologies and media.

Hidden challenge: The Emperor in the Hidden Challenge House gives the will, the authority and a power that helps one build one's empire, or find an adequate activity and one's place to work. However, it is not easy and it's also not easy to see why it's not easy. Becoming aware of one's skills and abilities and finding were to work and use these skills is a challenge.

Soul Intention and natural temper: Elodie's soul intention is to master herself, her life and to live according to what her heart tells her. Number 11 (Strength) as Natural Temper gives Elodie the ability to be well centered in her heart and body, to be self confident, to have courage, to fight to victory, to trust her instinct, to express the power of love, to strike a balance between power and love, to be fully independent while being connected to others and to use Heart Strength, which is what is symbolized by the number, in a very efficient manner.

Motivation: Number 4 (The Emperor) as motivation number means that she is strongly motivated either to build and run her own empire or two help run someone else's empire.

Self-realization: Number 18 (The Moon), which is there three times in Elodie's Birth Diamond (with her official birth date), appears here only as Self-Realization, Fulfillment or Life Axis Number. This number suggests here that Elodie's possibilities of accomplishing her destiny are connected with an ability to promote life and well being, to manage fears and emotions, to make people dream or to help them accomplish their dreams, to help children, to connect with the general public or with wemen or to activities linked with liquids, water, food and other recovery values that help life go on.

Birth Diamonds of some famous people.

It is very interesting to do some biographical research and match what is found with the houses of the Birth Diamond so as to see how that person expresses his or her birth Diamond.

YOUR BIRTH DIAMOND

AMANDA   TAPPING

28 / 8 / 1 9 6 5

House 10

12

House 12 | House 11 | House 9

11 | 6 | 21

House 1 | House 2 | SR | House 8 | House 7

10 | 18 | 3 | 8 | 13

House 3 | House 5 | House 6

11 | 4 | 18

Intention

41

House 4

7

Self Relization

21

The Diamond's Foundation

Your hidden facets

Your visible core

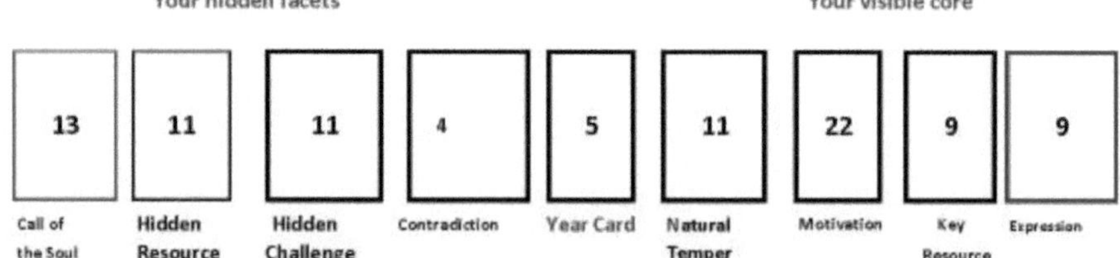

YOUR BIRTH DIAMOND

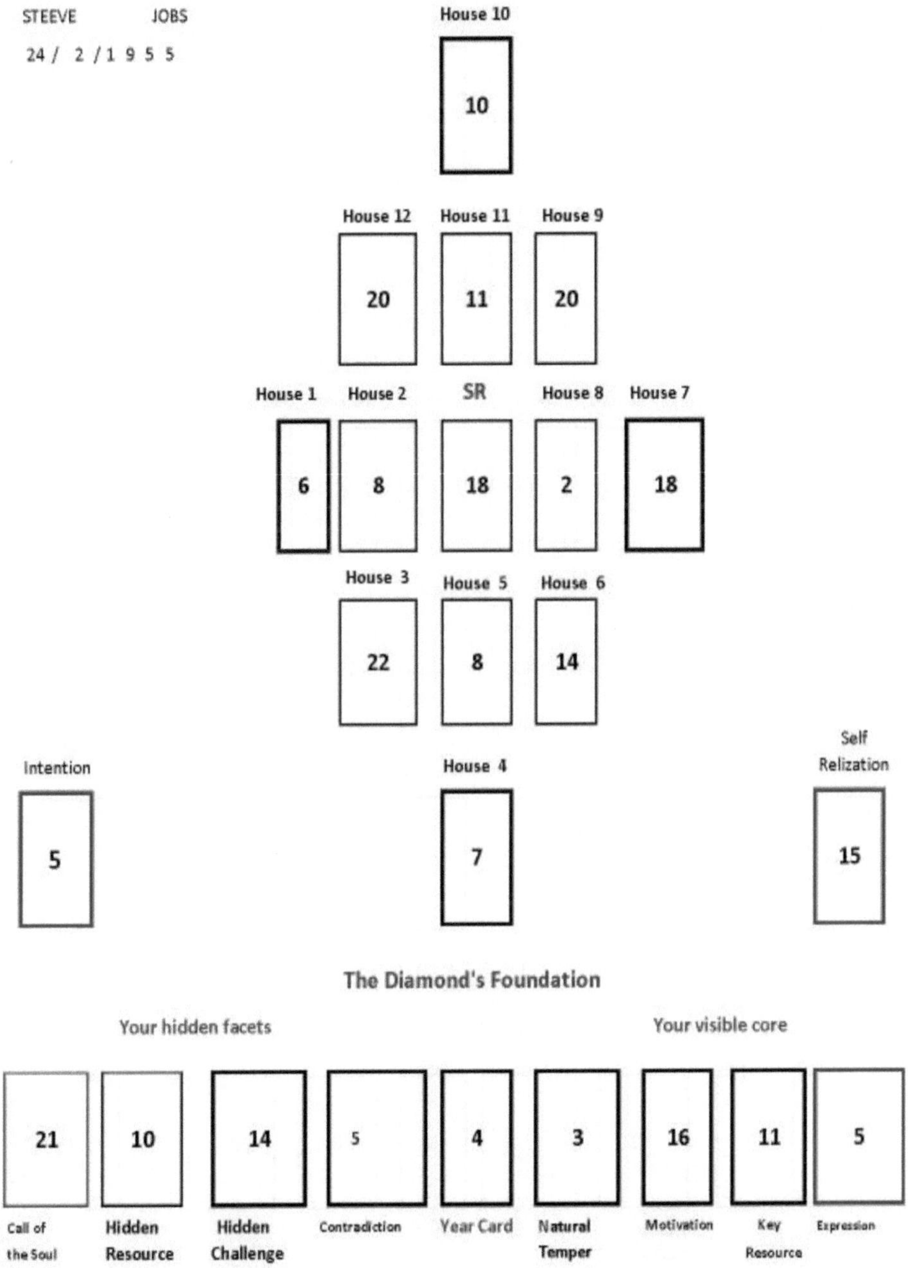

STEEVE   JOBS

24 / 2 / 1 9 5 5

House 10

10

House 12 — 20

House 11 — 11

House 9 — 20

House 1 — 6

House 2 — 8

SR — 18

House 8 — 2

House 7 — 18

House 3 — 22

House 5 — 8

House 6 — 14

Intention

5

House 4

7

Self Relization

15

The Diamond's Foundation

Your hidden facets

Your visible core

21	10	14	5	4	3	16	11	5
Call of the Soul	Hidden Resource	Hidden Challenge	Contradiction	Year Card	Natural Temper	Motivation	Key Resource	Expression

YOUR BIRTH DIAMOND

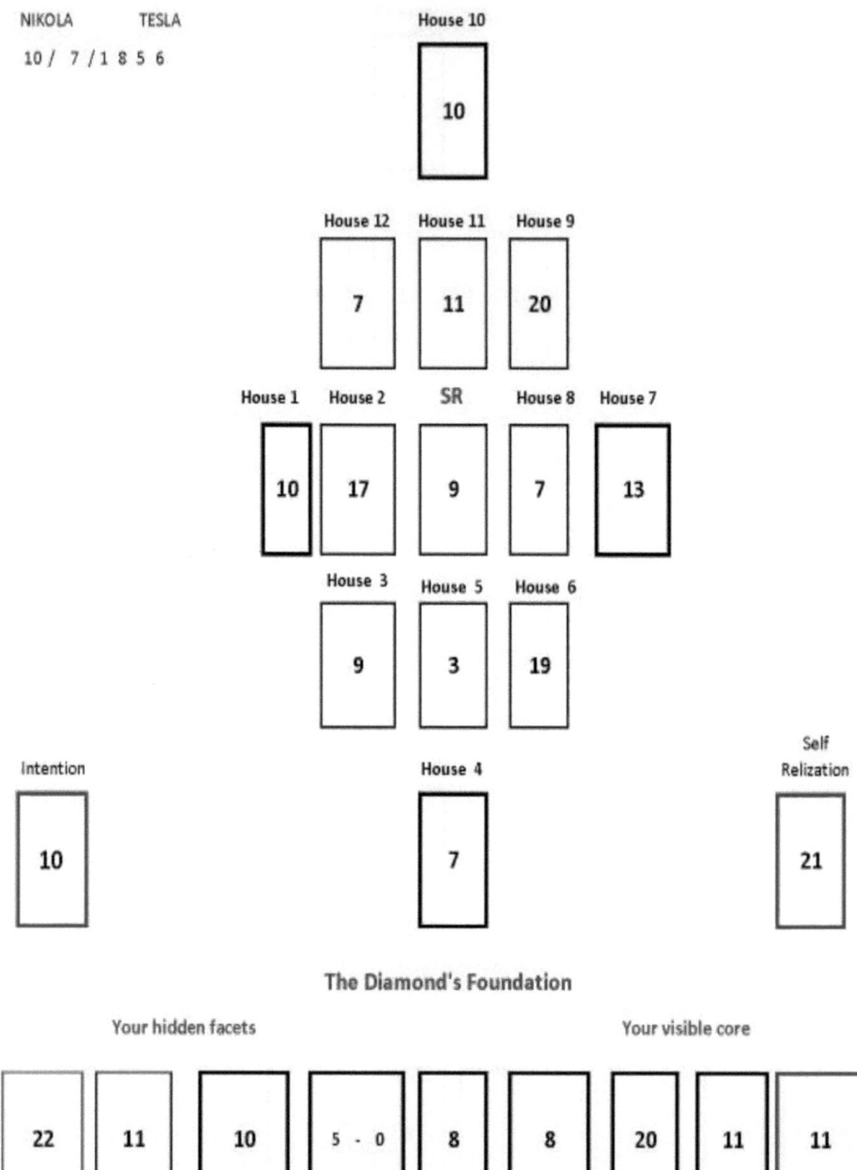

156

YOUR BIRTH DIAMOND

RANI   MUKHERJEE

21 / 3 / 1 9 7 8

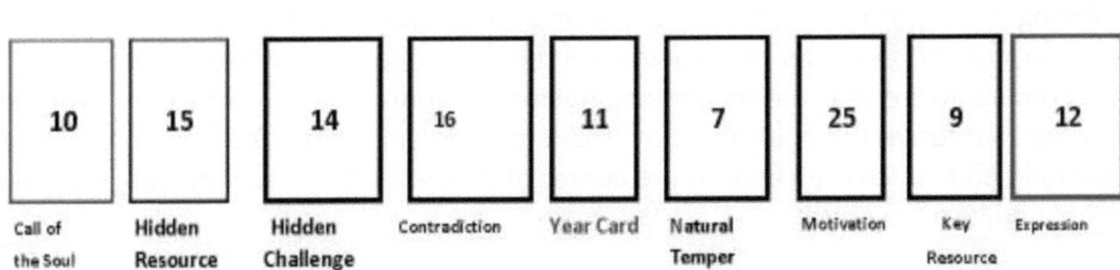

House 10

4

House 12 — **13**   House 11 — **17**   House 9 — **7**

House 1 — **21**   House 2 — **6**   SR — **10**   House 8 — **3**   House 7 — **4**

House 3 — **10**   House 5 — **10**   House 6 — **12**

Intention — **14**

House 4 — **5**

Self Relization — **16**

The Diamond's Foundation

Your hidden facets

Your visible core

10	15	14	16	11	7	25	9	12
Call of the Soul	Hidden Resource	Hidden Challenge	Contradiction	Year Card	Natural Temper	Motivation	Key Resource	Expression

157

Chapter 7: Others aspects of the Birth Diamond.

The spiritual origins of the name « The Birth Diamond »

This short text describes the foundations and essence of spirituality. It talks about "The Source of all Life", about a human beings embodiment into the world of matter and the returning path towards light and towards reconnection with "The Source of all life and light".

Before becoming embodied in a physical body, every human being existed as a spiritual being living in spiritual worlds. This spiritual being was then both male and female in one body and it lived in unity with its creator, the Source. Many spiritual beings, when they approached the worlds of matter, chose to experience these worlds. Because life is created this way, the consequences of this choice to experience matter are a splitting in two separate male and female bodies, a fragmentation of the soul in numerous and independent parts and an almost total disconnection with the Source.

Two antique symbols of the Source in China and Mexico

To most people living on earth, this reality is still veiled and totally unknown. But in every human being, there is a part of the soul that remembers where it comes from and knows all this, more or less consciously. And just like the salmons in the ocean have an instinct to go back were they come from, the human soul also wants to become reunited, to go back "Home" and to reconnect itself with its creator.

The path to return "Home" thus implies:

- Re-assembling together the different parts of the soul and living each part in full consciousness. The soul grows through life and action and it blossoms through silence and meditation
- Creating equilibrium between the masculine and feminine energies within us.
- Acting in conformity with spiritual laws and spending part of one's time doing spiritual activities in order to work toward reuniting one's self with the Source.
- Becoming aware that the reconnection with the Source can be done only with the master soul force, the spiritual body, made of love and light, whose shape is like a diamond and which is located at the center of the heart. This reconnecting with the source is like a new birth.

This is why this tool as called the Birth Diamond. To access one's Diamond, one needs to experience every facet or house of the Birth Diamond.

Numerology and the Birth Diamond:

If numerology is one of your passions, you will surely recognize, in the birth Diamond, the following different houses extracted from numerology.

- The Life Path (House 10) is the sum of the day, month and year of birth.
- The soul call is the sum of all vowels from first and last name.
- The Natural Temper or Natural Personality is the sum of the inner wealth (day+Month) and the outer wealth (Month+year)
- Expression number is the total value of all the letters in the first and last name.
- A person's Self Realization number is the sum of her expression number and her life path.

Certain numbers, existing in the practice of numerology, do not exist in the Birth Diamond. Here are three major numbers you can look into when analyzing a Birth Diamond if you feel it is wise to do so.

Heritage Number: This number helps to describe your family heritage. It is calculated by adding up all the letters in the family name. It can be combined with the analysis of House 4 in the Birth Diamond.

Personal Evolution Number: It describes how your personality evolves. It is calculated by adding up all the letters in the first name. It can be combined with the analysis of Houses 10 and 12 in the Birth Diamond.

Outer Achievement Number: It is calculated by adding up all the consonants of the first name and last name. It can be combined with the analysis of Houses 9 and 10 and the Self-Realization number in the Birth Diamond.

The 12 challenges and the 12 resources used in traditional numerology:
The resources are found by adding up two numbers amongs the day, month and year of birth and by reducing if the number found is above 22.
There can also be a way of calculation without reducing as will be shown below. The challenges are found by substracting two numbers amongs the day, month or year of birth. There can thus be more resources and chalenges. Quite often you end up with the same number. Three of the the resources (Houses 2,3 and 5) and challenges (House 7 and hidden challenge) are found in the birth Diamond. You can thus consider the other resources and challenges as extra hidden resources or challenges if the numbers found are different than the ones you find with Houses 2, 3, 5 hidden challenge and House7. Example for date of birth 11/01/1967:

Resource 1: year+month witout reducing. 1967+1=1968=24=6
Resource 2: year+month reduced. 5+1=6. **(House 3)**
Resource 3: year reduced and month unreduced. 5+1=6.
Resource 4: year unreduced and month reduced. 1967+1=1968=24=6.
Resource 5: day+year without reducing: 11+1967=1978=25=7.
Resource 6: day+year reduced: 2+5=7
Resource 7: day unreduced and year reduced: 11+5=16. **(House 5)**
Resource 8: day reduced and year unreduced: 2+1967=1969=25=7.
Resource 9: day+month witout reducing. 11+1= 12. **(House 2)**
Resource 10: day+month reduced.2+1=3.
Resource 11: day reduced and month unreduced: 2+1=3.
Resource 12: day unreduced and month reduced: 11+1=12.
So here numbers 3 and 7 are extra resources.

Challenges: You subtract the smallest number from the biggest.

Challenge 1: year-month witout reducing. 1967-1=1966=22.
Challenge 2: year-month reduced. 5-1=4. **(House 7)**
Challenge 3: year reduced and month unreduced. 5-1=4.
Challenge 4: year unreduced and month reduced. 1967-1=1966=22.
Challenge 5: day-year without reducing: 1967-11=1956=21.
Challenge 6: day-year reduced: 5-2=3
Challenge 7: day unreduced and year reduced: 11-5=6. **(Hidden Challenge)**
Challenge 8: day reduced and year unreduced: 1967-2=1965=21
Challenge 9: day-month witout reducing. 11-1= 10.
Challenge 10: day-month reduced.2-1=1.
Challenge 11: day reduced and month unreduced: 2-1=1.
Challenge 12: day unreduced and month reduced: 11-1=10.
So here numbers 1, 3, 10, 21 and 22 are extra challenges.

Two special other year cards: You can experiment the following: For each year, add your expression number (first and family names), your house 10 (date of birth) and the universal year. Another option to explore is to add your first name, the four family names of your grandparents, house 10 and the universal year.

The Birth Diamond of a couple:

By adding, for each house, the numbers of Male and Female partners, you can build the couple's Birth Diamond. The couple's house 1 then becomes the couple's confidence, strength and image, house 2 concerns the couple's wealth and joy, House 3 the couple's adaptability and communication processes, house 6 the couple's recurring difficulties, house 7 shows how the couple relates to others and their main challenge and so on. You can explore! It can be quite surprising!

Meditation and Birth Diamond:

Earlier in this book, we described coaching as a process to get effective results in real life and how the Birth Diamond can be used as a tool for coaching. Since very ancient times, words and pictures with symbols having a specific meaning have been used as tools to visualize and to meditate so as to trigger certain states of being.

Meditation is a process with the following steps:

- sitting comfortably
- closing the eyes and relaxing all the muscles in the physical body
- breathing in a natural manner and deeply
- emit the intention to find the deep inner self
- seeking, being and observing a happy, calm, joyful and vibrating state of being, free from any thoughts, desire or fear
- observing intensively what happens inside while ignoring any thought or picture that eventually pops into the sphere of awareness by just letting go their own way
- seeing that you are the observer and that you are pure awareness, a spark of awareness connected to "The Source of all Life"
- coming back to the "normal" or usual state of being when the vibrating and blissful state naturally lowers and fades away.

This process helps you contact your deep self and create a state of well being.

You can experiment, while being in a state of meditation; visualizing a number of your Birth Diamond and eventually the house it occupies so as to feel the energy of the number, alone or with the house. You can then use the energy of the number to create a certain state of being or to help you achieve your goals in daily life. You can also inwardly pronounce visualize and observe key words related to numbers/numbers. Here again you can explore.

Astrology and Birth Diamond:

Crossing numbers: In the astrological system, the twelve astrological signs and the twelve houses, who embody in solid matter the twelve signs, are organized in six opposite pairs or axis. House 1 is opposite House 7 (I and the other). House 2 is opposite House 8 (personal wealth and collective wealth, pleasure and sex, birth and death or embodiment in matter and departure from the world of matter). House 3 is opposite House 9 (communication and assertion in the world). House 4 is opposite House 10 (home and career). House 5 is opposite House 11 (personal expression and group expression) and House 6 is opposite House 12 (technical intelligence and faith, adapting to matter and adapting to spirituality, traumatic cycle and ancestors), just as in the Birth Diamond. Each axis makes up a whole, a totality. The birth diamond an interesting way to go from one house to the other and to unite each axis. If you add up the two numbers making up the axis, you obtain a number that summarizes the axis and the keys to make the best of all of what the axis symbolizes. If you subtract one number of the axis from the other, you obtain what can be called crossing numbers. If one of the numbers, obtained by addition or subtraction, already exists if the Birth Diamond, then the house it occupies will be a key to incorporate, assimilate and make the best of the axis.

Numbers and the four elements: The astrological signs and their houses are organized according to the four elements: Fire, Earth, Air and Water. Fire symbolizes action. Earth symbolizes organization in the world of matter. Water symbolizes intimate relationships and Air symbolizes communication and social relationships. You can analyze the individual numbers in the three fire houses (1, 5 and 9) to get information about how and what the person does. You can also add up the three fire numbers. The number obtained will show how the person globally handles and expresses her fire element. You can do the same thing with the other three elements.

Derived houses: This is a 2000 year old astrological technique that was used very often in ancient times. The 12 astrological houses are designed to enable classifying everything. Each house can therefore be related to a wide variety of symbols for this or that. These symbols are called significants. Here is an example of how derived houses work. Money is represented by House 2 or House 2 is one symbol (significant) of how a person earns and handles money. Couple and partnership are represented by House 7. Now how do we get information about the couple's financial situation? By using derived houses. In this case we look at the second house after House 7 (which is house 8). House 8 then becomes couple's money of financial situation. The third house after house 7 (House 9) then tells us how the couple communicates and adapts. This derived house system is really worth experiencing.

Degrees of planets in astrological signs: Planets circle around the sun along a horizontal axis in cyclic patterns. The starting point of each cycle is where the northern hemisphere spring equinox takes place, at zero degrees of Aries. The circular strip or zodiac is divided into 12 sections called astrological signs. As there are 360° in a circle and 12 signs, each sign is 30° broad. A planet is then always at a specific degree within a sign. A planet in a sign can be compared to the hour needle of a clock. Then the earth spins around itself in 24 hours and planets seem to travel across the Earth's sky. We have a second cycle that begins at sunrise and it is divided into 12 sectors or houses. The minute needle of our imaginary clock would be the position of a planet in a house or sector. It can then be very interesting to consider the specific degree of each planet in its sign and to connect what the number of the degree symbolizes, as seen in this book, with what the planet symbolizes. You then have a needle showing seconds on our self-knowledge clock. What you will find can be very explicit and surprising. The first degree, starting from 0 to 1, is connected with number 22. Research is open!

Exemple: If your sun is 20.05 degrees in any sign you will tend to focus on delivering messages or data that change people's lives. If your moon is 7 degrees in any sign, you need to set goals, to implement strategies and to get results to experience wellness. If Venus is 5 or 23 degrees in any sign, you need to find the right teechings, to teach, to live a meaningfull life to experience joy, pleasure, harmonious relationships and to earn money. If Jupiter is at 00.40 degrees in any sign, then you need to express your uniqueness to blosomm and thrive. And so on...

Hope you enjoyed this book!

Kind regards

Erik Jackson Perrin

The Birth Diamond - Classical Display

Date of Birth :
First Name :
Family Name :

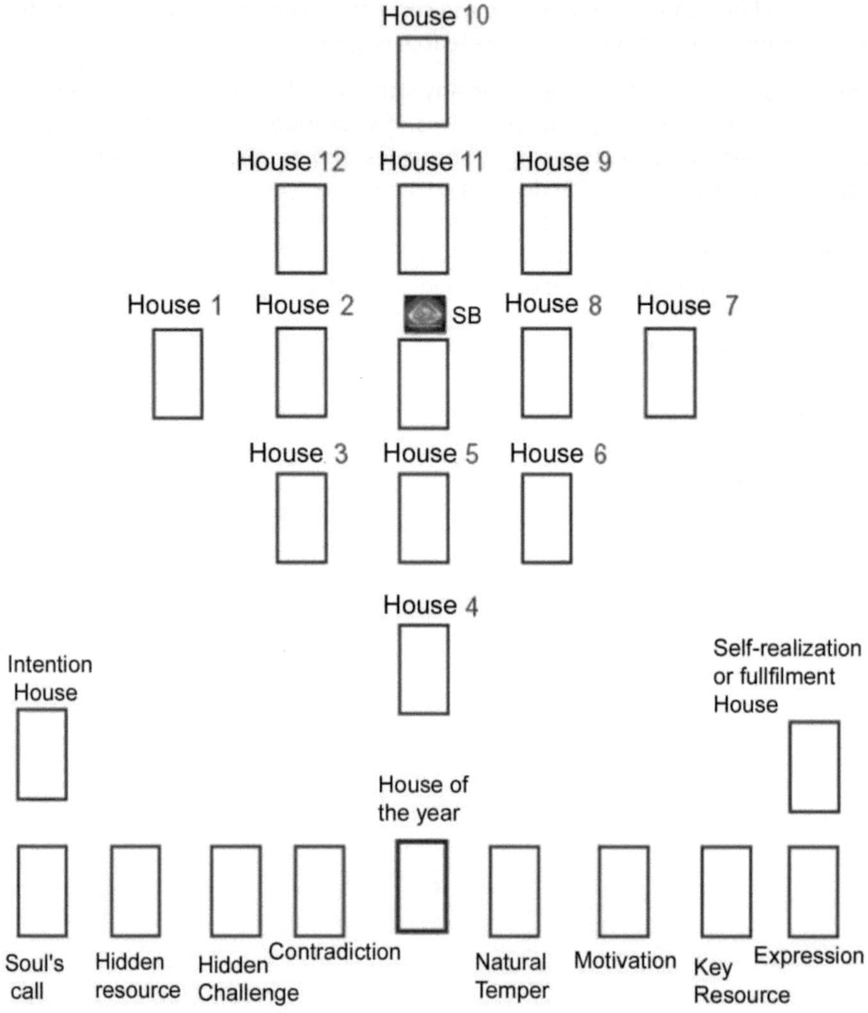

Creation : Eric Jackson PERRIN

The Birth Diamond - Classical Display

Date of Birth :
First Name :
Family Name :

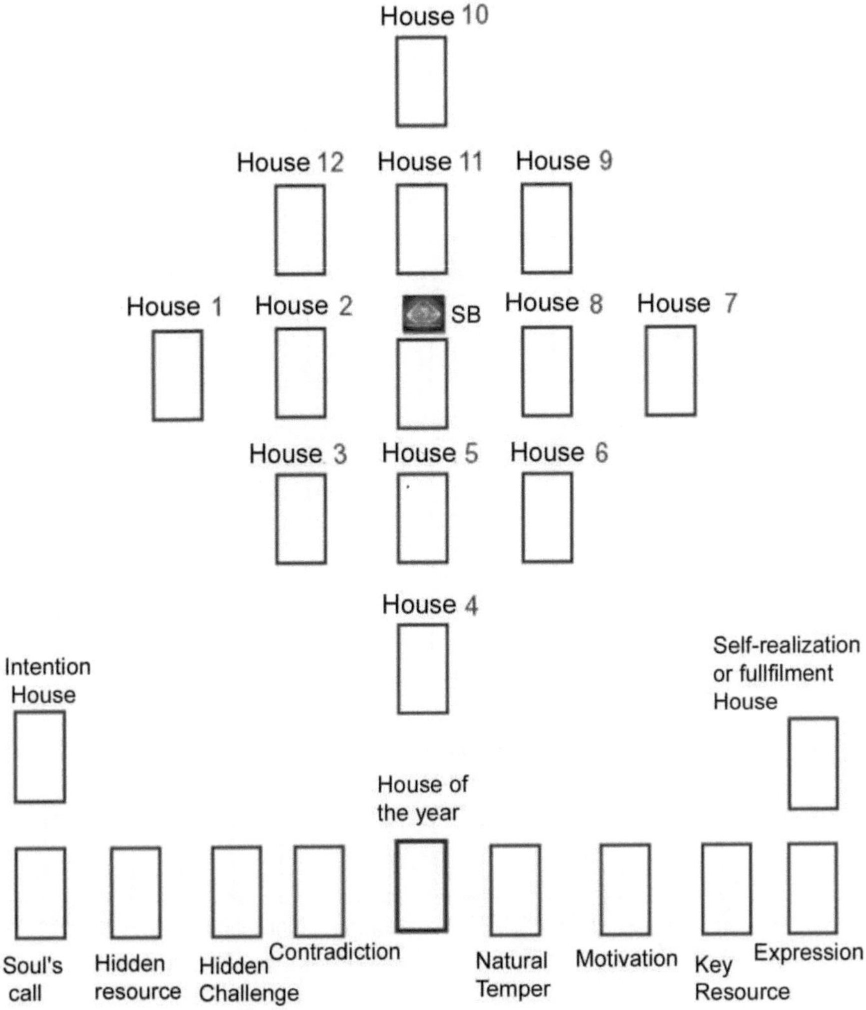

Creation : Eric Jackson PERRIN

The Birth Diamond - Classical Display

Date of Birth :
First Name :
Family Name :

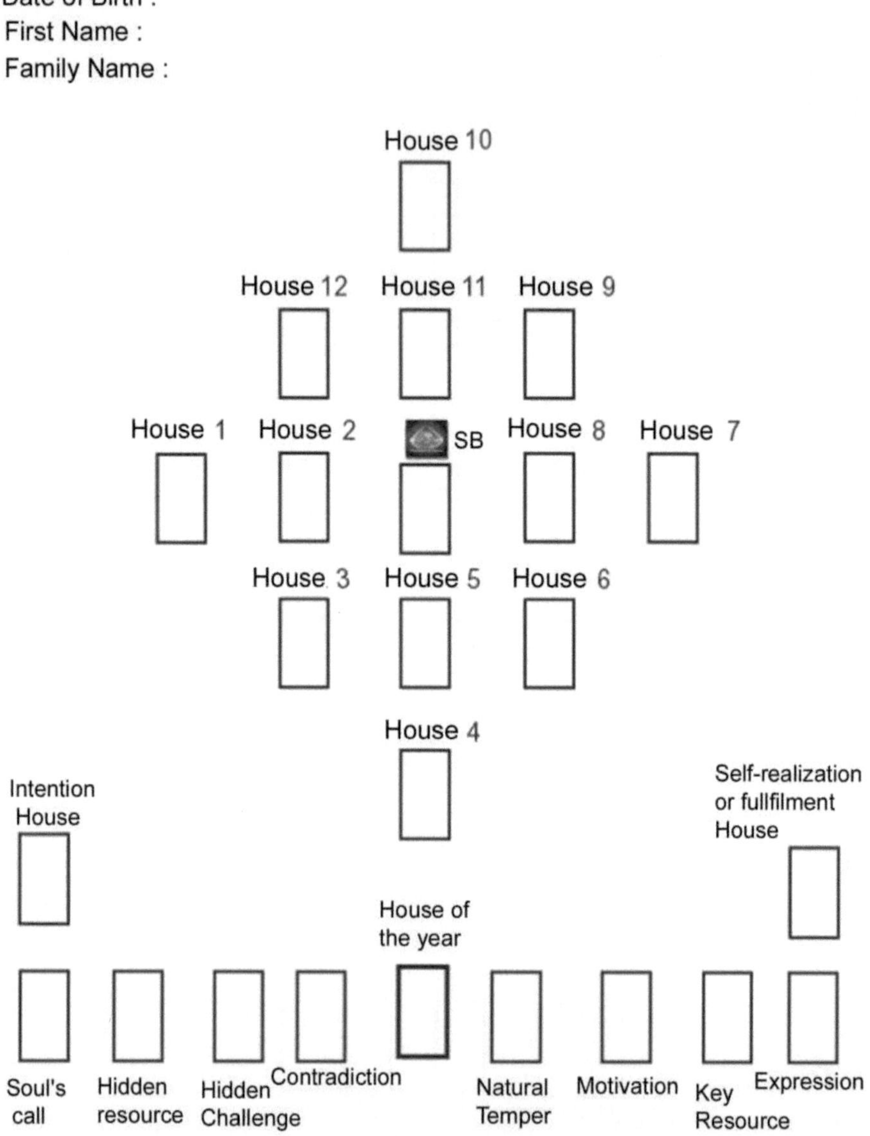

Creation : Eric Jackson PERRIN

166

Applied Numerology

The Birth Diamond© Workbook

Hindu and Sufi Evolutionary Sacred Karmic Numerology

****

For self-knowledge, consulting, Employment counseling and more...

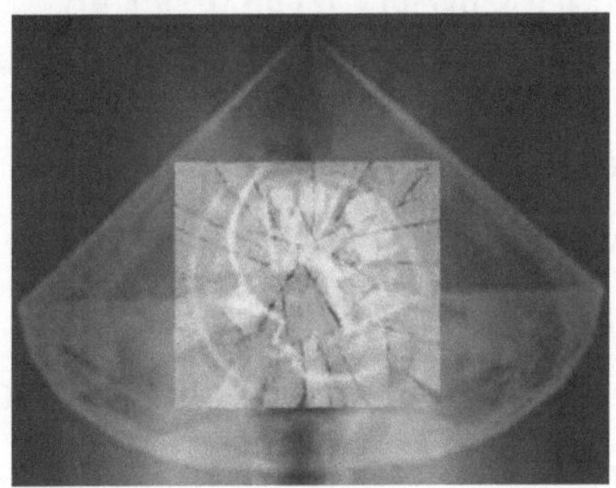

By Eric Jackson PERRIN

Legal information

© 2012 –2022 Eric Jackson Perrin
www.coaching-evolution.net

Published by Eric Jackson Perrin
69300 Caluire et Cuire – France

Printed in Germany by BoD – Books on Demand
ISBN: 979-10-94871-911

****

Summary

Introduction: Practicing Birth Diamond Numerology

The Source of all Life chose me to create and promote this wonderful self-knowledge tool for everyone so that each person can see their inner GPS, their evolution plan and their pathway to become the best version of themselves, serve life and contribute to creating a better world, here on planet Earth. Humanity will only be still here in 400 years if everyone on the planet does his/her best to do so!

The Birth Diamond can be of great help for self-knowledge. It can also be very useful to choose a job or to confirm a choice that has been made. It can help gain a better understanding of others and thus improve relationships. It can also help gain access to ancestral memories or memories of past lives so that any karmic emotional disturbances can be thrown away and so that these memories can be part of present day life in full awareness and in a way that that helps you thrive. The Birth Diamond can also allow you to structure time by allowing you to see the number that colors your year and the four time periods that structure your life.

This practical workbook was created as a support to interpret a Birth Diamond Chart. Professional practice of the Birth Diamond is for people who have taken the Birth Diamond Basic Course with me or with another teacher. Personal practice is for everyone.

The Birth Diamond chart is made up of numbers that live in houses. There are two ways of dealing with number. The most common way is to use the first 22 numbers and to use the images of the Italian Tarot to visualize what the numbers ate about. You then work in mode 22 and add any number above 22 so that 24 would then equal 6 (2+4). The second way is to use the first 24 numbers and to use the 24 German Runes to explain what the numbers are about. This second way is dealt with in my book about runes. You then work in mode 24 and add any number above 24 so that 25 would then equal 7 (2+5) and 31 would be 3+1=4.

How to describe and talk about the Birth Diamond

A simple way to talk about it:
-A self-knowledge tool based on numerology. A numerology based tool that uses keywords. A treasure map. A map of who you are.
-A set of keys with which you can open many doors.
-A coaching tool that enables you to become more aware and to do what can bed one to succeed at all levels in your life. A tool to make the Diamond that you are shine.
-An inner settlement with 24 houses in which you must live !
-The GPS of your inner life so that you can become the best version of yourself...

A deeper way to talk about it:
-A map of your soul, a map of your soul's structure and of how your soul works.
-A personal development tool that shows how your soul became fragmented upon embodiment in matter and how you can gather up the different parts of your soul and move forward on your path to enlightment.

What can it do ? Life coaching and personal development coaching!
COACHING = choosing/specifying a goal, becoming aware of why it's important, finding resources to achieve it, do what can be done and checking out results.

3-Comparing the Birth Diamond with the « Référentiel de Naissance »

Both systems use Tarot as a visual tool to express keywords and both used numerological formulae that come from Indian numerology.

Differences between the Birth Diamond and the « Référentiel de Naissance"

	BIRTH DIAMOND		**« Référentiel de Naissance »**
1	Created in 2011-2012	1	Created in 1981-1982
2	24 houses	2	13 houses
3	based 50% on astrology+50% on numerology	3	No connections with astrology
4	Takes first name +family name into account	4	Does not take your first name and family name into account
5	House meanings come from astrology and numerology - The first 12 houses are the same as the 12 houses used in astrology	5	House meanings come more or less from Tarot

The Birth Diamond is more modern, complete and relevant than the « RN ».

Memory Houses: Family and past lives (Karmic) memories can mostly be seen in houses 4,6,7,8,12, soul call, hidden resource, hidden challenge, contradiction and key resource houses.

The Birth Diamond - Classical Display

Date of Birth :
First Name :
Family Name :

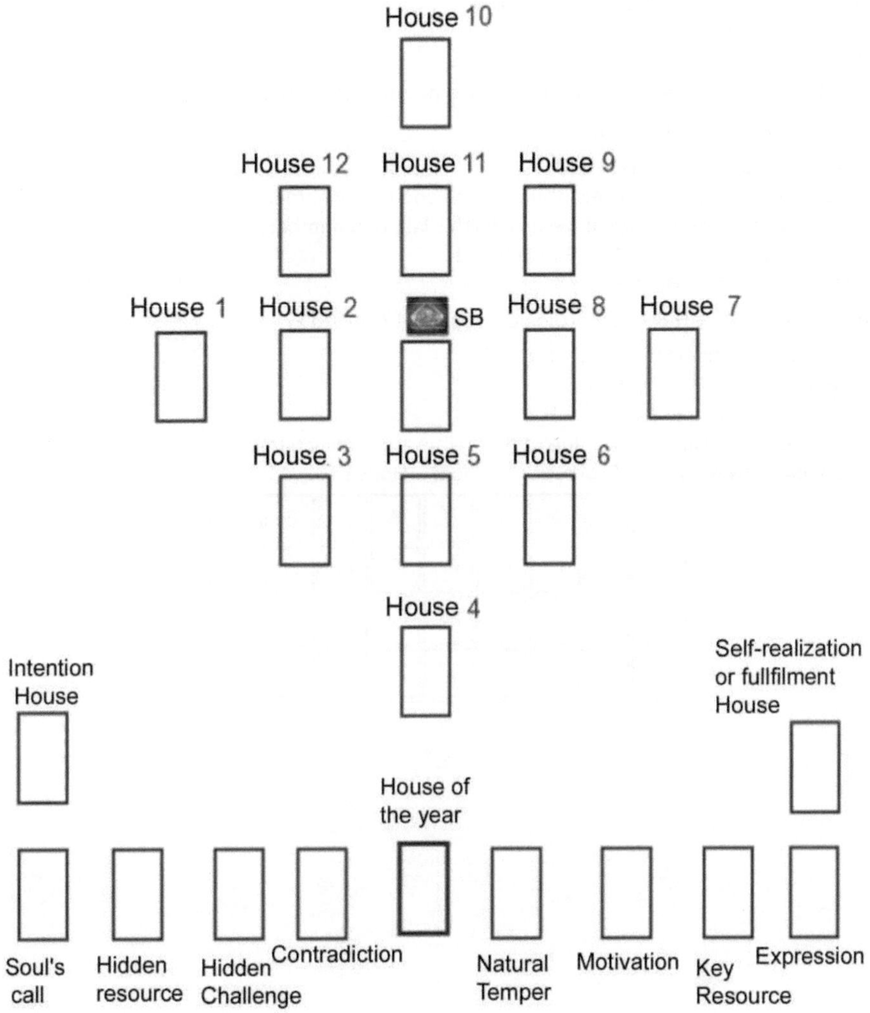

Creation : Eric Jackson PERRIN

TECHNICAL FILE – PUTTING TOGETHER THE BIRTH DIAMOND

Birth Diamond's core

HOUSE 1: Day of birth. HOUSE 8: Month of birth

HOUSE 9: year of birth. (1968 = 1+9+6+8=24 and 2+4=6)

HOUSE 10: Day + Month + Year.

HOUSE 2: H 1 + H 8. **HOUSE 3:** H 8 + H 9.

HOUSE 7: H 8 – H 9. HOUSE 5: H 2 + H 7

HOUSE 6: 22 – M 5. HOUSE 4: H 6 + H 7+ H 9

HOUSE 11: H 1 + H 8 + H 9 + H 10.

HOUSE 12: H 2 + H 8 + H 10

CENTER OF THE DIAMOND: Source of brilliance number: H 2 + H 10.

The Birth Diamond's foundation

Soul Intention number: H8+H9+H10

Soul's call number: Sum of vowels of first name and family name.

Hidden resource number: sum of year of birth's last two numbers

Hidden challenge number: H 1- H 9 or H 9- H 1

Contradiction number: H6+H7

Annual number: H 1 + H 8 + numerological year (2017=2+0+1+7).

Natural temper number: H 1+ H 8 + H 8 + H 9.

Motivation number: H 1 + H 5 + H8.

Key Resource number: H 2 + H 10 + H 11

Expression number: Numerical value of first name and family name.

SELF-REALISATION NUMBER: Expression number + House 10

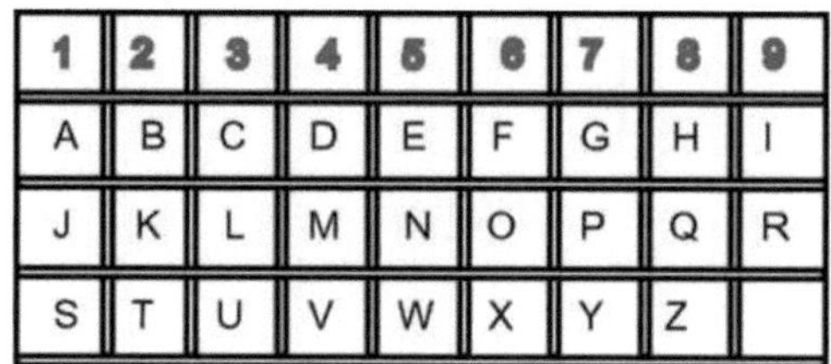

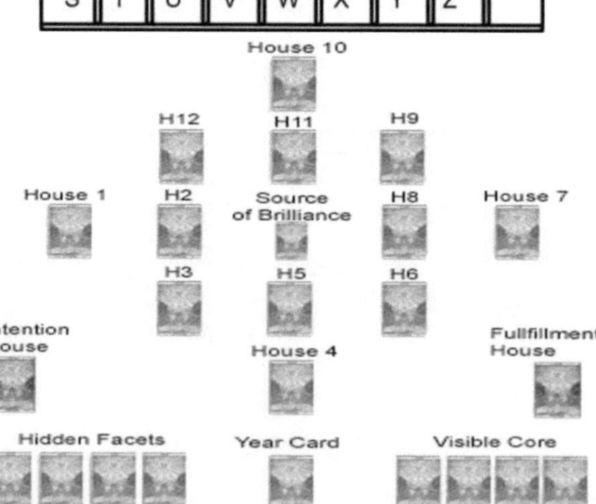

Chapter 1: Key words for interpreting the Birth Diamond chart
Start with house key words and follow with number key words

House 1 **Aries House** **Male Strength and sword**	In order to act and exist, to feel self-confident and strong, to be assertive and efficient, you need to…
House 2 **Taurus House** **Female wealth and joy**	In order to be joyful, to feel pleasure, to earn and handle money and to create a happy life on earth, you need to…
House 3 **Gemini House:** **Intelligence, adapting**	In order to listen, hear, communicate, be on the move, have fun, trade and adapt to your surroundings, you need to…
House 4 **Crab House:** **Parents heritage, being well at home**	In order to see and use correctly the skills, qualities and qualifications that your parents forced you to develop due to what they were or were not, and to feel well in your home, you need to…
House 5 **Lion House:** **Expressing your Heart, love, deep identity, what you really want…**	In order to become aware of who you are, of your identity, of what you really want, express your heart and your creative power, to love and feel loved, you need to…
House 6 **Virgo House:** **Repeating, becoming an expert, serving, repetitive issues**	In order to repeat so as to become an expert so as to serve life so as to adapt technically to the world of matter, you need to… In order to get out inadequate repetitive behavioral patterns, you need to…
House 7 **Libra House:** **relationships, partnership, main challenge, what need to be rehabilitated**	In order to interact with others, create harmonious social relationships, a harmonious life as a couple, to play a role in society, you need to… In order to find your balance, to rehabilitate yourself, to express harmoniously what you tend to reject and to overcome your major challenge, you need to…
House 8 **Scorpio House:** **spiritual quest, going from crisis to passion, sex life, being aware of life hereafter out of body experiences, enlightenment**	In order to experience your spiritual quest (what you are always looking for first in the outside world and then inside yourself), to fight for enlightenment you need to… In order to live a happy sex life, to create a healthy relationship with life hereafter, to go from a state of crisis to a state where you express your passion, you need to… You very deeply need to…

House 9 **Sagittarius House:** finding one's place in the world, , business purpose, thriving	In order to go beyond your parents hopes and live your own life, to express your authority, be legitimate, explore the world, find your place in this world, play your economic role within society, be successful and blossom, you need to...
House 10 **Capricorn House:** pathway towards inner peace, evolution, inner peace	In order to grasp the teachings that will help you become wiser, to grow, become more mature, encounter your deep inner truth and move forward towards your inner peace, you need to...
House 11 **Aquarius House:** inner freedom, mandatory solutions	In order to free yourself (from false beliefs, family influence, society, ancestral memories, past life memories and ignorance), to implement the compulsory solutions that will work out for you and to create a better world, you need to...
House 12 **Pisces House:** ancestral memories, going from suffering to bliss and delight	What causes you to suffer is due to... One of your most important ancestral memories can be described through a need to... To be relieved from suffering and freed from inadequate ancestral memories, to experience delight, bliss and communion with the divine, you need to...
House 13 **Source of brilliance House:**	In order to succeed, be the best version of yourself and to shine bright like the sun, you need to...
Intention House:	You have come to Earth to satisfy a need to... In order to implement your ideal lifestyle, you need to...
The Soul's Call House: your soul's deep needs	If you do not satisfy a deep need to...then your soul calls you, yells and shouts. In order to feel well you strongly need to... In order to satisfy the deep needs of your soul, it is required that you...
Hidden resource House:	The hidden resource that would be wise using can be used though a need to... The seed within you that can become a wonderful tree is linked to an ability to...
Hidden challenge House:	You more than likely, until you do some work on yourself, find it difficult to... The hidden challenge or spine in your foot that you need to overcome and transform into a resource or magic key is linked with a need to...

Contradiction House:	Where you are the most gifted for but where you find all the excuses not too is liked with an ability to… The contradiction that you must overcome and the lever that you can implement is connected with the ability to… The roots of your issues are due to a tendency not to express a need to…
Current year House:	This year, you have the opportunity to satisfy a need to… This year, it will be necessary to…
Natural temper House:	To feel well and to be natural, you need to… You have a natural tendency to… You are the type of person who tends to… When you feel well and natural, you have the ability to…
Motivation House:	In order to be motivated, you need to… What acts as a fuel for you is a need to…
Key Resource House:	The magic rod, joker or key resource that you have allows you to be able to… You have strong abilities to… To make your jocker, magic rod or key resource work, you need to…
Expression House:	To write your life's history, express what you have come on Earth to do and accomplish your destiny or life mission, you need to…
Achievement House:	To achieve complete self-realization and to go from writing your life story to being your legend, you need to

Using reversed phrases: Many people understand the reversed mode better than the direct mode so you can experiment it. What I call the reverse mode goes as follows: Instead of saying, in order to 'bla bla bla' you need to 'da da da' you can say if you don't have "da da da" then it's difficult for you to express 'bla bla bla'.

Exemple: Lover in House 1: In order to feel self-confident and be assertive, to need to have a choice, softness, harmony, kindness, colors, beauty and to feel connected with others. Reversing that would be: If you don't have a choice, if there is no beauty, harmony, kindness, colors and connections with people and love, it is very difficult for you to feel self-confident, to act and to be assertive. Do you see this?

THE NUMBERS'S KEY WORDS

1 **The juggler** **The magician** **The apprentice** **The smart guy**	-Act with joy, be assertive, live a busy life - Use/express your creative power - Find the appropriate tools and use them efficiently -Express your inner child, work with children, have fun, be a gamer or a game master -Have the energy, motivation and enthusiasm to start new things **Tools: intention, games, creative activities, crafts, trade, work on the inner child.**
2 **The High Priestess** **The seer** **Eternal Feminity** **The Popess** **The keys of wellness keeper**	-Implementing wellness for body and soul. -Find the right information, the right keys, storing and handling them, veiling or unveiling, becoming free from family secrets, doing paperwork -Work on your subconscious, beliefs, souvenirs, seeing what is invisible, deepening -Prepare what needs to be, give birth to someone or to a situation, express what you feel, use imagination and faith -Experience unity, partnership and strong emotional connections (intimacy). -**Tools: creative visualization, flower elixir, books, working on the grandmother-child relationship…**
3 **The Empress** **The organizer** **Smartness** **Adapting**	-To be listened to, to be heard, to communicate, to express yourself with authority, smartness and style -Synchronize your feelings, thoughts, words and actions, being coherent -Learn, understand, get organized efficiently, handle every parameter existing in your environment, being a super mother/assistant that takes care of everything -Be legitimate, put events into shape, trade -To be on the move, to adapt and to feel adapted -Do business and handle communication **Tools: communication, movement, creative activities, working on the mother-child relationship**

4 **The Emperor** **Power of verb** **The builder** **Authority** **Power**	- Express your authority/power with self-confidence - Take your place and play your economic role - Build your empire or play a role in someone else's empire, be legitimate - Build, structure, organize, manage a structure, the world of matter and a specific territory - Make sure the law is applied, ruling, leading, taking office, exercising power, framing - **Tools: games and building, working on authority and the relationship to the father**
5 **The High Priest** **The expert** **The teacher** **The pope** **The guide**	- Give a meaning to events, connect earth and sky, have faith - Master data systems, rituals and be an expert, feel legitimate - Find the right teachings, incorporate them and teach others, express your ability to educate - Express benevolence, protect, bless, unite, formalize - Advice, provide guidance, reassure, instil confidence - Explore philosophies, cultures, teachings - Experience travelling with body and/or mind - Be a doctor for the body and/or soul - **Tools: teachings, meetings, rituals**
6 **The lover** **The artist** **The flame** **The right choice** **Joy**	- Create connections with people, socialize, experience partnership, be in love - Express artistic abilities, sensitivity to beauty and make your life a work of art - Listen to your true desires so as to make choices that bring you and others joy, the right choices, create joy, beauty, harmony - See and explore different options, serve - Express your senses, desires, sensuality, create events - **Key phrase: my feeling of happiness does not depend on other people's happiness, i create form to experience joy, i leave fiction behind to live in reality** - **Tools: art, colours, chromotherapy, creative activities, partnership**

7 **The chariot (car)** **The coach** **The General** **The entrepreneur** **The sportsman or woman** **The goal/target** **Logistics** **Victory**	-Set a relevant goal or target, a specific destination, -Implement the appropriate organization or logistics, the right strategy and then go, act, move, undertake the appropriate steps and formalities -Obtain results, victories, reach your destination, be quick and efficient, travel, deliver -Be alike a general leading his troops to battle, go out on a mission, be motivated and exited -Authorize yourself to act and succeed, start, move forward, take control and be in control -Work within the corporate world or the world of sports -**Tools: work on goals, targets, organization, results and motivation.**
8 **Justice** **Rightness** **Truth** **The sword** **Civilization** Civilization keeper **Working together** Public administration **The joy of sharing**	-Order, justice, rightness, truth, be right and do what is right for you -Balance, harmony, beauty and structure (dance/decoration) -Socialize, connect people together, experience partnership, share in a state of joy Follow the rules, be legitimate, express abilities to handle legal affairs -Play a role in society by working in a public administration, a social structure or a club -Be and live in harmony with the order of things **key phrase: I stop wanting to be perfect, i do my best so I'm okay** **Tools: dance, decoration, focusing on how you feel when things are right**
9 **The time keeper** **The building site** **The site manager** **The architect** **The path** **The hermit** **The deep inner**	-Question, seek your deep inner truth, move forward and experience inner peace, deepness, wisdom -Be an architect, be in a building site like situation, manage building sites, build your temple, have a long term vision, structure, work on structure - time, simplicity, serenity, use plans/symbols/schemes - Get to the essential points right away, experience the essence of people, life and things, inner silence, meditation, abandon what no longer needs to be -**key phrase: God can only exist when you are in a state of joy and serenity**

truth **Inner peace**	-**Tools: questioning techniques, gemstones, meditation, yoga, geobiology**
10 **The wheel of fortune** **Wheel of destiny** **Cycles** **Service** **Adapting technically** **The Technician** **Making things work right**	-Understand how life, people, cycles, motion, events and things work - Do what is needed to make the wheel of life turn around the right way, start off a new cycle -Repeat so as to become an expert so as to serve life so as to adapt technically to the world of matter -Use a technical and practical intelligence -Be set like clockwork and make things work out -Experience tools and processes required to adapt -Leave repetitive patters behind so as to start off again differently, take cycles into account -Be connected to plants, animals, deal with health and hygiene matters -Use numbers, symbols and preciseness (woodwork, printing, accountancy, numerology, astrology, clockwork) -Be an analyst or technician who serves life -try your luck, satisfy your curiosity **Tools: numerology, astrology, plants, animals, working on cycles**
11 **Strength** **Creativity** **Mastering** **Power of Love** **Vision** **Organisation** **Success** **Wildness**	-To be centred in your heart and in your body -To embody the vision of the best version of yourself, to have a clear vision and translate it into relevant goals, efficient organization and success -Express your creative power and the power of love -Listen to your heart, do what you want, do what you love and love what you do, be passionate - discipline, be the master of your life, be self reliant, manage and master the wild animal that lives within you and be patient **Key phrase: when one truly wants one finds the means and when one does not truly want one finds excuses.** **key phrase: anger is a disorganized motion of the soul who is offended because it has not accepted something that was unavoidable given the circumstances** **Tool: working on vision and ideal, the heart, cardiac coherence, symbols and love, being creative**

12 **The hanged Man** **Suffering** **Ancestors** **Forgiveness** **Spirituality** **Clairvoyance** **Delight** **Inspiration** **Collective needs** **The mystic** **The healer** **The prophet**	-Free yourself from your genealogical tree, untie the knots within you and free yourself from bonds of loyalty -Get out of chaos, wandering, passivity, immobility, being a victim and suffering -Go from suffering to bliss, delight and communion with the divine, live according to spiritual values -Feel delighted and bring delight to the world -Turn your points of view and beliefs around or upside down and see things differently -Express charity, compassion and forgiveness -Express your gift of clairvoyance, be inspired - Bring relief to people's suffering and misery -Meet the needs of the community -Let go, accept what is, give a meaning to life, express unconditional love, live according to your dreams and aspirations and turn them into reality **key phrase: I, first and last name …, i give back to my ancestors what belongs to them, with love and respect, and i live my own life, I forgive and move forward** **Tools: working on ancestral memories, family constellations, forgiveness, unconditional love, faith, meditation and past life memories**
13 **The unnamed** **The investigator** **The revealer** **The keeper** **Safety agent** **Security officer** **Death** **The reaper** **Boatman of souls** **Rebirth** **The phœnix**	-Handle problems or damage claims, manage crisis, safety issues or insurance policies -Accompany the dying, provide care and nurturing to those at the end of life, accompany job seekers or people in crisis - Experience your essence -Eliminate, discharge, release, detoxify and de-pollute -Work on structures, joints, bones and teeth -Transform/make things changes by working on causes -Use and manage mediumship and/or clairvoyance -Work and balance subtle energies. Work with X-rays -Implementing and expressing a conscious relationship to life hereafter and being aware of one's eternal life -Relieve pain, go from depreciation and playing dead to expressing your passion and being lucid and genuine. Get to the essential points right away -Regenerate yourself and rise from your ashes

	- Be initiated to the secrets of life and death **- Tools: subtle energies or out-of-body experiences, learning to die consciously and happily, Mayan astrology, Chinese medicine and change protocols, karmic memories**
14 **The Angel** **Temperance** **Network master** **He who fixes** **He who connects** **Will of the sky** **A better world**	- Be connected, manifest the will of the universe, of the Source of all life - Express a psychological/technological intelligence that is able to find solutions, help, repair things or people and create a better world - Create networks of friends, customers or people, experience group activities, - Bring about progress and hope, create new concepts, manage projects, use computers, internet, social networks - Communicate, balance, harmonize, heal, express human values, adapt to the modern world - Be free, liberated from family, social pressures and old limiting schemes, be self-reliant and independent. - Have sufficient air and space, focus on the sky, travel by plane or spaceship, use hi-tech equipment, create movies **- Tools: psychotherapy, angels and healing strategies**
15 **The passionate** **The saboteur** **The master of metal** **The blacksmith** **The financier** **The Prince of matter** **The devil** **Pan**	- Be passionate, do what makes you feel passion and feel passionate about what you are doing - Feel under pressure, put pressure on yourself and others - Work with metal and forge objects or people - Handle problems, issues, crisis or safety issues - Seduce, manoeuvre, captivate, intrigue - Go from a crisis-like situation and a tendency to do sabotage to being authentic passionate - Be scareless, bold and daring - Go from being scared and a slave-like situation to a state of live, light and a master-like situation - Enjoy the world of matter, earn money, spend money, live a satisfying sex-life, use your personal power to serve life **Tools: live your passions, work with metal, learn to manage the saboteur, work on tantric sexuality**

16 **Change in structures** **The tower** **The House of God** **Sun bolt** **Lightning** **Liberator** **Dynamite stick** **A shock**	-Work on structure or building sites and implement changes in structure (through awareness or relocation) -Dive inwards and lock yourself up in a tower in order to find the light of God, experience enlightment and reconnect to the source of all life so as to live in harmony with the universe and the Will of God -Stress, shock, explode so as to upset or free what needs to be freed and so as to get out of any confinements -Express a psychological or technological intelligence so as to adapt to the modern world and its complex data systems, be enthusiastic/excited -Use languages, formulas and symbols, generate inner freedom and awareness using speech -Build tower and manage property/real estate -**Tools: Eye movement liberation technique, Tipi technique, kinesiology**
17 **The star** **Joy/delight** **Abundance** **Beauty** **The fairy** **Supplies management**	-Handle resources and supplies -Experience and create joy, delight, beauty, harmony, sweetness, happiness, inspiration, abundance, blossom -Create wellness of body and soul through naturopathy, kinesiology, massage, haircare, skincare -Express your senses and create a happy life of earth. -Be a fairy, a star, give your life to life in a state of unconditional love and devotion. -Live close to nature -Get back up after having being put on your knees -**Tools: abundance constellations, art, singing, gardening, kinesiology, massage, naturopathy, astrology**
18 **The moon** **The mother who takes care of life** **Memory cleaning** **Nourishment** **Emotions**	-Go from unwellness, sadness and emotional stress to wellness by purifying/working on water, food, memories, by nourishing yourself or others correctly, by doing what makes you feel nourished, by clarifying and by expressing your emotions, by taking care of yourself and of life, by knowing how to recharge yourself and by following your natural rhythms with fluidity -Express your sensitivity, your faith and your imagination so as to create a nice and joyful life -Be a mothers who nurtures others

Using imagination to create **Wellness** **Clarify** **Nurture**	- Create a home, manage houses/flats/estates, feel well in your home, take care of children or adults, tell stories -Live your dreams, making things flow smoothly -**Tools: Tarot, work on water and food, express the inner child or work with children, tell stories, awakened dreaming, intuition, imagination**
19 **The sun** **Expressing love** **will of joy** **Creations** **The Horse** **Experiencing God** **Best version of yourself** **Success** **The Radiant**	-Happily be the best version of yourself -Be your ideal, your vision, your values, implement your goals, efficient organization and success -Lead, reign, rule, govern, be visible, shine, promote, enhance, be well known, noticed, recognized, admired -Express your creativity, your generosity, fatherly love and gratitude, be ready, willing and able -Express your inner child, educate children -Listen to your heart, express love, experience special relationships and partnership, be someone's sunshine -Do what you love and love what you do -Experience God, the light of God, be a light to the world - Bring joy and happiness to others, be positive -**Tools: creative activities, working on the heart, love and gratitude, coaching**
20 **Messenger of God** **Propagandist** **Judgement** **The tomb** **The Archangel** **The shaman** **The healer** **Project manager** **Quantic healer**	-Get out of the tomb of past lives and ancestral memories and give yourself a second chance -Deliver messages, though speech, sound, music or vibrations, that bring about change, healing, liberation, regeneration, rebirth and revival -Handle complex projects and highly modern technologies -Announce, present, promote, advertise, publicize, spread communicate through speech, writing, radio, TV, internet - -Create movies and TV documentaries/shows -Elevate your vision and embody a multidimensional, awakened, shamanistic or therapeutic vision - Awaken your awareness to life hereafter and to Reality -**Tools: kinesiology, family constellations, shamanism, la sound therapy, short therapies**

21 **The world** **World citizen** **The engineer** **The president** **The traveller** **Space** **The ocean** **Serve the Source** **of all life**	-stretch yourselves to the utmost, express your full potential, come to something, succeed, achieve -Be anchored and well rooted in the world of matter -Be joyful and implement abundance -Gather all parts of yourself, express the power of love, be the best version of yourself, embody your ideal vision -Set goals, get organized and succeed -Embrace a higher vision, go from sabotage to expressing your passion, fight for light and a better world -Express a psychological/technological intelligence that is able to find solutions, help, repair things or people and create a better world -Explore space, travel, be connected to foreign people and lands, take your place in the world -Use and express your authority and power, play your economic role, master the world, dance your life - Devote your life to serve life and people while being connected to the Source of all life - Embody love and wisdom -**Tools: travelling, working on abundance, gathering yourself together, be the best version of yourself, I Ching**
22/0 **The fool** **The genius** **Cutting edge** **person** **The Chameleon** **The free electron** **The free and** **happy person**	-Live/avoid living according to your past lives or ancestors -Move beyond family, educational and social structures so as to express your uniqueness and the genius within you -Experience freedom, be a free electron, be a free and happy person, live as if everything was possible -Take care of handicapped or maladjusted people or of geniuses -Pack your bags and go out explore new lands, new quests and adventures, explore new options, be on the leading edge, enchant or re-enchant the world, places and people -**Tools: quantic therapies, trips and journeys, cutting-edge activities, chromotherapy, wish-board, freedom**
23 **data structures**	-Promote a heritage from ancestors or past lives -Free yourself from any remaining past life memory or ancestral memory -Disassemble et reassemble yourself, disappear and reappear somewhere else

splitting apart **reconstituting** **Heritage** **Sanctuary** **Quantic** **dimensions**	-Splitting apart old structures so as to create new ones -Create and promote a sanctuary, a place where change takes place, set in motion and reach a safe place -Express yourself from Origin and connection to the Source of all life -Work with the infinitely small, the quantic dimension, cells, data structures (genetics), portals and vortexes -Optimize your legacy and live the best destiny possible
24 **Eternal light** **Daylight** **Return of the light** **Forever New** **Happy You**	-Bring or create new and clear landmarks, guidelines and a new vision based on love, awareness and creativity -Enhance awareness and the return of light and love -Make light and love triumph, enlighten -Implement a new cycle of growth -Make all potentials blossom; bring about joy of life, prosperity and abundance. Make the light come back -Shine like the sun, radiate, be a light bearer -Live united with the Source all life and serve it

Numbers 23 and 24 are used when interpreting the BD with Runes

Cards existing twice: A certain amount of tension is required to express the card. **A same card in two different houses connects the two houses. One can thus make sentences using what the two houses symbolise instead of sentences that combine a house and the number in the house. EXAMPLE: House 1 = House 3. Direct sentence:** In order to act and exist, to feel self-confident and strong, to be assertive and to be efficient, you need to (House1) feel that people listen to you, you need to talk and communicate, you need motion, you need to understand, to do some trade and to adapt to your surroundings. **Reversed sentence:** If you feel that people don't listen to you, that nothing moves, that you don't have your say and that you can't adapt then you completely lack motivation, self-confidence and the energy to be assertive. Do you see this?

The Cross Spread

Position 1: Describes the consultant, what should bed one, what is positive and beneficial.
Position 2: Describes issues, what should not be done, what should be avoided.
Position 3 : Describes what comes from the outside and impacts the situation, the advice **to** adapt and evolve and heavenly intervention, the path of evolution.
Position 4 : Describes the answer, the outcome and what will happen.
Position 5 : Describes the meaning, the teachings and what is at the heart of the situation.
Position 6 : Describes how things evolves, the « and then what happens».

3 1 5 2 4 6	**Position 1 + position 2= hidden things existing here and now.** **Position 3+ position 4= hidden things that will exist in the future.**

Interpreting key 1: Harmony between a number and the house it's in.

A house is an inner space that seeks to express its needs. It will use the number existing in it to fulfill its needs. If the house and the number match well, the house's needs can be easily fulfilled but if this is not the case it may then be difficult to satisfy the house's needs and a positive way to express the number in the house will have to be found/implemented/experienced to fulfill the house's needs.

HOUSE	PLANET	Numbers well placed	Numbers not well placed	Neutral Numbers
1	Mars and SUN	1-7-11-19-21	2-6-8-9-16-18-13-15	OtherN
2	Venus/MOON	2-3-4-5-6-17-18-19-21	7-9-11-12-13-14-15-16-20-22	10
3	Mercury	3-10	9-13-15-16	OtherN
4	MOON	18	9-12-13-15-16	OtherN
5	SUN	5-11-19-21-6	NO NUMBERS	-
6	Mercury	10	Other Numbers	-
7	Venus/Saturn	6-8-19	Other Numbers	-
8	Pluto	2-9-11	Other Numbers	-
9	Jupiter	5-7-21	10-13-15	OtherN
10	Saturn	4-8-9	13-15-16-18	OtherN
11	Uranus	14-16-20	12-13-15	OtherN
12	Neptune	5-12-20	3-10-13-15-16	OtherN
Source of Br	SUN	11-19-21	NO NUMBERS	OtherN
Intention H	SUN	11-19-21	NO NUMBERS	OtherN
Soul Call H	MOON	All numbers	NO NUMBERS	-
Ressource H	Venus	All numbers	NO NUMBERS	-
Challenge H	Mars	NO NUMBERS	13-15-16-20	-
Contradiction	Saturn/Jupiter	NO NUMBERS	13-15-16-20	-
Year Card H	Uranus	All numbers	NO NUMBERS	-
Natural Temper	MOON	All numbers	NO NUMBERS	-
Motivation H	Mars	7-11-19	NO NUMBERS	-
Key Resource	Uranus	All numbers	NO NUMBERS	-
Expression H	Jupiter	All numbers	NO NUMBERS	-
Fullfillment H	SUN	11-19	NO NUMBERS	-

Interpreting key 2: Interpreting by connecting two different houses occupied by two identical numbers. This brings interessing data. Sentences are built by connecting the key words of each house. **Example:** Number X in House 2 and in Contradiction House. **Interpretation:** If you want to be joyfull, to feel pleasure, to earn money and to create a happy life for yourself, you need to overcome your contradiction.

Chapter 2: Job counselling

The cards found in the houses below are all options and solutions to find a suitable job, serve life, thrive, blossom and be the best version of yourself.

The Houses concerned with job counselling

The 3 major work houses	
House 3 **Gemini House**	House that allows you to communicate, learn, express your intelligence, trade and adapt to your surrounding world
House 6 **Virgo House**	House that allows you to repeat and organize data so as to become a technical expert so as to serve life and adapt to the world of matter
House 9 **Sagittarius House**	House that allows you to express your authority and personal power, take your place in the world, find the right teachings, experience social integration, thrive, blossom and experience fulfilment
House 2 **Taurus House**	House that allows you to feel joy, earn money, handle and manage money/resources and to express one of your main resources
House 11 **Aquarius House**	House that allows you to create a better world. This house is always a solution that can bring about freedom and satisfaction
Key resource House	House that allows you to express your inner genius, your key resource, a natural gift you can always call upon if you don't know what to do with your life.
Expression House	Your life mission and the story of your life

Trades/professions/jobs and the first 22 numbers

KEY WORDS: NUMBERS AND JOBS

1	Entrepreneur, jobs that require using creative power, company employee, craftsman, merchant, shopkeeper, salesman, sales representative, travelling salesman, freelancer, actor, magician, writer, gamer, player, entertainer, public letter-writer, working with children
2	Therapist, psychologist, librarian, writer, printer, developer of information carriers, data manager, public servant, primary school teacher, teacher, trainer, instructor, doctor, physiotherapist , midwife, pediatrician, dietician, nutritionist, naturopath, psychic, seer, ,babysitter, keeper, custodian, caretaker, caregiver.

3	sales representative, shopkeeper, sales assistant, press officer, task officer, executive secretary, journalist, office clerk, editor, manager, emissary, ambassador, businessman, business woman, jobs related to data management and co-ordination of information, program coordinator, jobs that deal with the public, jobs where one has to move around a lot, jobs requiring the use of numbers, white collar occupations, postman, football or tennis player, psychomotrician, kinesiologist, physiotherapist, language specialist.
4	company director, chief executive officer, business executive, leader, team manager, project manager, department head, chief officer, politician, supervisor, businessman, foreman, builder, real estate agent, property manager, building site manager, site foreman, police officer, soldier, defense serviceman, administrator, prefect, minister, president.
5	Counselor, adviser, professor, teacher, university lecturer, lecturer, consultant, guide, doctor, physiotherapist, priest, friar, abbot, healer, notary, lawyer, therapist, psychologist, coach, expert, tour operator, travel organizer, tourist guide.
6	Craftsman, fine arts, artist, designer, jobs related to promoting colour/beauty and connecting people, dancer, jobs related to bringing joy to others, flowers, decoration, guidance counsellor, marriage counsellor, beauty counsellor, fashion professions, tailor, seamstress, dressmaker, beautician, aesthetician, make-up artist, people who help others make happy choices, radio or tv hosts (with the angel or archangel), jobs related to public relationships like press officer/attaché or communications officer.
7	Jobs related to transport, travelling and vehicles (taxi driver, driver, truck driver, heavy equipment operator, sales representative, service technician, garage owner, tyre centre, car dealer), jobs related to logistics and supplies, planner, event organizer, business activities, company executive, sportsmen and wemen, ambassador, conqueror, jobs related

	to defense and military, general, coach, counselor, jobs related to horses.
8	Jobs related to law, justice, rules, courts and judiciary (lawyer, clerk, notary, usher, bailiff), jobs related to civil service and public service (mayor, prefect, administrative agent), jobs where the use of numbers is required (accountant, management controller, statistician), jobs related to human resources, jobs related to creating order and physical or psychological balance, jobs related to promoting civilization and public relationships, decoration and dancing (beauty with structure).
9	Architect, scholar, researcher, jobs related to the past (historian, archeologist, archivist), jobs where one asks a lot of questions, solitary activities, explorer, difficult jobs, jobs related to the building industry, plumber, activities in religious and monastic institutes, jobs related to old people, gerontologist, scientist, philosopher, builder, mountain guide, climber, scout, pathfinder, ski teacher, therapist, farmer, geologist, geophysicist, dowser, geobiologist, mountaineer, yoga/meditation teacher, mineral collector, mineralogist.
10	Jobs requiring organizing commercial information (sales assistant, supplies, sales management, shopkeeper), the use of knowledge and data (data manager, schoolteacher), technical knowledge (technician, engineer, inventor,) technology and preciseness (clockmaker, making or using very small components, micro technology) or dealing with motion or health and hygiene (health technician, pulmonologist, naturopath, physiotherapist), travelling (driver, car dealer, mechanic), using numbers (accountancy, numerology), jobs related to finance and money (banker, financier, poker player), jobs implying the use of plants (pharmacist, herbalist, Bach or other flower remedies advisor), jobs related to ecology and taking care of nature and the environment, jobs related to cleaning, jobs related to books and printing.

11	Liberal professions, self-employed people, leaders, managers, officers and executives, masters in their crafts, jobs requiring physical and/or moral strength, bravery and fighting (police officer, bodyguard, security officer), will power and love, sportsmen and wemen, sports coach, firemen, sea rescuers (with the hanged man), tamer, trainer, animal handlers and breeders, jobs requiring the use of creativity, jobs requiring organization abilities, jobs related to bringing light and heat, jobs requiring a very strong commitment.
12	Jobs related to health and the relief of suffering and misery (doctor, nurse, auxiliary nurse, caregiver, anesthetist, stretcher bearer, paramedic, ambulance driver, rescuer), jobs requiring personal sacrifice and total commitment, jobs related to the sea and fishing (nautical and maritime occupations, fisherman, sailor, lifeguard, protector of marine life), jobs related to alcohol or relieving addictions (oenologist, barman), jobs related to dreaming and bringing delight (harp player), to advertising and marketing, to travel and discovering, jobs related to using images, imagination and sound (sound therapist, actor, movie maker), jobs related to religious activities (priest), jobs related to spiritual growth and wellness (psychic, seer, yoga teacher, soul therapist, preacher, sophrologist, hypnotherapist, astrologer).
13	Jobs related to bringing about change and supporting change (job advisor, employment agent, coach, end-of-life care provider, energy therapist), to guarding, keeping and safety (investigator, security officer, police officer, detective, soldier), to bones, teeth and meat (dentist, osteopath, butcher, surgeon), to death and life hereafter (palliative care, funeral services, cemetery keeper, forensic doctor, medical examiner), to detoxification and cleaning, to disposal of waste and to waste management and recycling (street sweeper, garbage collector), to initiation and spiritual awareness (yoga teacher, spiritual guide), to bridges, mines, gates, doors and windows, to seeing the secrets of life and death (chemist, fuel maker, radiologist, psychic, psychoanalyst), to the secrets of the past (historian,

	archaeologist).
14	Jobs related to fixing and helping (Therapist, psychologist, social worker, human relationships counsellor, technical counsellor, facilitator, mediator, special instructor, worker in complementary medicine, healer, magnetizer, acupuncturist, repairman, jobs related to the movie industry (filmmaker, radio staff and TV staff, actor), jobs related to communication, phones, internet and networks (human resources employee or manager, operator, call centre employee), jobs requiring the use of electricity, computers, science and technology (electric appliances professional/builder/seller, electrician, technician, network technician, engineer, computer programmer/engineer, software creator), jobs related to cleaning, jobs related to bringing spiritual awareness and delight (Angel, therapist, harp player), jobs related to the sky, to space, to sci-fi, to airports and airplanes (aviation technician, pilot, stewardess, air traffic controller, airport staff).
15	Jobs related to industry, metal, mines, gates and doors, chemistry and the use of fire, jobs where there is a strong pressure, jobs related to crisis management, jobs earning a lot of money, jobs requiring working in the dark, underground or at night, illegal jobs related to drugs, smuggling, sex or prostitution, jobs related to banks and finance, tax controller, butcher, exorcist, politicians (with the pope, emperor or justice), jobs in secret organizations, jobs related to safety, customs officer, agent, criminologist, policeman, bodyguard, security officer, psychoanalyst, psychiatrist, therapist.
16	Jobs related to the building industry (Mason, bricklayer, architect, real estate agent, builder, building site manager), jobs related to dealing with disasters (fireman, emergency personnel, natural disasters management), healthcare personnel, radiologist, house, car or ship breaker/wrecker, mover, psychologist, therapist, repairman, repairer, jobs requiring electricity and modern technology(electrician, computer programmer or engineer, network technician,

	mathematics or physics teacher), cosmonaut (with the star), artificer, electric appliances professional/builder/seller, jobs related to bringing spiritual awareness (Angel, therapist), jobs related to the sky, to space, to sci-fi, to airports and airplanes (plane maker, air traffic controller, airport staff), highly specialized jobs.
17	Jobs related to the wellness of body and mind, to beauty and fashion, to nature/ecology and to managing resources and supplies (asset and capital management, water management, food, wood, earth, sand etc), to production, creating wealth and abundance (production planner, supplies technician, buyer, purchasing manager), to creating joy and happiness, painter, sculptor, singer, poet, dancer, perfume maker/seller, hairdresser, aesthetician, make-up artist, decorator, designer, massage artist, top model, star, landscaper, landscape architect, horticulturist, florist, practitioner in complementary medicine, naturopath, kinesiologist, homeopath, biologist, organic food grower, gardener, agro-business jobs, jobs related to the stars (astronomer, astrologer, cosmonaut).
18	Jobs with family members, jobs performed from home, jobs in public places, caretaking jobs, jobs related to trade especially food and water (cook, restaurant owner, restaurant and hotel staff, baker, brewer, barman), jobs related to real estate and housing (promoter, moving company, trustee, guardian, maintainer), jobs implying the use of imagination and creative power (storyteller, writer, poet, musician, designer, drawer, artist), jobs related to children, family and social welfare (nanny, schoolteacher, pediatrician, family counselor, social security officer), jobs related to animals, night jobs, jobs related to the sea (lifeguard, sailor, protector of marine life), jobs related to sleeping, jobs related to the past, jobs related to biology and life, jobs related to exploring the subconscious, jobs related to bringing wellness.

19	Jobs related to educating/training children and adults (jobs in training centers, teacher), jobs implying the use of creating power, jobs with human relationships, jobs with a very strong commitment, liberal professions, established professions, cardiologist, ophthalmologist, jobs related to light, lighting, solar energy and heat (heating installer/engineer), jobs related to management and leadership, jobs related to entertainment (comedian, actor, producer, stage director), jobs related to beauty (top-model, make-up artist, image counselor), retail in luxury goods/premium goods and jewelry, jobs consisting in helping people become the best version of themselves, bringing self-knowledge, awareness and love.
20	Jobs related to speaking or writing (Speaker, media officer, radio, TV, audiovisual and internet professions, journalist, newscaster, webmaster, preacher), jobs where one is in relation with the general public, jobs related to communication and advertising, jobs related to music and sound (musician, sound engineer, sound therapist), jobs related to very advanced technologies and complex projects management, (scientist, engineer, inventor), jobs related to giving birth (midwife), jobs requiring an ability to judge and give council (members of the courts, lawyer, judge), jobs related to cleaning, jobs related to tourism and travelling to unknown places and dimensions, jobs related to healing (awakener, shaman, healer, therapist, kinesiologist).
21	Jobs related to leadership (director, chief executive officer, minister, president), to human resources, to teaching, to logistics, planning and supplies, to imports, exports, customs officer, jobs related to the hotel and restaurant industries, to tourism and travelling, to translating, to large retail, to business, to forestry and environment occupations, to sports, liberal professions, jobs where one becomes famous, jobs related to art and crafts, to science and engineering, highly qualified jobs, architect, jobs related to politics, jobs in very large companies or in international bodies, jobs related to dancing, jobs related to healing and finding God.

<table>
<tr>
<td>22/0</td>
<td>Atypical, off the standards and unclassifiable jobs, jobs implying the use of one's creative power, jobs related to data management, independent artist, independent trades, jobs where one spends a lot of time travelling (sales representative, delivery man, driver, postman, traveling merchant, ambulance driver, taxi driver, train driver), traveler, explorer, inventor, revolutionary, avant-guarde jobs, prophet, hobbyist, do-it yourself jobs, jobs related to helping either geniuses or handicapped/unadapted people, jobs related to mental health (therapist/healer, psychiatrist, specialized teacher or educator, quantum touch healer), jobs related to animals (veterinary, groomer, dog instructor, zookeeper, animal psychologist), jobs related to special artistic activities (clown, Biodanza teacher, actor, player, designer, style counselor).</td>
</tr>
</table>

Chapter 3: Comparing Enneagram, numbers and planets.

ENNEATYPE	Definition	PLANET	Numbers
TYPE 1	**Idealistic Perfectionnist**	SUN	19 11 8
TYPE 2	**Helper Motherly**	MOON	18 2
TYPE 3	**Fighter Warrior**	MARS	1 7 4 3
TYPE 4	**Artist Healer**	VENUS URANUS	6 17 8 14 16
TYPE 5	**Observer Sage**	SATURN	9 16
TYPE 6	**Technician Phobic**	MERCURY PLUTO	10 13 15
TYPE 7	**Epicurean Traveler**	JUPITER VENUS	5 21 6
TYPE 8	**Master Chief Controler**	PLUTO SUN	15 13 4
TYPE 9	**Mediator Caretaker**	VENUS NEPTUNE	12 20

Chapter 4: LIST OF FAMOUS PEOPLE TO PRACTICE BD

A great way to learn how to master the Bith Diamond is to analyse charts of people who know or have known (close relatives). You can also study famous people's Birth Diamond charts by comparing their lives to their numerological structure. Here is a short list to show you the idea. You can check the connection between work houses (3/6/9 etc) and their work lives.

ARCHITECTURE: GUSTAVE EIFFEL: 15/12/1832/19H47 GMT/DIJON.

ASTROLOGIE : ANDRE BARBAULT : 01/10/1921/17H/ CHAMPIGNELLES / FRANCE.

CINEMA FEMALES: AMANDA TAPPING: 08/8/1965 ESSEX UK.

CINEMA MALES : HARISON FORD: 17/07/1942/06H45 GMT/CHICAGO.

CINEMA IN FRANCE : LUC BESSON: 18/03/1959/ 13h45/PARIS.

MUSIC: JONH LENNON: 09/10/1940/0H58 GMT/LIVERPOOL.

COMPOSITEURS CLASSIQUES : WOLFGANG. A. MOZART : 27/01/1756/20H/SALZBURG.

COMICS-STORY TELLERS: HANS. C. ANDERSON: 02 / 04 / 1805 / 1H / ODENSE. DENMARK.

DICTATORS: OLIVER CROMWELL: 05/05/1599/03H30 GMT/HUNTINGTON GB.

GUIDES IN SPIRITUAL EVOLUTION: BÔ YIN RÂ: 25/11/1876 / ASCHAFFENBOURG. Germany.
P. YOGANANDA: 05/01/1893/20H40/GORAKPUR INDIA.
SRI SRI RAVI SHANKAR : 13/05/1956 BAIDYABATI INDIA 14h00

INDUSTRY AND TRADE: HENRI FORD: 30/07/1863/14H20/GREENFIELD.
BILL GATES: 28/10/1955. STEEVE JOBS 24/02/1955 SAN FRANFISCO CALIFORNIE 19H20.

LITTERATURE IN FRANCE: JULES VERNE: 08/02/1828/12H/NANTES.
RENE BARJAVEL: 24/01/1911/3H30/ORANGE.

LITTERATURE IN THE WORLD: ISSAC ASIMOV: 02/01/1920/PETROVOCHI / EX URSS.
MARION ZIMMER BRADLEY: 03/06/1930 ALBANY USA 09H00

MEDICAL IN FRANCE: MAURICE MESSEGUER: 14/12/1921/16H30/CALEYRAC ST CIRQ.

MILITARY/JUSTICE: CLIFF MONTGOMMERY: 17/10/1920/8H30 GMT/NEBRASKA.

FASHION/DESIGN/PERFUME: CHRISTIAN DIOR: 21/01/1905/ 01H25/ GRANVILLE.
YVES ST LAURENT: 01/08/1936/19H45 GMT/ ORAN/MOROCCO.

ARTISTS/PAINTERS/ PHOTOGRAPHERS / SCULPTORS : SALVADOR DALI : 1/05/1904/8H45/FIGUERAS.
EDOUARD MANET : 23/12/1832/19H/PARIS. CLAUDE MONET : 14/11/1840//PARIS.

PHILOSOPHY AND SPIRITUAL AWARENESS: GEORGES GURDIEFF: 13/01/1877/21H25 GMT/ALEXANDROPOL. RUDOLF STEINER : 25/02/1861/23H15/KRAJEVIC.
KALIL GIBRAN: 06/01/1883/04H30 /BECHARE/LEBANON.

PSYCHOLOGY / PSYCHOANALYSIS.
SIGMUND FREUD : 06/05/1826. CARL. C. JUNG: 26/07/1875.
JEAN PIAGET : 09/08/1896/00 H 45 /NEUCHATEL.

POLITICIANS/LEADERS IN THE WORLD
VLADIMIR POUTINE: 07/10/1952, 09h30 St Petersburg. (PRESIDENT OF RUSSIA).

REVOLUTIONNARIES : CHE GUEVARA : 07/06/1928/2H/ROSARIO ARGENTINE.

SCIENTISTS/ INVENTORS/ RESEACHERS: NICOLAS TESLA: 10/07/1856 CROATIE

SECTS: HELENA BLAVATSKI: 12/08/1831/01H47/MOSCOU. (FONDATRICE THEOSOPHIE).

SPORTS : RAFAEL NADAL: 03/06/1986 MANACOR Espagne 18H00 (TENNIS)
NADIA COMANECI : 12/11/1978 ROUMANIE AS 22 SAG

TRAVELERS/EXPLORERS : NICOLAS HULOT: 3 0/04/1955/07H50 GMT / LILLE. (REPORTER).
NIEL ARMSTRONG: 05 / 08 / 1930 / 05 H 10 GMT / WAPAKONETA /OHIO / USA
ALEXENDRA. D. NEEL : 24/10/1868/5H/PARIS (EXPLORATRICE CENTENAIRE).

SEERS : EDGAR CAYCE : 18/03/1877/15H/LOUISVILLE/KENTUCKY USA

Chapter 5: The 4 or 5 life slices

The Birth Diamond's annual card reveals the atmosphere of the year. Another cycle can be found by adding your entire birthdate (house1+house8+house9) your entire name (expression house) and the current year. I have also seen some people add the first name, the four names of the four grandparents, the date of birth and the current year. Classical numerology reveals 4 or 5 mains periods of life. I like to call them time slices. Each time slice has its number and a specific length.

Slice/Achievement number 1 = Day + month of birth **Number in House 2 in the BD**	**Time span 1:** The first time slice goes from birth to 12 times 3 minus the life path number (house 10) which here is reduced to a number between 1 and 9 so that 10 and 19 are equal to 1 for example. This number describes childhood and youth.
Slice/Achievement number 2 = Day + year of birth **(coincides most times with House 5 of the BD)**	**Time span 2:** It starts at the end of time span 1 and lasts for 9 years. It describes the first part of adulthood.
Slice/Achievement number 3 = Achievement number 1 + Achievement number 2. **(coincides most times with motivation house of the BD)**	**Time span 3:** It starts at the end of time span 2 and lasts for 9 years. It describes the second part of adulthood.
Slice/Achievement number 4 = Month + year of birth **House 3 of the DN**	**Time span 4:** It starts at the end of time span 3 and lasts for 9 years. It describes the third part of adulthood.
Slice/Achievement number 5 = Achievement number 3 + Achievement number 4.	**Time span 5:** It starts at the end of time span 3 and lasts for 9 years. It describes the time of retirement.

The 4 "thirteen year" Mayan Cycles

Being aware of what phase you are in within the 13 year Mayan cycle may help you focus and organize each year. These cycles as described in my book Practical Mayan Astrology.

Age							
0	0						
1	1	14	1	27	1	40	1
2	2	15	2	28	2	41	2
3	3	16	3	29	3	42	3
4	4	17	4	30	4	43	4
5	5	18	5	31	5	44	5
6	6	19	6	32	6	45	6
7	7	20	7	33	7	46	7
8	8	21	8	34	8	47	8
9	9	22	9	35	9	48	9
10	10	23	10	36	10	49	10
11	11	24	11	37	11	50	11
12	12	25	12	38	12	51	12
13	13	26	13	39	13	52	13
A beginner		**An apprentice**		**An explorer**		**A master**	

What age you are when you begin each 9 year time sequence depending on your Life Path

The 9 life paths	Time Slice 1	Slice 2	Slice 3	Slice 4	Slice 5	Slice 6
Life Path1	0-35	36	45	54	63	72
Life Path2	0-34	35	44	53	62	71
Life Path3	0-33	34	43	52	61	70
Life Path4	0-32	33	42	51	60	69
Life Path5	0-31	32	41	50	59	68
Life Path6	0-30	31	40	49	58	67
Life Path7	0-29	30	39	48	57	66
Life Path8	0-28	29	38	47	56	65
Life Path9	0-27	28	37	46	55	64
Life Path10	0-26	27	36	45	54	63

9 year cycles

The 9 sequences	Slice 2	Slice 3	Slice 4	Slice 5	Slice 6	Slice 7	Slice 8	Slice 9	Slice 10	Slice 11	Slice 12
1	10	19	28	37	46	55	64	73	82	91	100
2	11	20	29	38	47	56	65	74	83	92	101
3	12	21	30	39	48	57	66	75	84	93	102
4	13	22	31	40	49	58	67	76	85	94	103
5	14	23	32	41	50	59	68	77	86	95	104
6	15	24	33	42	51	60	69	78	87	96	105
7	16	25	34	43	52	61	70	79	88	97	106
8	17	26	35	44	53	62	71	80	89	98	107
9	18	27	36	45	54	63	72	81	90	99	108

7 year cycles

The 7 sequences	Slice 2	Slice 3	Slice 4	Slice 5	Slice 6	Slice 7	Slice 8	Slice 9	Slice 10	Slice 11	Slice 12
1	8	15	22	29	36	43	50	57	64	71	78
2	9	16	23	30	37	44	51	58	65	72	79
3	10	17	24	31	38	45	52	59	66	73	80
4	11	18	25	32	39	46	53	60	67	74	81
5	12	19	26	33	40	47	54	61	68	75	82
6	13	20	27	34	41	48	55	62	69	76	83
7	14	21	28	35	42	49	56	63	70	77	84

The needs of each time slice are related to the key words of the slices number.

Chapter 6 : Cards when balanced and unbalanced

Nombre	Well integrated/established	Unbalanced
CARD 1 : THE MAGICIAN	I act with joy, confidence, energy and efficiency so as to achieve my goals. I express my intentions, my creative power and my inner child in the present moment to start new things and to be assertive, brave, with intelligence, enthusiasm and the right tools. I find the right tools, improvise and learn how to use them.	I may have difficulties starting things, feeling motivation, having sufficient energy, setting myself in action, feeling brave, knowing what to do or how to do it, expressing my inner child, feeling joyful and enthusiast, finding the right tools or knowing how to use them. Impatience, lack of experience, illusions. Issue with a child.

CARD II : THE HIGH PRIESTESS	I see memories within the invisible worlds. I wait. I give birth to. I find and give the keys and the right information for the wellness of body and soul. I unveil. I look deep within. I hide. I handle data. I use imagination and faith to create and bring about wellness.	I may have difficulties unveiling or not hiding things, having faith, expressing my emotions, using my imagination, giving birth to myself, making things come true, seeing in the invisible worlds, finding the right keys and freeing myself from secrets.Family secrets. Issue with a grandmother.
CARD III : THE EMPRESS	I listen to people. I hear them. I synchronise my thoughts, my feelings, my speech and my actions. I express myself with authority, intelligence and elegance. I communicate. I adapt. I put things into shape. I organise my surroundings. I take care of everything.	I may have difficulties getting appropriate education, learning, understanding, feeling listened to, communicating, telling the truth and adapting. Problem with being a woman or with one's mother. Mental confusion. Speech is confined. Lightness, flimsiness, superficiality, issue with the mother.
CARD IV : THE EMPEROR	I express my authority, my ability to organise things and my power in order to take my place, build my empire or contribute to someone else's empire. I structure, frame, make things happen and sometimes forbid. Self-confidence, stability, legitimacy, rigour and work power.	I may have difficulties feeling self-confident, expressing authority or accepting other people's authority or the rules of society, feeling legitimate, taking my place and building my empire. Inertia, rigidity, confinement, authoritarianism, materialistic, violence, problem with territory or with the father.
CARD V : THE HIGH PRIEST	I learn to master a data system and spiritual laws. I find, incorporate and give back the right teachings. I find my place in society. I give meaning. I bless. I give people permission to succeed. I protect, reassure, formalize, unite and give advice with benevolence and spiritual strength.	I may have difficulties giving meaning to events, having faith, understanding how to organise my life, accepting the educational system, finding, incorporating and giving back teachings, getting the right education, feeling protected by life. Dogmatism, intolerance, inflexibility, abuse of power, fanatism, bad advice, lack of benevolence, proselytism.
CARD VI : THE LOVERS	I listen to my true desires and to other people's desires to make the right choices. I express my social intelligence, my charm and my artistic abilities to serve, create beauty, joy and harmony. I choose. I relate to others. I commit and I love. Partnership.	I may have difficulties centering in myself if I centre too much on others, listening to my true desires, making the right choices, expressing artistic abilities, committing myself to a relationship and living in harmony with others. Hesitation. Lack of maturity, fashion victim, naiveness, emotional dependency.
CARD VII : THE CHARIOT	I look inwards, check things up, set goals, take the necessary steps, find the appropriate means and strategy and organization to as to succeed and obtain victory. I take charge of things. I express my entrepreneurial spirit. I manage projects and I move about.	Difficulties looking inward, setting relevant goals, motivating myself, finding my way, mastering my trajectory, expressing my power/entrepreneurial spirit, implementing the right strategy and organisation and succeeding. Functional blockages. Obstacles. Impulsiveness. Excessive speed. Burnout.
CARD VIII : JUSTICE	I become aware of life's underlying order and of the law of equilibrium. I create rightness, order, beauty + structure, truth, harmony, art, contracts, organizations and legitimacy to contribute to civilization. I weigh, decide, adjust and apply. Discipline, rigor.	Difficulties finding my place in civilization, being orderly, right, truthful, balanced, seeing what is right, accepting laws, contracts, order and structures. Unfairness. Bias and partisanship. Procedural. Harshness. Victimisation. Illegalness. Karma. Misunderstanding of life and its underlying order.

CARD IX : THE HERMIT	I handle time and set long term goals, isolate myself, question, look inwards, seek and search and move forward, slowly but steadily, with simplicity. I build and handle building sites. I make my way towards my deep inner truth, I evolve towards inner peace, I become wise, I bear and share light. Happy loneliness. Deepness. Reality	Difficulties handling time, seeing the long term, looking inwards, being truthful and simple, questioning, seeking, isolating, showing respect, walking on, evolving towards inner peace and showing wisdom. Abandonment injury. Shyness. Restraint. Austerity. Ascetism. Slowness. Stubbornness. Heaviness. Weighed down. Loneliness. Sadness.
CARD X : THE WHEEL OF FORTUNE	I express a technical, practical and organizational intelligence, a sense of dealing with numbers/data and an understanding of cycles to get out of old patterns, try my luck, take charge of my life, repeat, become an expert, serve, deal with plants, animals or health issue and adapt to the world of matter. Destiny.	Difficulty getting out of old patterns, understanding how life and abundance work, setting myself into motion, stopping constant thinking, being practical, repeating so as to be an expert, adapting to the world of matter, taking care of my health/pets and making things turn the right way. Blocks, misfortune. Karma.
CARD XI : STRENGTH FORCE	I centre myself in my heart, focus on my vision, on the vision of the best version of me and translate it into an ideal, into relevant goals and efficient organization. I find the appropriate means and I succeed. I connect myself to the Source of all life, express self-confidence, creative power, my will and the power of love so as to master and be autonomous and so as to heal. Clarity.	Difficulty accepting people and events, as they are, being centred in body and heart, loving myself and others, having a clear vision, handling my strength, my aggressiveness and my inner violence, setting goals, finding the appropriate means, expressing my will and personal power, being autonomous and succeeding. Power based relationships. Pride. Meanness. Cruelty. Boastfulness. Violence. Lack of patience. Anger.
CARD XII : THE HANGED MAN	I reverse my beliefs and points of view, open up to spiritual reality and to unconditional love, accept situations and people as they are, let go, give meaning, commune, blend, bring relief to the worlds sufferings and misery, free myself from past lives memories and ancestral memories, forgive, transcend, delight people and places and heal with prayer, faith and christic love.	Difficulty becoming free from ancestral and past life memories and ghosts, taking spiritual reality into account, accepting situations and people as they are, meditating, letting go, escaping/recovering from chaos, turmoil, vagrancy, passivity, immobility, victimization, disease, suffering and fear of humiliation/betrayal/suffering. Escapism. Addictions. Plaintive. Autistic. Lethargy, Withdrawism. Blocs and knots. Depression.
CARD XIII : DEATH	I dive into emptiness, into darkness, deep down so as to clearly see invisible subtle energies and to access my inner being and eternity. I become aware of my true eternal identity and of the world hereafter. I become lucid and authentic. I learn to change, to let go of the past, to leave, to get rid of what is no longer needed, to die and become reborn, to rebuild myself, to regenerate and to rise from my ashes.	Difficulty getting out of a state of ignorance, emerging from the shadow, from one's grave, from misery, reject, despair and pain, stepping across vacuity and emptiness, seeing behind appearance, being lucid, letting go of the past, embodying, feeling safe, having faith in life, stopping a tendency to downgrade, sabotage and playing dead, changing, regenerating and experiencing my deep inner truth. Genetic code or identity issue. Issue with a dead person/karmic memory
CARD XIV : THE ANGEL	I connect with « the Source of all life » and I use my intuition, my logic, my abilities to communicate, my sincerity, my purity of heart, my human values, a	Difficulty connecting with the universe, making things flow, implementing harmony, using a psychological/technological intelligence, working within a group/network,

	psychological and/or technological intelligence and my ability to manage projects to do networking, to work within a group, to find solutions, repair, help and heal, bring hope, implement progress and independence/freedom, bring about serenity and great success and contribute to create a better world.	finding solutions, repairing, healing, making progress, becoming free and self-reliant, getting out of what is hypothetical and virtual, embodying, adapting to the modern world, having enough energy, setting goals, using modern technology, managing complex situations/projects, becoming independent, helping others and being an angel.
CARD XV : THE DEVIL	Lucid, passionate, bold and fearless, I see clearly in the dark, know how to reveal each person's dark side and to create suspense and emotion. I am connected to my instincts, my nose, my deepest drives and urges. I express my need to earn money, to live a happy sex life and to express my personal power which I humbly use to serve life so as to master the world of matter. I forge metal and life. I seduce and cast spells on people. I manoeuvre, act tactically and dominate with a very sharp intelligence and a highly efficient organization.	Difficulty getting out of a state of ignorance and fear, illegitimacy and perversity, jealousness and possessiveness, slavery and obsession, of relationships of dependency or always complicated situations, emerging from the shadow, from misery, despair and fear of betrayal, seeing behind appearance, being lucid, feeling safe, having faith in life, stopping a tendency to downgrade and sabotage, changing, expressing my personal power, working with metal, living a happy sex life, doing what makes me feel passionate, getting paid, spending money and mastering the world of matter.
CARD XVI : THE TOWER	I look inward and confine myself in my tower or temple so as to increase my awareness, awaken, become awareness of awareness, connect with the Source of all Life, experience God and explode in bliss. This salutary shock then allows me to upset, deconstruct et rebuild, reconnect, liberate and heal what needs to be healed and experience enlightment, a spiritual experience and a new vision. I use a psychological and technological intelligence and an intelligence of structures to find solutions, repair, master languages, liberate using speech and adapt to the modern world.	Difficulty asking deep questions, connecting with my spiritual self and with the Source of all life, becoming aware and awakening, looking inward to experience God, liberating using speech, breathing, getting out of confinement, get back on feet and on track after a shock or a fall, not exploding, not being stressed, using a psychological or technological intelligence to adapt to new situations, master languages, getting organised efficiently and to adapt to the modern world, networking and evolving in harmony with the laws of universe. Blindness. Stress. Emotional shocks. Violence. Unpredictable. Insanity. Accidents or disasters.
CARD XVII : THE STAR	I connect myself to the source of all joy, to Eternal Feminity, to unconditional love, to fairies, to the truth, to Mother Earth, to nature and to the stars. I embody, express my sensuality, my intuition, relational intelligence, my ability to produce and I implement beauty, joy, harmony, peace of heart, abundance, grace and life. I bring joy, happiness, hope, inspiration, delight and spiritual love in the hearts of people. I find and manage resources so as to live happily on Earth.	Difficulty rising back up again after having been down or brought to my knees, connecting with nature, with the stars, with the Source of all joy and of all life, embodying, seeing beyond form, not abusing earthly pleasure and overeating, getting out of illusions and naïveness, not being lazy and over emotional, incoherent and stupid. Difficulty setting goals, setting myself in motion to get things done, having enough energy, being brave, adapting to change and to the unknown and living my life as if it were a work of art.
CARD XVIII : THE	I make things flow. I create and perpetuate life by expressing motherly love, by being natural and kind, by	Difficulty emerging from the dark and from a bad dream, from anguish and a state of unconsciousness, from emotional

MOON	following and living my dreams, resourcing myself through safe haven activities (water, food, sleep, music, household activities and family relationships). I go from a state of unwellness to a state of wellness by working on corrupted memories, by cleaning up my past, by nourishing myself on all levels, by expressing my emotions and feelings, my imagination and my intuition, by making sure everything is clear, by taking care of myself and other, by creating intimate relationships and by being life happily living itself.	dependency and being overemotional, from incoherence and disorder, from illusions and hallucinations, denial and lies. Difficulty expressing my emotions, managing my fears, avoiding emotional blackmail, expressing motherly love, giving birth, living harmonious family relationships, healing my emotional wounds and grief, going from a state of unwellness to a state of wellness, resourcing myself through safe haven activities, cleaning up upset memories, nourishing myself at all levels, using my intuition and my imagination and taking care of myself, my home and of other people.
CARD XIX : THE SUN	I succeed in life by living in my heart according to my heart, by being connected to the Source of Love and to other people's hearts, by expressing fatherly love, generosity and gratitude, by being aware of being aware, by embodying positive attitudes, by highlighting myself, by expressing my inner light and my vitality, by giving light and education to children living in ignorance, by being committed, by sharing, by creating special relationships and partnerships, by building a nice life, by setting relevant goals, organizing myself efficiently and finding the means to succeed, by mastering what needs to be mastered, by expressing the best version of myself, by bringing joy and happiness to others and by shining like a Sun living in unity with God and the Source of all Life.	Difficulty connecting with my heart, loving myself/other and accepting other people's love, connecting to others, living special relationships, highlighting myself, expressing my creative power and my willpower, having a good image of myself or giving a good image of myself to others, seeing things clearly and expressing myself clearly, being a positive, warm hearted, generous person, not being selfish, individualistic and self-centered, not needing to be highlighted by the gaze of others, expressing my authority without behaving like a complete monarch, not being over attached to luxury, not acting like a megalomaniac, being self sufficient, setting the right goals, finding the means to succeed, getting organized efficiently, building a nice life, living happily, being the best version of myself and shining like a Sun.
CARD XX : JUGEMENT	I uplift my vision; develop a multidimensional and sacred vision of the human body, soul, mind and spirit and of time and space. I express the power of faith and prayer. I manage complex projects. I call upon and use very modern and innovative technology possibly linked with sound, images, vibrations or speech. I deliver messages that bring about revelations, change, a second chance, liberation, awakening to life hereafter, the ability to rise from one's ashes and a rebirth, a renewal, a resurrection in a new body and a new life. I free myself from past lives and ancestral memories so as to stop being confined in a tomb and so as to live my true life/destiny.	Difficulty not judging, misjudging and condemning others or humanity, being aware if signs, not fealing guilty, not living in a dream, not being confined in a tomb of ancestral or past lives memories, not living a lie, uplifting my vision, becoming aware of what is sacred, having faith and calling upon the power of prayer, vibrating with love, handling complex projects, using innovative technology and new web orientated technologies, revealing myself to myself, deliver the correct messages, becoming aware of life hereafter, changing, liberating, adapting to the unexpected and to new people/situations, giving myself or others a second chance, healing and rising from my ashes to be reborn/resurrect and live my true life/destiny.

CARD XXI : THE WORLD	I express all my potential, go at the end of myself. I embody with joy into matter so as to create abundance. I set goals and implement the efficient organization so as to succeed. I battle to uplift my soul and my vision and to express my personal power. I use my psychological and technological intelligence so as to find solutions, repair, implement progress and create a better world. I get the appropriate education so as to succeed. I open up to the world and to foreign lands. I express my personal power and play my part in the world and take laws and rules into account. I gain access to spiritual laws, to wisdom and to the centre of my spiritual body. I become and express love and wisdom.	Difficulty getting out of my world or not choking in my world, broadening my horizons, increasing scope and expanding, expressing my personal power and taking my place in the world, embodying in the world of matter and implementing abundance, not being snatched and overwhelmed by the world, setting relevant goals and getting organized efficiently, getting the right education, not being over complicated, succeeding, uplifting my soul and my vision, using my psychological and technological intelligence, networking and making friends, adapt to the modern world, being open to foreigners and to new worlds, respecting territories, laws and rules, getting access to universal laws, being a loving and wise person, expressing all my potential and going to the end of myself.
CARD 22 OR 0 THE FOOL	I get off beaten tracks, go beyond usual frames and landmarks, step out of systems and structures or organizations so as to connect myself with the universe, with the stars, with my ancestors or my past lives and to the magical power of faith and imagination so as to express my uniqueness, my creative powers and my genius. I master the world of form and of matter. I serve life in my own way. I take care of handicapped people or of geniuses. I create my own reality. I break free from past life or ancestral memories and break the bonds of karma. I travel in search of new adventures. I bring delight to people and places. I return to live in the house of God and become a truly free and happy person living in a state of grace. I go where no one has ever been. I'm at the leading edge of trends and technology and contribute to creating a new and better world.	Difficulty getting out of the small mind and freeing myself from past life or ancestral memories, breaking the bonds of karma, going beyond form and illusions, getting off beaten tracks, stepping out of organizations, systems and structures, going beyond the ordinary, use the magical power of faith and imagination so as to express my uniqueness and the genius within me, getting appropriate landmarks, understanding how people and society and life works, getting structured and organized, finding my place in society, adapting to the modern world, not living on the fringes of society, being aware of my rights and my duties, being a responsible person, growing up, not being confused, not going astray, not being illogical and incoherent, not being mad, not doing crazy things, not being ill-adapted, inappropriate, unsuitable or handicapped, liberating myself from false beliefs and living as a free and happy person on Earth.

Chapter 7: Working with the spirit of animals

You can call upon animals that symbolize the different numbers and learn to feel how the spirit of an animal, in relationship to the number you want to work on, can help you or your patient embody qualities linked to it. You can also use animal figures or toys.

	animal 1	animal 2	animal 3	animal 4	animal 5	others
Number 1	otter	horse	ram	monkey	dragon	-
Number 2	owl	cow	turtle	cat	beetle	night animals
Number 3	dog	falcon	magpie	butterfly	crane	bobcat
Number 4	reindeer	bull	eagle	beaver	elephant	powerful animals
Number 5	buffalo	elk	deer	horse	migrating animals	
Number 6	doe	sheep donkey	bird	duck	rabbit	cute animals
Number 7	tiger	cheetah	jaguar	leopard	thoroughbred	hunters
Number 8	white crane	big birds	heron	ants	elegant animals	
Number 9	bear	goat	elephant	camel	desert/mountain animals	
Number 10	monkey	fox	coyote	squirrel	parrot	rat
Number 11	lion	peacock	swan	dog	-	-
Number 12	dolphin	salmon	whale	sea lion	walrus	squid
Number 13	crow vulture	night butterfly	polecat lizard	crocodile	phœnix	earthworm
Number 14	seagull	albatross	gull	giraffe	wild geese	unicorn
Number 15	wolf jackal	boar rat	bat	spider lemur	snake scorpion	dangerous animals
Number 16	rooster	gannet	seagull	termites	-	chocking animals
Number 17	hummingbird dove	donkey cow	frog	giraffe	rabbit	squirrel
Number 18	cat	crab	wolf	crayfish	meerkats	turtle
Number 19	horse	swan	prairie dog		-	famous animals
Number 20	eagle	phœnix	-	-	-	siren
Number 21	whale	horse	bull	eagle	lion	jaguar
Number 22	chameleon	seagull	cat	-	-	strange animals

Chapter 8: THE BIRTH DIAMOND OF PAIRS

Adding up numbers in two same houses:
This shows what the pair requires to express itself in the outside world.
Substracting numbers in two same houses: This can sometimes also be done.
This shows what the pair requires to express itself within the privacy of the pair, between partners.

House 1 of the pair: What your relationship needs in order to be confident and assertive. The image it shows in the outside world.

House 2 of the pair: What your relationship needs in order to be in a state of joy, to feel pleasure, to earn money, to create abundance and to live happily on earth.

House 3 of the pair: What your relationship needs in order to listen and hear, communicate, set itself in motion and adapt to its suroundings.

House 4 of the pair: What your relationship needs in order to feel well at home and to become free from the past.

House 5 of the pair: What your relationship needs in order to love, define it's identity, do what it loves doing and what it wants.

House 6 of the pair: What your relationship needs in order to serve, to become free from unadapted repetitive schemes. Potential repetitive challenges that the relationship may face.

House 7 of the pair: What your relationship needs in order to be balanced and to live in harmony, to exist as a pair and to overcome any difficult karmic memories.

House 8 of the pair: What your relationship needs in order to thrise sexually, to experience tantric love. The relationship's spiritual quest. What the pair is looking for deep down.

House 9 of the pair: What your relationship needs in order to express its autority and power, to find it's place in the world, to play its economic role, to travel, to experience philosophy, teachings and to thrive.

House 10 of the pair: What your relationship needs in order to move forward towards its deep inner truth and find inner peace. The relationship as a building site so it can become a sacred temple.

House 11 of the pair: What your relationship needs in order to experience freedom and to create a better world.

House 12 of the pair: What could be a cause of suffering and what your relationship needs in order to avoid suffering, to become free from ancestral memories, to be deligghted and to experience God.

Source of Brilliance House: What your relationship needs in order to succeed, radiate and manifest abundance.

Intention House : What the relationship's intention is.

Soul Call House: The relationship's deep needs that should be taken into account.

Hidden Resource House, Hidden challenge House and Contradiction House : The relationship's hidden resource, hidden challenge and contradiction

The pair's yearly House: The pair's yearly atmosphere and what the relationship focuses on during the year.

Natural Temper House : The pair's natural temper and what the pair needs to feel good.

Motivation House : The pair's motivations.

Key Resource House: The relationship's key resource

Expression House and Fulfilment House: What the relationship needs to live its life, to accomplish its destiny,to blosom and to achieve fulfilment.

Chapter 9: TRAINING SESSIONS to learn the BIRTH DIAMOND TOOL

DAY 1 :

1: Secret history of Italian numerology (Tarot), German numerology (Runes) and Chinese numerology (I-ching) and spiritual foundations of numerology and the Birth Diamond

2: Learning the card's key words

3: Question symbols, the cross tarot spread and other spreads

DAY 2 :

1-History of the Birth Diamond - Origin – Why the name « Birth Diamond »?

2-How to talk about the BD – What if the BD? What can it do?

3-How do you calculate it? How does it work? How do you display it?

4-Comparing it with the "Référentiel de Naissance"

5-Explaining how to calculate the most important houses, The 3 storey structure "Asgard-Midgard-Uttgard" and Identifying difficult houses/resourcefull houses.

6-Interpreting numbers in houses

7-Cards found twice, three times, four times, five times or more.

8- Pairs adding to 22, 17, 13 etc.

9- Using Birth Diamond numerology to choose/find a job.

10- Using Birth Diamond numerology to choose a partner, understand/accept/love your partner and create a happy relationship.

11- A technical concept: octaves and harmonics

12- Make a list/print out BD of 20 known people to get living landmarks

13- Using the practical workbook – Working with animal photos or figurines

14-Softwares and 15- For those who master astrology.

Chapter 10: Comparing Tarot Cards, I-Ching and Runes

Tarot and I-Ching

1-The Magician: CREATIVE POWER

2-The High Priestess: RECEPTIVITY

3-The Empress: DIFFICULT BEGINNINGS (adapting)

4-The Emperor: Inexperienced youth (The master and the pupil)

5-The High Priest: STRATEGIC WAITING

6-The Lovers: CONFLICT

7-The Chariot: THE ARMY

8-Justice: CIVILISATION

9-The Hermit: HANDLING WINTER

10-The Wheel: THE RIGHT CONDUCT (making things work right)

11-Strength: STRENGHT OF HEART OR PEACE

12-The Hanged Man: DECLINE

13- Death: COMMUNITY WITH MANKIND

14-The Ange : GREAT SUCCESS

15-The Devil: HUMILITY

16- The Tower (House of God : ENTHUSIASM

17-The Star : FOLLOWING (your star)

18-The Moon: FIXING THE CORRUPTED
19-The Sun: POSITIVE DRIVE (of the sun)
20-Jugement (the Archangel) : SACRED VISION
21-The World: LAW AND PUNISHMENT
22-The fool: FORM OR GRACE
23: BREAKING APPART and 24: RETURING TO ORDER

Tarot and Runes

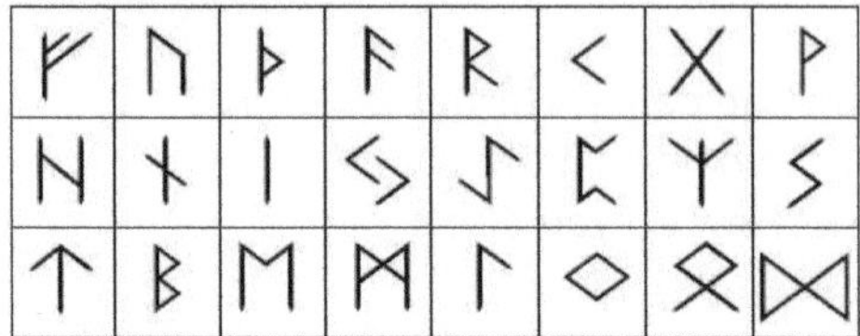 Row 3 or third Aett from 17 to 24...

1-The Magician : **RUNE 1**-FEHU-CREATING WEALTH

2-The High Priestess : **RUNE 2**-UR-FEMALE POWER

3-The Empress : **RUNE 3**-THORN- ADAPTING

4-The Emperor : **RUNE 4**-AS-POWER EXPRESSED)

5-The High Priest : **RUNE 5-**RAIDH-JOURNEY OF BODY AND MIND

6-The Lovers : **RUNE 6**- KEN-TORCH OF LOVE

7-The Chariot : **RUNE 7**-GYFU-UNITY IN ACTION-BEING A GIFT FOR LIFE

8-Justice : **RUNE 8**-WYN-JOY OF SHARING AMONGST MEN

9-The Hermit : **RUNE 9**-HAGL-HAIL-BEING ONE'S ESSENCE

10-The Wheel : **RUNE 10**-NYD-What is required, destiny, constraints

11-Strength : **RUNE 11**-ISA-ICE, WILL POWER, POWER OF LOVE/LIGHT

12-The Hanged Man : **RUNE 12**-YER-THE GOOD HARVEST

13- Death : **RUNE 13**- EIH-YEW-DEATH

14-The Angel : **RUNE 14**-PERTH-A TOOL TO CONSULT THE GODS

15-The Devil : **RUNE 15**-EOLH-ELK REED-PROTECTION AGAINST EVIL

16- The Tower (House of God) : **RUNE 16**-SIGL-SUNBEAM OR LIGHTNING

17-The Star : **RUNE 17-** TIEW - SKY GOD

18-The Moon : **RUNE 18**-BERKANO-BIRCH TREE-LIFE AND WELLNESS

19-The Sun : **RUNE 19**-EH-HORSE-INNER UNITY WITH THE GODS

20-Jugement (the Archangel) : **RUNE 20**-MAN-THE GREAT MAN (father of mankind) and THE GREAT DEPARTURE (awakening)

21-The World : **RUNE 21**-LAGU-WATER-RETURNING TO THE OCEAN

22-The fool : **RUNE 22** - ING-GOD OF FREEDOM-EXPERIENCING ALL OF ONE'S POTENTIAL

23 : I-CHING=BREAKING APPART - **RUNE 23**: LEGACY – EXPERIENCING/REACHING ORIGIN

and 24 : I-CHING=RETURING TO ORDER **RUNE 24**- DAYLIGHT RETURNS.

Chapter 11: Harmonics and octaves

This is a research chapter. A Harmonic = a number, existing the the Birth Diamond chart, multiplied by 1, 2, 3, 4, 5 etc. Harmonics come both from music and astrology. I realised they could be used with the Birth Diamond numbers thanks to my friend Virginie D. An octave is a specific harmonic where numbers are only multiplied by 2. An Octave = a number, existing the the Birth Diamond chart, multiplied by 2.

In music, a number is a frequency and when multiplied by 2, you get the same note with a higher pitch. In the natural A432 Hz scale or range for example, the frequencies 2-4-8-16-32-64-128-256 and 512 Hz all give a C tone whiles frenquecies 3-6-12-24-48-96-192-384 and 769 Hz all give a G tone. One can thus connect the 24 numbers existing in the Birth Diamond to frequencies!

Astrology takes into account the degree on wich a planet is located. This degree is relative to a position called the vernal point which is the zero degree of Aries. It is then possible to multiply the value the the harmonic we seek to explore. If your Sun is located at 20° Capricorn for example, then thats the 290th degree from zero Aries. To find the second harmonic, then you multiply 290 by 2=580. You subtract 360 and you get 220 which brings you to 10° Scorpio. The first harmonics can be found for all planets and angles of the astral chart. They often do this in India. Applied to the Birth Diamond, there are two choices. You can multiply each number by 2 and do this up to 7 times. You would then find the first octave, the second octave and so on. The other possibility is to multiply the 24 numbers by some number between 3 and 12 and to do this a certain number of times.

The original Birth Diamond equals the first harmonic and the fisrt octave. To get the second harmonic/octave, you multiply each of the 24 numbers in the 24 houses by 2. To get the third octave, you multiply what you previously found by two again and so on. To get the fifth harmonic, you multiply the original numbers by 5 and so on. To interpret, i supose and this needs to be checked, that we need to refer to what the number you are multiplying by simbolizes, either by comparing it to an astrological house or to a tarot card. For example, the second octave tells us about ressources to use and memories to clean up.

The third octave or harmonic tells us about what is required to adapt by using one's brain/mind. The fourth octave/harmonic would be about origins, wellness and reconecting with the Source of all life if we refer to astrology and expressing one's power and building one's empire if we refer to Tarot. The fifth octave/harmonic has to do with expressing your heart and identity, love and the ability to guide and be guided. The sixth harmonic/octave has to do with either technical intelligence, service, health, recurrent issues or with joy, feelings, being an artist and love.

The seventh octave/harmonic has to do with relationships, partnership and with what needs to be balanced and with what can therefore be a major challenge.

The eight harmonic/octave has to do with inner quest, initiation, crisis and passion.

The ninth harmonic/octave has to do with dharma, expressing one's power in the outside world, the economic role played and possibly with looking within and handling building site like situations to move towards one's deep inner truth so as to find inner peace.

The tenth harmonic/octave has to do with one evolution path towards inner peace and wisedom if we refer to the tenth astrological house and with understanding life and cycles, becoming an expert by repeating, serving life and adapting to the world of matter if we refer to the tenth Tarot Card.

The eleventh harmonic/octave refers to becoming free from whatever hinders progress and to contributing to create a better world if we refer to the eleventh astrological house and to being the best version of one's self, embodying one's vision, setting goals, getting organized efficiently and succeding if one refers to the eleventh tarot card.

The twelfe harmonic/octave refers to how to get out of suffering and misery, setting on a spiritual path, becoming free from ancestral memories and/or past lives memories and experiencing deligth, bliss and God.

One way to graphically show the first harmonics/octaves of the Birth Diamond is to put them, for each of the first 12 houses, around a circle as below. The circle on the left shows the first five octaves while the circle on the right shows the first 7 harmonics. A second set of circles is then required for houses 13 to 24. The example below if for a person named Jack Riceson Renpri date of birth 11th january 1976.

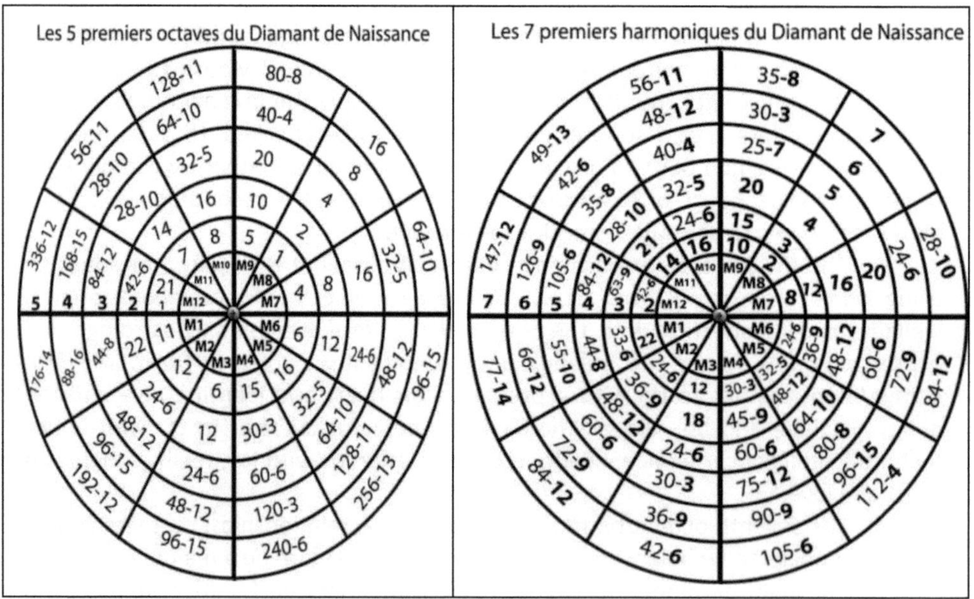

Chapter 12: Connections between numbers, stars, planets and stones

PLANETS	NUMBERS	ASTRO LOGICAL SIGNS	*Bach Flowers*	**Examples of Gemstones**
MARS	1 7 4 3	**ARIES**	Impatiens, agrimony Clematis	Red Jasper, garnet, ruby, haematite
VENUS	6 17	**TAURUS**	Red chestnut Wild Rose	Carnelian, amber, saphire, orange calcite
MERCURY	3	**GEMINI**	chestnut bud white chestnut	Sulfur, blue calcite, chalcedony
MOON	18 2	**CRAB**	Honeysuckle Walnut	Moon stone, howlite, Pink quartz, Selenite
SUN	11 19	**LEO**	Chicory, Elm, Vine Water violet, Larch	Imperial Topaz Rock Crystal, citrine, agate
MERCURY	10	**VIROE**	Crab apple, cherry plum	Fluorite, malachite, shungite, Olivine,
VENUS	6 8	**LIBRA**	Centaury, Olive, Pine, Sclérantus	Rodochrosite, kunzite, chrysocolla, Manganocalcite
PLUTO	13 15	**SCORPIO**	Aspen, Beech, Willow Mustard, Rock rose	Obsidian, tourmaline, septaria, Tiger's eye
JUPITER	4 5 7 21	**SAGITARIUS**	Oak, Vervain, Wild oat	Jade, aventurine, labradorite
SATURN	9 13 16	**CAPRICORN**	Cerato, Larch Mimulus, Rock water	Fossilised wood, Onyx, haematite, stibine
URANUS	14 16	**AQUARIUS**	Gorse, Heather, ornbeam, sweat chestnu	Sodalite, azurite, lapis-lazuli, pyrite, angélite, zircon
NEPTUNE	12 20	**PISCES**	Holly, star of Bethléem Gentiane	Amethyst, aquamarine, sugelite, smocked quartz, purpurite, charoïte

Chapter 13: Yearly Birth Diamond and progressed Birth Diamond

The yearly Birth Diamond

The yearly Birth Diamond starts at the date which is your birthday of the current year. Example: If today is 12th May 2022 and your date of birth is 12th November 1977, then the year you are in started 12th November 2021 and we take this date as if it was your birth date. You can then do a Birth Diamond just like the one based on the real birth date except here, it is just for a year. Many cards in houses will be similar to the original Birth Diamond but some will be different.

The progressed or symbolic Birth Diamond

Just as with astrology, you can consider that there is a symbolic relationship between one day of your life and one year of your life. If you want some information concerning your fortieth year then you can check out the forties day after your birth date. Example: If you were born 11th august 1986 then the fortieth day after that would be 19th of September 1986. You then calculate and built the Birth Diamond for that specific day and consider that it will tell you many things about your fortieth year. Check it out!

Chapitre 14: Chakras, planets, sounds, essential oils and gemstones

CHAKRAS COLOURS	PLANETES	Music Note	Examples of stones	Huiles essentielles
1-ROOT RED BROWN I survive, I live, i take root, I become assertive	**MARS SATURN PLUTO**	**C** 128/256 /512 Hz	Red Jasper, garnet, ruby, haematite Fossilised wood, Pyrite, Black Tourmaline, Septaria, Obsidian, Tiger's eye	Basil, Thyme, Cinnamon, Savory, Angelic, Tea Tree, Spruce, Clove, Black peper, Helichrysum
2-SACRED ORANGE I feel mye motions, I enjoy, I take care of	**MOON VENUS**	**D** 144/288 /576 Hz	Carnelian, amber, saphire, orange calcite	Sage, Jasmine Benzoin, Orange, Patchouli, Bergamot, Ylang Ylang, Tangarine
3-SOLAR YELLOW I accept/recover my power I take my place	**SUN JUPITER MERCURY**	**E** 162/324 /647 Hz	Imperial Topaz citrine, agate, Sulfur, Jade Aventurine	Lemon, taragon, Roman Chamomile, ginger, lemon verbena, Lavander, Geranium, Laurel
4-HEART/LUNGS GREEN/PINK I open my heart, I love/share, Joy and Gratitude	**SUN VENUS MERCURY**	**F** 171/342 /686 Hz	Agate, Rodochrosite, Kunzite, Pink quartz, Manganocalcite, Labradorite, Olivine	Cedar wood, Rose, Lemon-grass, Rose wood, Santal, Myrrhe, Black spruce Hemlock, Fragonia.
5-THROAT LIGHT BLUE I free myself I express myself I communicate my emotions	**VENUS MERCURY JUPITER**	**G** 192/384 /769 Hz	Blue Calcite, Saphire Angelite, Turquoise Apathite, Chrysocole Chalcedony, Fluorite, Malachite, shungite	Eucalyptus, Mint Myrtle, Niaouli Pine apple Ravintsarra, Sage, Coriander
6-THIRD EYE DARK BLUE J'ouvre ma vision Je m'éveille à la Réalité	**MOON SATURN URANUS NEPTUNE**	**A** 108/216 /432 Hz	Onyx, Stibine Sodalite, Azurite, Lapis-lazuli, Zircon, Meteorites	Sage, Rosemary Italian Helichrysum Hyssopus, Valerian, Mint, Immortal
7-CROWN PURPLE/GOLD/WHITE I connect myself with the universe, I express THE SOURCE OF ALL LIFE	**SUN NEPTUNE PLUTO**	**B** 121/242 /485 Hz	Rock Crystal, Amethyst, Aqua marine, Sugelite, Smoked quartz Purpurite, Charoïte	Incense, juniper Angelica, Lavander Myrrhe, Nard Fir, Cypress

The Birth Diamond - Classical Display

Date of Birth :
First Name :
Family Name :

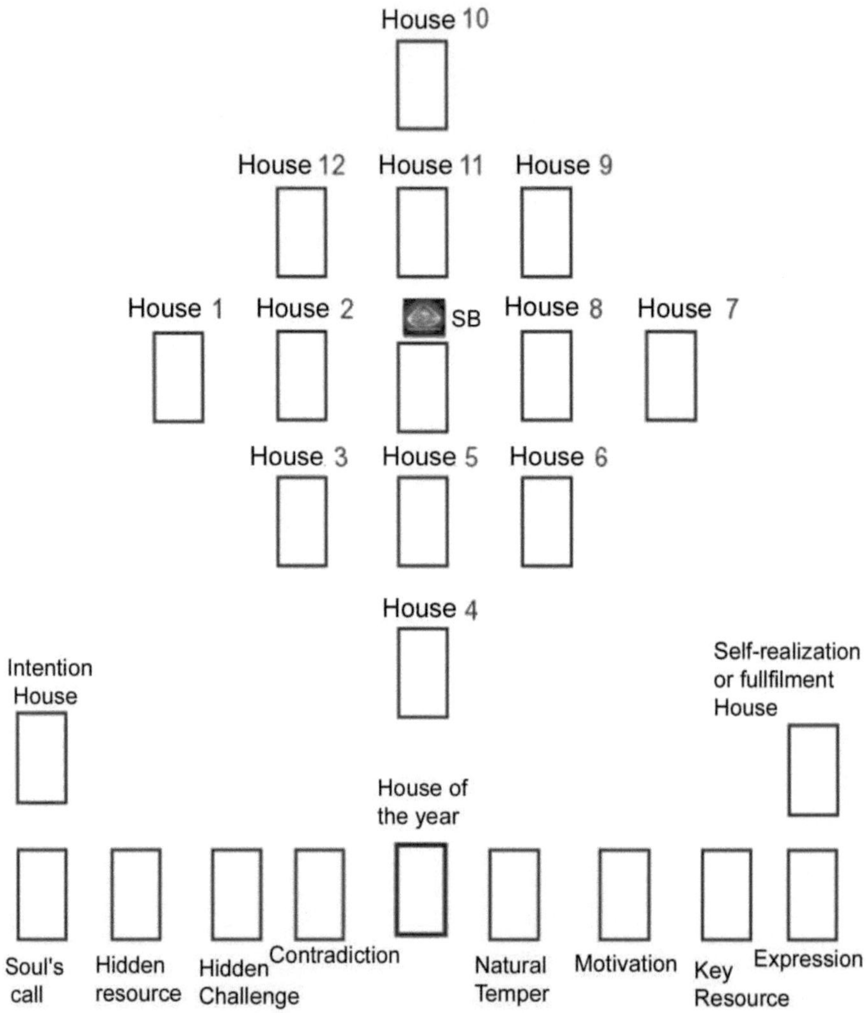

Creation : Eric Jackson PERRIN